Celebrating a Century of the American Anthropological Association

Edited by Regna Darnell and Frederic W. Gleach

Celebrating a Century of the AMERICAN

NTHROPOLOGICAL ASSOCIATION

Presidential Portraits

American Anthropological Association, *Arlington VA*

University of Nebraska Press, *Lincoln and London*

A·M·E·R·I·C·A·N
ANTHROPOLOGICAL
ASSOCIATION

The illustration credits on page 361 constitute an extension of the copyright page.

Library of Congress Cataloging-in-Publication Data

Celebrating a century of the American Anthropological Association : presidential
portraits / edited by Regna Darnell and Frederic W. Gleach.
    p. cm.
  Includes bibliographical references.
  ISBN 0-8032-1720-X (cl : alk. paper)
    1. American Anthropological Association—History. 2. American Anthropological
Association—Officials and employees—Biography. I. Darnell, Regna. II. Gleach,
Frederic W. (Frederic Wright), 1960– III. American Anthropological Association.

GN2.C393 2002
301'.09—DC21

                                                                    2002022195

Contents

Editors' Introduction

For most visitors to the American Anthropological Association offices in Arlington, Virginia, a memorable feature is a wall of the conference room where meetings are regularly held. Displayed on this wall are the official portrait photographs of all the AAA presidents—77 men and women who have served over the organization's first century. The recognizability of the subjects varies considerably: Franz Boas is known to all, but a young Margaret Mead may be difficult for many to identify. Some of the subjects may remain a puzzle even after the name is checked with the photograph.

This volume brings the experience of visiting the "Wall of Presidents" to all members and friends of the AAA. Each portrait is reproduced and accompanied by a biographical sketch written for the occasion.

Curiosity about the identities of the portraits and the persons behind them brings to life the history of professional anthropology in North America. Disciplinary histories involve not just the ideas and institutions of a discipline, but the people who populate those institutions and debate those ideas. Historians of anthropology can argue over various lists of the "most important" anthropologists, but the roster of AAA presidents provides an illuminating sample of American anthropologists; each was chosen by the membership to lead the AAA, and each reflects some of the dimensions of the discipline and of the larger world surrounding it. Their biographies, encompassing careers in anthropology as well as illuminating their personae, present a history of anthropology that complements the more typical accounts.

A century of professional history offers a time depth easily accessible to oral history. Our living elders, whether presidents or not, describe the early years of the AAA and anthropology in North America through their memories and those of their teachers. Through the transmission of these professional genealogies, the merely anecdotal becomes significant in a larger context of professional socialization. Each contemporary anthropologist stands at a particular and unique point in disciplinary history. Over a career, one's relationship to the presidents and other distinguished colleagues tends to become increasingly personal; we go from reading the works of our elders, to seeing them presenting papers at the meetings, to sitting around talking with them over a drink or a meal. Through the stories that are told, we come to know something even of those long dead. One could argue that we are still a small and relatively intimate discipline that values our grounding in face-to-face relations; each anthropologist has a web of relations and an intellectual genealogy, with all of these overlapping to constitute the larger whole of the discipline.

The centennial of the AAA, virtually coinciding with the turning of the millennium, provides an excuse to take stock of where we have been as a profession and where we are going. However arbitrary the calendric scale, there is a psychological reality to a century that cries out for closure. As Stephen Jay Gould observed, "All the world loves a centennial; we can't resist the temptation to celebrate something clean and even in a ragged and uncertain world" (1983:11).

In 1998 then-president Jane Hill appointed a AAA centennial executive commission (CEC) consisting of Regna Darnell (Western Ontario), chair; Lee D. Baker (Duke), Jennifer Brown (Winnipeg), Raymond DeMallie (Indiana), Frederic W. Gleach (Cornell), Richard Handler

(Virginia), Jonathan Marks (North Carolina, Charlotte), and Stephen O. Murray (Obregon Institute); Richard Handler later had to step down due to obligations at Virginia. AAA officers serving ex officio are Jane Hill (Arizona), Louise Lamphere (New Mexico), Don Brenneis (California, Santa Cruz), and Carole Crumley (North Carolina). Bill Davis, executive director, and Susan Skomal, director of publications, have represented the AAA.

President Hill also invited a longer list of disciplinary elders and experts in anthropological history to serve on a larger AAA centennial advisory commission, which has met at the annual meetings since 1999. Others have also been added as warranted, and there are currently over 60 members of the advisory commission. Many of these individuals have been invaluable in defining projects and contributing their personal perspectives on the century.

The Presidential Portraits Project was among the first commitments made by the CEC. It offered an ideal combination of celebratory potential and documentation of disciplinary history. We envisioned every practicing anthropologist and every anthropology student with professional aspirations in North America (and perhaps even beyond) wanting to have such a record in their personal library. Celebration, we suggest, is not incommensurable with historicism; presentist relevance and ongoing interpretation of the past are best supported by the description of persons and events in the context of their times.

Most of these biographical sketches have been written by members of the CEC. The 21 "living legends" have provided feedback on the presentation of their biographies but were not asked to write their own. We are grateful to the former presidents, who have cheerfully cooperated to make this project successful.

In the course of researching and writing this volume we have also been helped by many individuals who were not members of the centennial commissions. Reference librarians and archivists at a variety of institutions in the United States and Canada responded to our questions and earned our thanks. Susi Skomal and the staff of the AAA office organized photographs and answered many questions as we worked on this project. Genevieve Ames, John Henderson, and Bernd Lambert also provided help at key points, and Vilma Santiago-Irizarry offered critical assistance during the editorial process. We would also like to acknowledge the ongoing assistance of Gary Dunham, who for some time has been far more than just an editor in working on the centennial projects.

There can be no question that the leadership of the AAA has worked for the common good of anthropology. Individuals may have been physical or cultural anthropologists, archaeologists or linguists; they may have worked in small-scale societies or urban centers; they may be categorized in a variety of ways, and may have had multiple specializations. But all were "Anthropologists." In the words of Charles Hockett (1979:640): "Those who claim the privilege of calling their work *anthropology* thereby also assume the responsibility of caring for the whole discipline, not just their favorite segment of it." The diversity of the discipline and the proper balance between specialization and a common identity have been discussed from the very beginning, and the debate shows no signs of abating.

Looking back a century often evokes a kind of nostalgia for a Golden Age in which things were simpler and more personal. Many contemporary anthropologists are nonplussed by the thousands of registrants at an annual meeting; it seems almost unbelievable that 40 people were invited to the first formal meeting in 1902, or that early meeting programs presented only one session at a time. Everyone present knew everyone else. American anthropology was perhaps very much like the small-scale societies in which most anthropologists were wont to conduct their fieldwork. In both parts of the analogy, however, we suspect a degree of wistful thinking. Both the AAA and its meetings, and the culture that anthropologists attribute to the "others" they study, are messier and less clearly bounded than we have sometimes acknowledged.

Imagined communities—whether local, national, or professional— extend the kinds of social bonds that arise from face-to-face interaction of known persons to others who share common interests or identities, and therefore become like oneself. Today, as a century ago, American anthropologists flock to the annual meetings and congregate in coffee shops, bars, meeting corridors, and hotel rooms to talk to old friends, meet new colleagues, and catch up on what others are doing. We are quintessential fieldworkers, valuing first-hand experience of one another's reported experiences and research results. We are professional snoops or gossips, at least in one mode. Margaret Mead is reputed to have quipped that her husbands may have been smarter than she was, but she was the one who always knew whose pig had died. Because we have maintained a commitment to personal networks as well as to the theories and ethnographic cases with which we work, our professional culture has not become impersonal. Some may manipulate the networks for personal gain, but for most, "networking" is about catching up with far-flung friends and colleagues.

Identities crosscut because most of us do more than one thing. Graduate school cohorts reassemble each year; most of us have ties of one sort or another to multiple academic institutions (and even if we don't, our friends do). Other linkages follow ethnographic-area lines, or involve theoretical or methodological perspectives. We meet colleagues on AAA committees and commissions, representing the 35 AAA sections that reflect the enormous variety of subjects in which anthropologists are professionally interested. Moreover, multiple section memberships are the norm, with many belonging to five or more. The numbers of internal divisions and participating individuals may have increased over the century, but we still feel a common bond as anthropologists.

Presidents and Representation

As this project progressed, many were startled not only by how well the biographies represented general trends in the discipline, but also by how well the presidents represented the subdisciplines and even the specializations within each subdiscipline (albeit with a substantial number of individuals crossing the traditional boundaries). Not surprisingly, this is especially true in sociocultural anthropology; the diversity within biological anthropology is less well represented among the presidents, but that range is at least reflected. Although the numerical balance certainly lies in sociocultural anthropology, this roughly reflects the proportions of membership in the AAA. There have been 46 sociocultural anthropologists (with the longest consecutive run, save two exceptions, between 1963 and 1982), 19 archaeologists (12 of them serving before 1937), six biological anthropologists (much more heavily represented in the pages of the *American Anthropologist* than in the AAA presidency), and six linguists (overrepresented for their proportion in the membership). While archaeologists, biological anthropologists, and linguists have separate associations that provide a primary professional identity for many practitioners, there is no alternative umbrella organization for sociocultural anthropologists. A number of presidents were practicing anthropologists, under one label or another, but this commitment does not lend itself to unambiguous classification across subdisciplines.

The gender balance among presidents has been disproportional in different ways at different times. The first among the 13 women to serve as president was Elsie Clews Parsons in 1941, followed by Ruth Benedict in 1947. Margaret Mead attained this honor in 1960; Frederica de Laguna and Cora Du Bois also served during the 1960s. Ernestine Friedl was the only women president of the 1970s. More recently, however, women have been prominent. Margaret Clark, Nancy Lurie, and June Helm presided in the 1980s, and in the final decade of the century Jane Buikstra, Annette Weiner, Yolanda Moses, Jane Hill, and Louise Lamphere served as presidents.

The ethnic and racial diversity of the AAA presidency has not been extreme. Several AAA presidents were born outside North America (Franz Boas, Frederick Hodge, Aleš Hrdlička, Nels Nelson, Edward Sapir, Diamond Jenness, Ernestine Friedl, and Francis Hsu). Particularly in the early years, when anthropologists were self-trained or trained in related fields, many of the presidents came from working class or farming families or were the children of immigrants (e.g., W J McGee, W. H. Holmes, Alfred Kroeber, Clark Wissler, George MacCurdy, John Swanton, Robert Lowie, Robert Redfield, Harry Shapiro, A. I. Hallowell, G. P. Murdock, Harry Hoijer, Sol Tax, Cora Du Bois). The first nonwhite president was Francis L. K. Hsu in 1978; the first black president was Yolanda Moses in 1996–97.

Many individuals other than presidents have served the association in various capacities. The annual meeting program, for example, acknowledges the contributions of *American Anthropologist* editors, distinguished lecturers, and award winners. Many more than the presidents have served on the AAA executive board and various ongoing committees, created and sustained the 35 sections and their publications, and participated in the annual meetings. In some serious sense, then, the presidents whose careers are celebrated in this centennial volume represent all of us and encapsulate our collective professional identity.

The Founding of the AAA

When the American Anthropological Association was organized in 1901, U.S. President McKinley had only recently been assassinated, the Oklahoma Land Rush was just under way, and oil had only recently been discovered in Texas. New U.S. President Theodore Roosevelt sparked controversy by dining with African American intellectual Booker T. Washington. The tallest building in New York City was 382 feet, a Broadway show was less than a dollar, and the principal U.S. export was hog products. Air-conditioners had not yet been invented. There were still four widows of Revolutionary War soldiers collecting pensions.

Anthropology as a field of study was not new, of course; its roots can be traced to the ancient Greeks, and its 16th- and 17th-century forms are well known (e.g., Hodgen 1964). In the 19th century anthropology blossomed, like many fields of scientific enquiry (e.g., Darnell 1998, Hinsley 1994); studies of American Indians were a critical part of the discipline's development, with Lewis Henry Morgan but the best remembered of many early scholars.

The first anthropological society in America was the American Ethnological Society of New York (AES), founded in 1842 by Albert Gallatin; this organization lapsed, but it was revived in 1899 by Franz Boas. In 1879 the Anthropological Society of Washington (ASW) was established. The American Association for the Advancement of Science (AAAS) created a section for anthropology in 1882 ("Section H"), later headed by many of the same people who were AAA presidents. Washington, New York, Cambridge (a less formally constituted group centered around Harvard faculty), and Philadelphia (largely through the scientific societies, although Daniel Brinton held a nominal appointment at Pennsylvania as professor of archaeology and linguistics) were the major centers for American anthropology, but the government- and museum-based anthropologists in Washington were not well represented in the AAAS. A national organization had been considered repeatedly in the late nineteenth century; in 1896, largely under the influence of Brinton, the AAAS began a series of regular "Informal Conferences" for members of the anthropology section, a compromise to appease those concerned that a separate national organization might weaken the AAAS (Boas 1902:804, McGee 1903:178–179).

The matter was discussed again in 1898, resulting in another half step: the *American Anthropologist* was relinquished by the ASW, and a new series was begun in January 1899 as a national journal. In the fall of 1901, following continuing correspondence between Boas and McGee, the ASW and AES sent delegations to the AAA Section H meeting in Chicago. Further discussion took place with McGee and J. Walter Fewkes representing the ASW, Boas, Livingston Farrand and George Grant MacCurdy representing the AES, and Stewart Culin, Roland B. Dixon, George A. Dorsey, Frank Russell, and Frederick Starr representing the AAAS. Although there was general agreement that a national organization should be established, there were different opinions within this group as to the form the organization should take. One major contingent, led by Boas, wanted a strictly professional society linked with the AAAS, which would limit membership; the other, led by McGee and Dorsey, wanted a more open and general association (McGee 1903:180–182).

Correspondence continued after the Chicago meeting, and several other anthropologists were consulted. McGee then apparently seized an opportunity, and in March 1902, with Culin, Dorsey, Fewkes, and Joseph D. McGuire, he filed incorporation documents in Washington DC; the more open form of association was created, but the founding meeting would be limited to 40. On 30 June 1902 in Pittsburgh, where the AAAS was meeting, the first meeting of the American Anthropological Association took place. Culin chaired the meeting, as chairman of Section H, and Dorsey was asked to be secretary. The members present constituted a nominating committee, and McGee was elected president (McGee 1903:183–186). There were initially 175 members elected, including 16 women (McGee 1903:191–192).

Continuity and Change in the AAA

The AAA was intended to represent all the subfields of anthropology, but through the twentieth century it became gradually more ethnological in membership; this may have been at least partly due to the presence of and increase in other societies specifically devoted to the other subfields (e.g., the Archeological Institute of America, the American Association of Physical Anthropologists, and the Linguistic Society of America), and more specialized journals (e.g., the *American Journal of Physical Anthropology*, *Anthropological Linguistics*, the *International Journal of American Linguistics*, and *American Antiquity*).

Structurally, the AAA remained relatively stable through its first four decades. Through the early years there remained a tension between Boas and the academically oriented members, largely in the Northeast, and the museum- and government-based anthropologists of Washington DC. The first seven presidents were carefully chosen not to allow either side to develop too much strength: McGee from Washington, then Putnam from Cambridge, Boas from New York, Holmes and Fewkes from Washington, Dixon from Cambridge, and Hodge from Washington.

Events of 1919–20 brought matters to a head. Boas publicly opposed U.S. involvement in World War I, and in 1919 he also publicly questioned the integrity of President Wilson and charged several American anthropologists with spying in Latin America under the guise of science. His letter, published in the *Nation*, triggered an explosion of pent-up anger directed at Boas, who increasingly controlled the discipline and marginalized the Washington and Cambridge factions. Holmes wrote a letter of censure against him. Boas was excluded from both the Council of the AAA and the National Research Council. Structurally, little changed in the AAA, but the tension between Washington museum anthropologists and New York and Cambridge academics was somewhat defused. By this time there also were more anthropologists in more centers, making the old binary opposition less sustainable. The nomination of W. C. Farabee as president in 1920 was a final compromise to restore harmony (Stocking 1968:270–307).

During World War II many, perhaps most, anthropologists had war-related responsibilities, whether directly in the armed forces or otherwise (Eggan 1943); among the AAA presidents this included Fay-Cooper Cole, Diamond Jenness, Ruth Benedict, Clyde Kluckhohn, Harry Shapiro, Fred Eggan, Harry Hoijer, Margaret Mead, Morris Opler, Alexander Spoehr, Frederica de Laguna, Cora Du Bois, Anthony Wallace, Edward Spicer, Richard Adams, Paul Bohannan, Conrad Arensberg, William Sturtevant, and Roy Rappaport. Discussion of the role of anthropology and links to government agencies, dormant since 1920, resumed at this time, and there was talk of establishing a new organization to work in concert with government bodies for the promotion of anthropology and the social sciences. Instead, the AAA was reorganized in 1946 with a small executive board that could act quickly on behalf of the membership, and two classes of membership: members and fellows—the latter being approved by the executive board as qualified anthropologists, rather than students or interested laypersons. Control of the AAA was in the hands of the fellows.

Also in 1946, for the first time, the annual meeting featured multiple concurrent sessions.

During the 1960s a new set of political issues roiled the AAA. The number of anthropologists had risen dramatically. Many were working for the United States and other governments, either directly as employees or indirectly through grant-supported research. As U.S. government policy, particularly foreign policy, diverged in the 1960s from the sentiments of many Americans (and people of other nations), anthropologists again began to question the propriety of different kinds of government-connected research. Shortly before the 1965 meeting it was disclosed that an anthropologist had been working with Project Camelot, a clandestine CIA-backed operation to destabilize the political situation in Chile and observe the effects. Voices were loudly raised before and at the annual meeting, and a special session was put together to discuss the situation. While some angrily opposed such work and wanted the AAA to take a stand, others felt that as a professional society the AAA should not be involved in political issues that individual members might or might not agree with; the *Fellow Newsletter* (the title at the time of the AAA newsletter) of this period contains much correspondence on the subject. The AAA Council sought to keep the focus on "the issues of access to foreign areas, the integrity of the field worker, and the effects upon field work of mission-directed projects supported by the government" (AAA 1966:770). Ralph Beals was appointed to chair a committee to investigate the matter, and eventually a code of ethics was adopted, the AAA's first.

This was not, of course, the first time the AAA was asked to take a public position on a matter of policy. As early as 1905 it urged governments to follow anthropological guidance in dealing with indigenous peoples; in 1938 a resolution was passed against racism, and in 1945 another resolution urged caution in the use of atomic energy. But the Project Camelot scandal, in the context of growing protests in the 1960s, was politically a different kind of situation.

As Charles Frantz noted, "The relevance of these newly-debated *external* concerns of the profession . . . is that they provoked more consciousness among members about their status and role *within* the Association as well. There was an increasing awareness of how uncoordinated the various specialized anthropological societies actually were when issues of common import arose" (1974:18).

In addition to the development of a code of ethics, a period of gradual restructuring of the AAA ensued, culminating in a major reorganization in 1983 with a new set of bylaws. The AAA became an umbrella organization for a collection of units, now termed sections; some sections began within the AAA, while others began as separate societies and merged into it. All members of any section are also members of the AAA, fostering both unity and diversity within the discipline.

The Imminent Demise of Anthropology?

As evident in the discussion above, there have been fractures within the AAA from its very inception. Museum-based vs. academic anthropology, physical (and sometimes archaeology) vs. cultural anthropology, scientists vs. humanists (and more recently postmodernists), evolution vs. historical particularism, and many other divisions have sometimes seemed to threaten to shatter the umbrella of Anthropology. But then, many anthropologists are members of multiple sections; we specialize in various ways, but most of us retain interests in the broader fabric of anthropology.

One of the most persistent dichotomies in classifying anthropologies and anthropologists has been the "pure" vs. the "applied." Even within the limited sample of AAA presidents, one sees a regular reinvention of terms for applied anthropology, an ongoing effort on the part of many scholars to overcome the dismissal of applied work as somehow less worthy than "pure research" and "theory." As Davydd Greenwood has written (e.g. 1999), this emphasis has worked to the detriment of anthropology: "Anthropologists too often confuse doing publishable work for doing socially meaningful work. Publishability is determined by intraprofessional networks and not by the social value of the work, and so publishing is really only a test of clout within these networks. The public, the government, and even most academic administrations know this, and the declining respect and funding for much scholarly work may be attributed, at least in part, to this knowledge." There is some tendency for the general public to perceive anthropologists as eccentric or flaky—bolstered by images in films, such as *Krippendorf's Tribe* (1998) and even the Indiana Jones series. Socially meaningful work is a tool to counter that tendency, in addition to its inherent value. Readers may be surprised to see how many AAA presidents over the first century have done applied anthropology of one sort or another.

The discipline and the AAA have also been shaken by the end of colonialism and the subsequent anthropological guilt trip. While some anthropology certainly was complicit in colonialism—and still is complicit in neocolonial and postcolonial political orders in many places—this is not true of all anthropology. Seeking knowledge of others is a virtually universal activity (see Helms 1988); the value of the practice derives from the intention and use of the knowledge. We would argue that our ambivalence about this history mandates a humanistic sensitivity to the immediate and potential uses of anthropological knowledge, rather than an abandonment of the discipline or its transformation into an overly reflexive exercise in narcissism. A nuanced reading of disciplinary history can help to avoid the excesses one sometimes finds (see Darnell 2001).

We perceive an unfortunate tendency in recent decades toward overly rigid, extreme positions, at least in public discourse; this may parallel trends in American society at large, where "sound-bite" journalism encourages simple, obviously opposable views. Like many of the presidents profiled here, we believe that science and humanism are both essential components of anthropology. The postmodernist critique of representation has value, as does scientific anthropology. But the rigidly intolerant extremes of both are often unproductive.

Perhaps complaining about our eminent demise has been one of the things holding us together all along. Or bickering about what is and is not anthropology. If nothing else, our self-flagellations certainly create an engaging show. Barry Michrina wrote of a nonanthropologist, curious about the *Darkness in El Dorado* furor, who talked with him at the 2000 meeting in San Francisco: "I did not expect to see my interviewer again, but two mornings later we met again in the Hilton lobby. . . . [H]e mentioned that he was leaving early the next morning and that he would miss seeing all the anthropologists. I told him that he should make a regular practice of attending our annual meeting, maybe sitting in on some sessions, and perhaps eventually presenting papers. His eyes brightened at the thought of future meetings, and he asked me where the next one would be held. However, he balked at the idea of presenting a paper to an audience of anthropologists. For him, studying them was enough." (2001:59) Humans really are interested in "others." And despite progress in other social sciences and humanities, and some notable mistakes and failures in our own discipline, anthropology remains the discipline most firmly committed to ensuring that all dimensions of human diversity are represented in understandings of the human condition.

Like the elders of an oral tradition, we socialize a new generation even as we employ rhetoric of dissolution and loss, in the hope that they will take up the responsibility of continuing the transmission. Certainly, there are new sections emerging, which on the surface suggest splintering of common bonds. But there is no intrinsic reason that a federation cannot provide an umbrella for large numbers of crosscutting constituent affiliations. While some have questioned whether it matters that we call the discipline "anthropology," our presidents have had a certain degree of faith in the discipline and its longevity—an optimistic view that the contributors to this volume share.

Celebrating a Century of the American Anthropological Association

W J McGee
1902–1904

William John McGee (who preferred "W J" without the periods) was born at the family farm in Farley, Iowa, on 17 April 1853. He was the fourth of nine children. His parents, James and Martha (Anderson) McGee, were of Scotch-Irish descent; both sets of grandparents were strong supporters of the American Revolution. A sickly child, W J sporadically attended a county district school until about age 14 and was then home schooled by an older brother from 1867 to 1874. Although his mother strongly encouraged education, McGee was largely self-educated; he read law, practiced in justice-court, taught himself mathematics, astronomy, and surveying, and corresponded with several distinguished scientists of his day. At around age 20 he worked at a forge and sold agricultural implements, patenting a commercially unsuccessful adjustable cultivator in 1874 with an older brother and a cousin. His only formal credential was an honorary LL.D. in 1901 from Cornell College in his home state.

In 1878 McGee began to publish in geology and joined the American Association for the Advancement of Science. He conducted a geological and topographical survey of northeastern Iowa from 1877 to 1881 and during that fieldwork became fascinated by the units of measurement in Mound Builder monuments. He went on to describe a cranial "peculiarity" distinguishing these early settlers from modern Indians. *Frederick Webb Hodge* described McGee's ethnological results as "characteristic of the period" but "untenable in light of present knowledge." Hodge's obituary mildly notes anthropological progress over the ensuing period (Hodge 1912:684).

McGee's description of upper Mississippi valley glaciation led Maj. John Wesley Powell to hire him in 1883 as a geologist for the U.S. Geological Survey, and McGee soon headed the Atlantic Coastal Plains Division. His decade of service ended with a transfer in 1893 to the Bureau of American Ethnology (BAE), also under Powell's direction. For both Powell and McGee, discipline labels were less significant than stretching budgets to support needed research. In 1894, in response to Powell's declining health, McGee's title changed from ethnologist to ethnologist-in-charge, making him the de facto head of the bureau.

Although his day-to-day work for the BAE was primarily administrative, McGee studied the Seri Indians of Tiburon Island in the Gulf of California and on the Sonoran coast in 1894 and 1895. He prepared a topological map of the island but his research ended when the Indians fled from his research party; his personal contacts were solely with Seris employed on mainland ranches. McGee also completed Siouan manuscripts after the death of James Owen Dorsey, collaborated with Dr. M. A. Muñoz of Peru on trephined skulls, and synthesized what was known about "primitive numbers" using the broad evolutionary framework that Powell had adopted from Lewis Henry Morgan.

Powell's death in 1902 removed political obstacles that had curtailed the scientific activities of the bureau. Smithsonian secretary Samuel Langley appointed *William Henry Holmes* of the National Museum to replace Powell and reorient the work "from theory to material collections for public display." These actions "effectively eliminated BAE leadership of American ethnology" (West 1992:23).

Considered heir apparent to Powell for a decade, McGee resigned in

1903 to head the anthropology department of the Louisiana Purchase Exposition in St. Louis. Despite organizing the World's Congress of Arts and Sciences in 1904, he was unable to muster continuing support for a public museum in St. Louis. After a brief period in the southwestern desert, he joined the Bureau of Soils in the U.S. Department of Agriculture and specialized in subsoil erosion and groundwater; he held this position until his death.

McGee was an enthusiastic supporter of scientific societies. He was a founder of the Columbian Historical Association and served as president of the National Geographic Society and vice-president of the American Association for the Advancement of Science. When the Washington Academy of Sciences was founded in 1898, McGee was the only person to join all 12 constituent societies.

With *Franz Boas*, he orchestrated the expansion in 1899 of the *American Anthropologist* from the organ of the Anthropological Society of Washington (ASW) to a journal of national scope. He served as president of the ASW from 1898 to 1900, and in 1902 he became the first president of the American Anthropological Association. Throughout this crucial period in the professionalization of American anthropology (Darnell 1998; Hinsley 1981) McGee represented the interests of government-sponsored anthropology, maintaining a balance of power in Washington against other major contenders such as *Frederic Ward Putnam* in Cambridge and Boas in New York.

McGee also embraced the nascent conservation movement and became vice-chairman and secretary of the Inland Waterways Commission established by President Theodore Roosevelt. He and Gordon Pinchot provided the intellectual force behind Roosevelt's ambitious conservation policy. McGee considered his conservation work to be applied anthropology in the interdisciplinary tradition of the BAE—that is, science in service of the public good. Following in the tradition of Powell's arid lands report of 1875, McGee emphasized human alteration of the natural environment and advocated government management of natural resources, providing a holistic plan for the Mississippi watershed as an ecological system. Lamentably, congressional resistance rendered Roosevelt's policies abortive.

Although McGee was not a player in the burgeoning of American anthropology after 1903, which took place primarily in universities, his role at the pivotal juncture between amateur and professional science and local and national scope cannot be underestimated. He supported public engagement with science and evaded disciplinary labels and titles rigidified by increasing emphasis on formal credentials. His political and entrepreneurial skills were considerable, and although the evolutionary theory he espoused was rapidly eclipsed after his departure from anthropology, in his own day McGee was highly respected for the quality of his scientific work. That he built a second successful career in a different field of government science attests to his abilities.

McGee married Anita Newcomb, the socially prominent daughter of America's leading astronomer, in 1888, despite her family's lack of approval (Emma McGee 1915). With his encouragement, Anita McGee obtained a medical degree and had a distinguished career in her own right. The couple had two children, but the marriage disintegrated and McGee thereafter lived at the Cosmos Club in Washington. He cataloged the progress of the cancer that claimed his life on 8 September 1912 at the age of 59. In the interests of science, McGee willed his body to a medical college for dissection. Though he requested no funeral, a service was held at Pinchot's home.

REGNA DARNELL

Frederic Ward Putnam
1905–1906

B orn in Salem, Massachusetts, on 16 April 1839, Frederic Ward Putnam was a member of an extended family that included some of New England's bluest blood. As an adolescent Putnam hoped to spend his life as a military officer and set his sights on West Point. He was tutored at home and never attended formal schools. This enabled him to pursue his interest in, and unusual talent for, natural history—especially local fish and bird populations. At age 16 Putnam wrote his first scientific paper, on the fish of Salem Harbor, and enlisted in the Salem Light Infantry. His catalogs of the fish and birds of Essex County opened the door to his first scientific job. In 1856 Putnam was appointed Curator of Ornithology at the Essex Institute of Salem. A year later Louis Agassiz invited Putnam to Cambridge to assist him at Harvard's Museum of Comparative Zoology (MCZ).

Putnam worked closely with Agassiz on ornithology and ichthyology. His peers at the (MCZ) included Edward S. Morse, Alpheus Hyatt,

Samuel H. Scudder, and A. S. Packard. During this period they established the *American Naturalist*. Although his lab mates were students at Harvard's Lawrence Scientific School, Putnam never enrolled in classes there; he studied exclusively with Agassiz. He was the last of Agassiz's students to fully embrace ideas of Darwinian evolution, which Agassiz bitterly opposed (Dexter 1979:168).

The Harvard Corporation conferred a bachelor's degree on Putnam in 1862 for his work with Agassiz. "The influence of Agassiz remained with him [Putnam] during his entire life. His love for his teacher and the respect and admiration for Agassiz's method of teaching were always favorite themes in his conversations with his own pupils. His never-ending lament was that his students found their knowledge in books rather than in specimens" (Tozzer 1935:127). Putnam's tutorial style of instruction enabled Alice C. Fletcher to receive professional training. As a woman, Fletcher could not attend Harvard. By working closely with Putnam at the Peabody Museum of American Archaeology and Ethnology, she was one of the first women to receive formal training in anthropology.

While Putnam's peers juggled classes, he sought various positions of scientific leadership, editorial responsibilities, and personal research. By his mid twenties, Putnam had served as the curator of ornithology, mammalogy, ichthyology, and vertebrates at the Essex Institute and the curator of ichthyology at the Boston Society of Natural History. In 1864 he took the helm at the Essex Institute as its superintendent and director for six years. The young Putnam developed a remarkable skill for service through leadership, research, fund-raising, and editing. His legacy for anthropology resulted from his skill in marshalling people and resources to build institutions simultaneously in multiple locations.

Putnam's service was not limited to science. At the outbreak of the Civil War, rumors that Southern sympathizers would seize the Cambridge arsenal led him to organize student volunteers to guard it. With great difficulty Agassiz persuaded Putnam not to enlist in the cavalry regiment that his cousin Pickering Allen was mustering.

In 1873 Putnam was chosen as permanent secretary of the American Association for the Advancement of Science (AAAS), a position he retained through 25 years of scientific professionalization. He also became the editor of its influential journal, *Science*.

Around this time Putnam began to focus more on anthropology and archaeology. He had had a long-standing interest in American Indian prehistory, and from 1875 onward he engaged in a systematic study of Pueblo ruins in California, Arizona, and New Mexico, and of mound structures in the Ohio valley.

The shift from zoology to archaeology was fortuitous. By the time Putnam began exploring archaeology in the Americas, George Peabody's 1866 endowment to Harvard for a museum and professorship in American ethnology and archaeology had grown sufficiently to fund this expansion. In 1875 Putnam was appointed curator of the Peabody Museum, a position he held for 34 years. Putnam provided new leadership, expanded the collections, constructed a new building, and initiated the *Papers of the Peabody Museum*.

Stitching together an impressive network of scientists and philanthropists, Putnam launched major archeological projects in the Ohio valley and in the ice-age gravels of New Jersey; he also undertook large-scale digs in Central America and in the Yucatán Peninsula. Although Peabody's initial endowment prescribed a professorship in conjunction with the museum, the Harvard Corporation did not confirm Putnam as its Peabody Professor until 1887.

In 1890 Putnam took a three-year leave of absence to head the ethnology department at the 1893 World's Columbian Exposition in Chicago. Putnam's goal for the exposition was to introduce anthropology to the American public. Although his anthropological building and exhibitions of "native" habitations along the midway were a resounding success by any measure, the grandiose scale of his original plans was compromised by competition from the Smithsonian's National Museum and the Bureau of American Ethnology (Patterson 2001). Nevertheless, Putnam fulfilled his vision of a grand exposition of objects from the Americas and beyond.

Putnam used the fair to establish a permanent natural history museum in Chicago. His initial pitch to Chicago's commercial club in 1891 convinced Marshall Field to endow the museum that bears his name, but Putnam's plans were usurped by others. Putnam reminded the fair's director-general that he was investing his time and energy in the advancement of science with the expectation of a permanent museum in Chicago. Ably assisted by George Dorsey and *Franz Boas*, Putnam employed more than 50 scholars and collected some 50,000 specimens—the nucleus of the anthropological collections of the Field Museum, which opened in 1894.

Within the year Morris K. Jesup invited Putnam to develop similar collections at the American Museum of Natural History in New York City, where he served as curator from 1894 to 1903. During these years Putnam and Boas launched the Hyde Expeditions to the Southwest and the Jesup North-Pacific Expedition.

In 1903 Phoebe Apperson Hearst and Benjamin Wheeler invited Putnam to establish an anthropology department and museum at the University of California, Berkeley. Hearst's endowment funded California Indian, Peruvian, and Egyptian ethnological and linguistic research. After a downturn in the financial markets curbed the ambitious scope of the museum, *Alfred L. Kroeber* developed the academic programs at Berkeley.

Putnam also contributed to the transformation from Section H of the AAAS to the independent and increasingly professional American Anthropological Association.

With prescient prose, Putnam wrote to his wife about the World's Fair ethnological exhibit, "I have hit the nail on the head" (quoted in Dexter 1970). Putnam used an apt metaphor; his career and contributions to anthropology are framed by building: he built institutions, developed archaeological standards, assembled scholarly organs, and supported students. Putnam died in Cambridge, Massachusetts, on 14 August 1915.

LEE D. BAKER

Franz Boas
1907–1908

F ranz Uri Boas, the dominant figure of 20th-century American anthropology, was born in Minden, Westphalia, on 9 July 1858, to a prosperous middle-class Jewish family. His father, Meier Boas, was a textile merchant; his mother, Sophie Meyer Boas, favored the political ideals of the failed 1848 revolution. On graduation from the gymnasium, Boas rejected a safe career in medicine and sought both scientific challenge and scope for his substantial ambition.

Boas entered the University of Heidelburg in 1877, moved to the University of Bonn to study physics, and then to the University of Kiel, where he studied geography with Theobald Fischer. He received his Ph.D. in 1882 with a dissertation on the optics of seawater. During his student years Boas moved from materialism to psychophysics, to geography, and ultimately to ethnology (Stocking 1968).

After a year's compulsory service in the Minden regiment Boas went to Berlin to prepare for an expedition to visit the Eskimos. He spent the entire year of 1883–84 in Baffin Island, living largely off the land. This field experience solidified his cultural relativism and his respect for the Eskimos. *The Central Eskimo* (1888) emphasized subsistence and material culture. Ethnology began to seem more urgent than geography.

Boas obtained a temporary assistantship at Berlin's Royal Ethnological Museum through Adolph Bastian. He earned a habilitation degree in geography and became a *privatdozent*, certified to lecture for student fees. In 1885 he began to study Northwest Coast (NWC) dance masks and the "wealth of thought" hidden behind them (Cole 2000:97). In his spare time he visited the Bella Coola Indians. Although his family wanted him back in Germany, he foresaw better opportunities in America with its less virulent anti-Semitism.

In 1887 Boas moved to New York City to become an assistant editor of the journal *Science*, enabling him to marry Marie Krackowizer, the daughter of an Austrian-born New York physician. He borrowed money from his uncle-by-marriage, New York physician Abraham Jacobi, for his first NWC expedition, to be repaid by profits from collecting. After 1888 Boas's NWC fieldwork was sponsored by the British Association for the Advancement of Science under the direction of Horatio Hale and by the Bureau of American Ethnology (BAE).

Psychologist G. Stanley Hall hired Boas as an underpaid-overworked docent in psychology at the newly established Clark University in 1889. During Boas's three years there, A. F. Chamberlain received the first American Ph.D. in anthropology. Boas's measurement of local schoolchildren caused a tempest in the local press. University founder Josiah Clark was appalled; Hall equivocated but the board supported Boas's academic freedom. Boas resigned in 1892 along with most of the faculty. Unlike others, he was not appointed at the new University of Chicago.

Boas became *Frederic Ward Putnam*'s assistant at the Chicago World's Fair, supervising physical anthropology and NWC ethnology. George Hunt's Fort Rupert Kwakiutls (now know as Kwakwaka'wakws) were the "standard tribe," but the exhibit was "more quaint than coherent" (Cole 2000:156). Between the panic of 1893 and Putnam's resentments over his marginalization from plans for a permanent museum at Chicago, Boas's expected curatorship at the Field Museum did not materialize at the end of the fair. *William Henry Holmes* of the BAE was hired over his head. Boas's 1894 vice-presidential address to the American Association for the Advancement of Science on "the human faculty as determined by race" provided a precursor of his later unmitigated antiracism.

Putnam, newly appointed curator of anthropology at the American Museum of Natural History in New York, offered Boas temporary work preparing NWC life groups. An unappealing offer from the BAE galvanized Putnam into cobbling a position between the museum and Columbia University, facilitated by an anonymous salary donation from Uncle Jacobi. Boas persuaded banking magnate Morris K. Jesup to sponsor a North Pacific expedition to Siberia and the NWC that promised to resolve the American Indian origin question. Although the Jesup Expedition produced critical ethnography from Berthold Laufer, Waldemar Jochelson, Waldemar Bogoras, and Leo Sternberg, the final synthetic volume never appeared, and Jesup withdrew support for fieldwork after 1902.

In 1898 Boas and *W J McGee* of the BAE orchestrated an expansion of the *American Anthropologist* from an organ of the Anthropological Society of Washington into a national journal. Boas revived the defunct American Ethnological Society, putting New York (his domain) alongside Cambridge and Washington on the map of anthropological centers. The founding of the American Anthropological Association (AAA) in 1902, however, defeated Boas's plan for restricting membership to credentialed, employed professionals. Nonetheless, he served as AAA president in 1907–08.

Boas's appointment as lecturer at Columbia became permanent in 1899, with Jacobi again providing funds. Columbia students pursued their field research under museum auspices until Boas's resignation from the museum in 1905.

Boas was a pacifist during World War I, placing internationalist science above nationalism. His public accusations of spying by anthropologists in Mexico earned him censure by the AAA in 1919. Thereafter, however, American anthropology was dominated by Boas and his former students (Darnell 1998, Stocking 1968). Boas shifted to an activist position when the Nazis rose to power during the final decade of his life. Although he was previously an assimilationist Jew, after he retired from Columbia in 1938 he worked extensively against anti-Semitism.

Boasian historical particularism coalesced as a critique of evolution, particularly its premature generalization, around the analytic distinctiveness of race, language, and culture (1911a), the title of his 1940 collected essays. History incorporated the standpoint of the observer, the "native point of view." Also in 1911, *The Mind of Primitive Man* asserted the anthropological commitment to the psychic unity of humankind, alongside details of particular cultural histories. Despite positivist criticisms of his purportedly atheoretical stance, Boas's psychological and historical approach remains deeply embedded in Americanist anthropological practice (Darnell 2001). He was both an intellectual and an institutional leader, consolidating the four-field definition of anthropology and the "redemptive value" of cultural relativism as methodology (Cole 2000:276).

Boas died at lunch with colleagues in the Columbia Faculty Club on 21 December 1942, in the arms of Claude Lévi-Strauss (Lévi-Strauss and Eribon 1991:37–38).

REGNA DARNELL

William Henry Holmes
1909–1910

William Henry Holmes was born on a farm near Cadiz, Ohio, on 1 December 1846. While he completed his normal-school education he taught in alternate sessions, preparing for his intended career as a teacher. From an early age he had shown a talent and a love for drawing, and at the age of 24 he took the money his father had advanced him for further education and went to Washington DC to work with Theodore Kauffman, an established artist there. In Kauffman's studio Holmes met the daughter of Joseph Henry, the secretary of the Smithsonian Institution; during Holmes's first visit to the Smithsonian he was observed sketching and invited upstairs to meet some of the scientists. Through these associations Holmes was appointed in 1872 as painter to F.V. Hayden's Geological and Geographical Survey of the Territories, working for seven years in Yellowstone, Colorado, Arizona, and New Mexico; he saw his first cliff dwellings at Mesa Verde in 1875 on one of these surveys, and was fascinated by "clambering in the dusty, smoke-blackened rooms of the ancient people" (Hough 1933:752).

In 1879 Holmes traveled to Italy and Germany to study art. He returned to join the new U.S. Geological Survey (USGS) as a "geological assistant." He served as a (USGS) geologist throughout the 1880s; on a trip to Mexico City in 1884 he happened upon an excavation at a brick factory that led him to recognize the principle of stratigraphic sequence in archaeology (Holmes 1885). Although Thomas Jefferson had recognized stratigraphy in his excavation of a Virginia burial mound, and it would take the later work of Manuel Gamio and *Nels C. Nelson* to make stratigraphy a regular component of archaeological work, Holmes's contribution remains noteworthy.

Throughout this period Holmes continued his artwork, producing illustrations for the first two volumes of the annual report of the Bureau of American Ethnology (BAE). He was made the honorary curator of aboriginal ceramics in the National Museum in 1882, and in 1889 he left the USGS for the BAE. He was then officially an archeologist rather than a geologist, and one of the responsibilities he received from bureau director John Wesley Powell was to counter the arguments for "Paleolithic Man" in the New World. This took several forms, but most notable was his detailed study of stone tools in the tidewater area of Virginia and Maryland (Holmes 1897), which won the $1000 Loubat prize in 1898 "for the outstanding contribution in the archaeological field during the preceding five years." The study confirmed Holmes's position as a significant figure in American anthropology.

Earlier, Holmes had received recognition for his Smithsonian exhibits at the 1893 World's Columbian Exposition in Chicago. He was one of the first to use life-size models in anthropology exhibits. Afterward Holmes was put in charge of the Field Museum, which included *Frederic Ward Putnam*'s and *Franz Boas*'s exhibits from the exposition. He returned to Washington in 1897 to head the anthropology department in the National Museum. Holmes and Boas had long had an antagonistic relationship, exacerbated by the Loubat prize (for which Boas was the runner-up). When Powell died in 1902 Holmes was appointed his successor as bureau head—over *W J McGee*, who had been acting director and who had ties to Boas. McGee deeply resented Holmes's appointment, and Boas strongly and publicly protested it, but to no avail. Holmes requested the title of chief rather than director and a lower salary than Powell's to indicate his lack of desire for the position. Boas and Holmes then perforce had to work together for many years; "Boas was hostile and Holmes slightly condescending," notes Mark (1980:160), but to some extent they were jointly responsible for many of the important works published by the BAE during this period. Even so, Holmes was shy and according to many not a particularly effective leader for the BAE, and at least partly responsible for its decline. In 1909 he resigned from the BAE to return to the National Museum.

The crowning blow in the Holmes-Boas relationship was the 1919 resolution of censure written by Holmes against Boas over his public opposition to World War I, to President Wilson, and to certain anthropologists he had characterized as spies. This resolution resulted in Boas's exclusion from the Council of the American Anthropological Association and from the National Research Council—where Holmes felt he was being squeezed out. Ironically, the resolution was among Holmes's last acts as an anthropologist; in 1920 he left the National Museum to head the new National Gallery of Art. His left leg had to be amputated above the knee in 1926, but he continued to work. He had married Katherine Osgood in 1883, and they had two sons; when he retired from the National Gallery in 1932 he moved in with one of his sons in Royal Oak, Michigan. He died there on 20 April 1933.

In addition to the 1898 Loubat prize, Holmes won another in 1920. He was a member of the National Academy of Sciences and many national and international professional societies in both the arts and the sciences. He served terms as president of the Washington Academy of Sciences and the National Institute of Fine Arts, as well as the AAA. Wiry and remarkable agile, he was also a noted mountain climber and was credited with several first ascents in the Rockies; two mountains were also named for him. He was a classic generalist, and he often said that "the broader your foundation, the better your results will be" (quoted in Hough 1933:754).

FREDERIC W. GLEACH

Jesse Walter Fewkes
1911–1912

J esse Walter Fewkes was born in Newton, Massachusetts, on 14
November 1850. He entered Harvard University in 1871 and graduated four years later with honors and as a member of Phi Beta
Kappa. He received his A.M. and Ph.D. from Harvard in 1877 and
then studied zoology for three years at Leipzig University, Germany.
He returned to work at the Museum of Comparative Zoology at
Harvard. Fewkes became widely known as a marine zoologist, publishing 69 works on the subject, but during a trip to California in 1888
he encountered Pueblo Indians along the route of the Santa Fe Railroad and became interested in ethnological studies.

Following Frank Hamilton Cushing's work with the Zunis, Fewkes
was appointed leader of the Hemenway Expedition in 1890. Cushing
was furious at being replaced, particularly by someone he viewed as an
unqualified newcomer with Harvard degrees. Fewkes first continued
to work with the Zunis but later shifted his research to the Hopis. He

was the first to use the phonograph to record and study Native American music (Fewkes 1890), testing it with the Passamaquoddies in 1889 and then taking it to the Zunis and Hopis in 1890 and 1891. He also studied Hopi ceremonies over the full course of the calendar year as one of his first projects with them, bringing to his ethnological research the sense of detail he developed in his work in the natural sciences. Fewkes edited the *Journal of American Ethnology and Archaeology* from 1890 to 1894, and was appointed to the Bureau of American Ethnology (BAE) in 1895, following Mary Hemenway's death in 1894.

Typical of the period, and particularly of research in the Southwest, Fewkes was actively involved in both ethnological and archaeological research. Archaeological interpretation was then still in its infancy, and Fewkes's study and knowledge of contemporary Pueblo cultures offered comparative data to make sense of the archaeological findings. Relations between Native peoples, cultural anthropologists, and archaeologists are today being rekindled in productive ways. The roots of this practice can be seen in the work of Fewkes and others in the Southwest.

From 1902 to 1904 Fewkes conducted archaeological and ethnographic research in Puerto Rico, Cuba, and other islands of the West Indies, resulting in a monograph published by the BAE (Fewkes 1907); he later returned to this area for further research (Fewkes 1922). His initial goal was to learn more about the prehistoric inhabitants of Puerto Rico, the recently acquired U.S. possession, but he quickly learned that in order to understand the island's prehistory it was necessary to consider the broader context of the Caribbean, South America, and the southeastern United States. Building on his experience in the Southwest, Fewkes consciously applied what he termed the historical, archaeological, and ethnological methods to this study, but the focus of his research was on the archaeological collections.

After a brief survey in eastern Mexico, Fewkes returned to work with the Puebloan cultures of the Southwest, and particularly with their connections to the archaeological sites of the area. Through the traditions of Hopi clans, Fewkes gained understanding of their origin stories and of the distributions of clan totems, and through his discussions with Hopis he was able to identify certain archaeological sites as named settlements. He also recognized the importance of naming them in his work "Hopi" rather than the then widely used "Moqui," the latter being a derisive Navajo term for them ("The Dead Ones"), the former their name for themselves ("Peaceful People").

In 1908–09 Fewkes worked on the excavation and restoration of Casa Grande in Arizona and Cliff Palace and Spruce Tree House in Colorado. Over several years in the 1910s he worked on the excavation and restoration of the Cliff Dweller sites at Mesa Verde in Colorado, following its transfer to the National Park Service. While Fewkes was not a great innovator in archaeological excavation, he was an early proponent of the potential educational and economic value of archaeological sites through their restoration, interpretation, and protection as national monuments. He was also a proponent of employing the knowledge of Native elders in this enterprise through ethnology. His vast archaeological collections are largely in the Smithsonian Institution.

Fewkes continued with the BAE throughout this period, and in 1918 he was appointed its chief. He retired from the BAE in 1928 due to illness. According to Hough (1934:267), Fewkes was "a likable, friendly man . . . [who] delighted to communicate his knowledge to all and common," although he also had his detractors. By the end of his career his methods seemed old-fashioned to some; he neglected developments in stratigraphic research, for example.

Fewkes was active in professional societies, and he received a number of honors. He was president of the American Anthropological Association in 1911–12 and a vice president of the American Association for the Advancement of Science in 1905 and 1912–13. While AAA president he worked to improve ties with other learned societies (partly to increase AAA membership), and he made operating funds available to the editor of the *American Anthropologist* for the first time. He also supported efforts to publish a comprehensive bibliography of Americanist anthropology.

Fewkes was made a Knight of the Royal Order of *Isabela la Católica* in recognition of his work at the 1892 Columbian Historical Exhibition in Madrid. The following year he received a gold medal, "*Literis et Artibus*," from King Oscar of Sweden for his scientific research. In 1915 he was awarded the degree of LL.D. by the University of Arizona for services in anthropology.

Fewkes was married twice. He married Florence George Eastman in 1883; she died in 1888. In 1893 he married Harriet Olivia Cutler. Fewkes died on 31 May 1930, following his wife by only a few weeks.

FREDERIC W. GLEACH

Roland B. Dixon
1913–1914

As a student of *Frederic Ward Putnam* and *Franz Boas* and a contemporary of *Alfred L. Kroeber* and Earnest Hooton, Roland Burrage Dixon exemplifies the shifts and tensions in anthropology at the turn of the 20th century. Born in Worcester on 6 November 1875 to Louis Seaver Dixon and Ellen R. Burrage, Dixon lived in Massachusetts his entire life, spent his career in the service of Harvard University, and died at his home in Cambridge in 1934. Prepared at the Hopkinson School in Boston, Dixon proceeded to Harvard University, earning an A.B. in 1897, an A.M. in 1899, and a Ph.D. in 1900. In 1901 Dixon was appointed instructor in anthropology at Harvard. Although a respected teacher, he is best remembered for his meticulous supervision of the Library of the Peabody Museum of American Ethnology and Archeology (beginning in 1904) and his service as the museum's curator of ethnology (beginning in 1912).

Dixon's career not only spanned the discipline's move from museum ethnology to academic institutions, but his diverse research also high-lights the advantages and liabilities of the four-field approach. Dixon began his formal anthropological training in 1897 when he was ap-pointed an assistant in anthropology at the Peabody Museum. His train-ing as an anthropologist coincided with the growth of ethnological museums and, at first, focused heavily on obtaining archaeological ar-tifacts for the ethnology collection at the American Museum of Natu-ral History, where Putnam was curator.

Caught between the social evolutionary theories of Lewis Henry Morgan and Edward B. Tylor and a diffusionist paradigm of culture history, Dixon's work with the Jesup North Pacific Expedition (1898–1905) was a mixture of artifact collection and cultural documentation. With encouragement from Boas, his supervisor, Dixon used the Jesup Expedition to expand into collecting folk tales, taking plaster casts of heads and bodies, and interviewing locals for ethnological informa-tion. In 1899, after taking a course in Indian linguistics at Columbia, Dixon put his newly acquired methodological skills to practice among the Maidus on the Huntington California Expedition.

Dixon's thesis on the Maidu language earned him Harvard's second Ph.D. in anthropology in 1900 and sparked a life-long interest in the diffusion of language and artifacts. In a recent reflection on Dixon's contribution to California ethnology, Bruce Bernstein suggests that Dixon's "collections are of continuing importance because of their generally good documentation, firm collection dates, and location of purchase" (1993:21).

Although Dixon continued to write about and systematically collect examples of indigenous Californian culture throughout the 1910s, by the 1920s he had enlarged his geographic focus to include Mongolia, Siberia, South America, Asia, and Oceania. Consequently, the subjects of Dixon's later publications ranged from comparative interpretations of Aboriginal myth and folklore, to physiological comparisons between populations throughout the world, to theories of migration. Dixon adopted Boas's four-field methodology and critiqued *Clark Wissler's* ren-dition of diffusion.

Although Dixon collected many types of data in the field, including physical measurements and plaster casts, his work prior to 1920 did not venture explicitly into physical anthropology. In 1923 he combined the physical data from his world travels with his interest in diffusion in *The Racial History of Man*. In keeping with the hierarchical and eugenic tone typical of his time, Dixon constructed his own typological scheme of physical traits (head size, face width, nose breadth, and cranial capacity) to suggest that most populations have long been racially mixed. The book was critiqued for its analysis of climate-determined character assessments and for the historical and geographic factors Dixon used to explain his typology (Kroeber 1936). Although Dixon was criticized for his methodology at the time, his use of multiple indices became the standard measuring procedure for physical anthropology.

In a shift from physical anthropology back toward material culture, *The Building of Cultures* (1928) examined the migration of people through the distribution of various cultural objects and forms, such as moccasins, horses, tobacco, the sun dance, and myths. Again analyzing trait complexes rather than a single cultural trait, Dixon outlined the text's paradigm and goals: "In the origin and growth of human culture there are three primary factors involved; those, namely, of environment, of diffusion, and of nationality or race … [Here] I shall endeavor to show in what fashion and to what extent each of these factors is active and how, through their interaction, the building of cultures takes place" (1928:5). Although Kroeber suggested that "Dixon's finest and richest vein of scholarship [was] developed in special papers on problems involving geographic, cultural, and historical comparisons" (1936:296), it was his geographically broad, hierarchically informed, and reductionist approach that became the focus of criticism (Moos 1975).

As a professor of anthropology, Dixon taught courses that have been described as "encyclopedic outpouring[s] of carefully organized information pertaining to primitive peoples and cultures" (Hooton 1935:773). Additionally, in the midst of tirelessly conducting research, analyzing data, supervising students and indexing anthropological sources for the Peabody Museum Library, Dixon also participated in public anthropology. Like many anthropologists of his era, Dixon was called on by the U.S. government for his expertise. In 1920 he compiled an exhaustive enumeration of native Californian languages and tribes for the Bureau of the Census. Additionally, he served as a member of the House Commission on the Political Conditions in Central Asia (1918) and the American Commission to Negotiate Peace (1919). Dixon also held membership in many professional societies, including the American Antiquarian Society, and he served as president of the American Folklore Society.

In his personal life, Dixon was a private and solitary man. Kroeber, one of his closest associates, described Dixon as a lover of the outdoors and a man of few intimacies—"a naturalist translated into a scholar in the field of culture history" (Kroeber 1936:297). Nonetheless, Dixon maintained a reputation as a "pleasant and courteous companion" (Hooton 1935:774), respected lecturer, and excellent supervisor of graduate students. "Dixon's most valuable pedagogical function was the supervision of the research of graduate students," Hooton writes. "He was a most exacting taskmaster, rigid in his insistence upon exhaustive bibliographical study, meticulous sifting of evidence, and the deduction of logical conclusions" (1935:773). Dixon was also described as "one of the most erudite ethnographers of all time" (Tozzer 1936:294).

KATHERINE LAMBERT-PENNINGTON

Frederick Webb Hodge
1915–1916

Frederick Webb Hodge was born in Plymouth, England, on 28 October 1864. At the age of seven he moved with his parents to Washington DC. He attended public schools, and then Columbian College (later George Washington University). After college he worked as a legal secretary in Washington, and then as stenographer for the U.S. Geological Survey. In 1886 he was chosen by Frank Hamilton Cushing as field secretary of the Hemenway Expedition, and left with Cushing in 1889. Hodge later joked that what he remembered best of that expedition "was the water he drank from the Hasayampa, that fabled tributary of the Gila whose waters are said to make one's speech super-factual" (Powell 1954:159). He was critical of Cushing's archaeological work but married his sister-in-law, Margaret W. Magill, in 1891.

Returning to Washington, Hodge was appointed to the staff of the Bureau of American Ethnology (BAE), where his knowledge of the Southwest was quickly put to use. When the bureau moved in 1893 Hodge was appointed librarian in addition to his other duties; he proceeded to catalog and rearrange the collection, and he expanded the exchange program to further develop the holdings. By the summer of 1894 Hodge was doing much of the editorial work for the BAE; his editorial and clerical abilities contributed to several of his most notable projects. He played a major role in founding the American Anthropological Association (AAA), and he edited the *American Anthropologist* from 1899 to 1914 (except for 1911, when he resigned and was replaced by *John R. Swanton*; he returned the following year when operating funds were guaranteed).

Hodge transferred to the Smithsonian Institution in 1901 to direct International Exchanges. He returned to the BAE in 1905, serving there as "ethnologist-in-charge" from 1910 to 1918, preferring that title to *William Henry Holmes's* "chief." During this period with the BAE he completed the work of editing *The Handbook of American Indians North of Mexico*, which was immediately recognized for its importance. It remains one of the most widely used works in American anthropology. While Hodge had editorial responsibility for many BAE projects, he had been working on the compilation of information for the handbook since 1893 and wrote many of the entries himself. In addition to BAE editor, Hodge also served as editor for Edward S. Curtis's landmark 20-volume set, *The North American Indian*, the narratives of Cabeza de Vaca and Coronado (in Hodge and Lewis 1907), and a number of other volumes and journals.

In 1918 Hodge left Washington to serve as assistant director and editor for the Museum of the American Indian, Heye Foundation, a position that allowed him to return to archaeological work in the Southwest. His most important work there was at the historic Zuni village of Hawikuh, one of the "Seven Cities of Cibola," excavated from 1916 to 1923. Hodge produced several small volumes on this work; the excavation report was published after his death. In New York Hodge also chaired the editorial board for "the first exhibition of American Indian art selected entirely with consideration of esthetic value" in 1930; the catalog published by the Exposition of Indian Tribal Arts in 1931 truly served as an *Introduction to American Indian Art* for many people. In 1932 he moved to Los Angeles as the director of the Southwest Museum and the editor of its publications; he retired from there in 1956 to Santa Fe, where he hoped to spend the rest of his years doing research and writing on the Southwest. He died just months later. Hodge was working on several projects at the time, including a study of the Apaches in connection with land claims for the Department of Justice.

Hodge was very active in professional and scholarly societies. They included, in addition to the AAA, the American Association for the Advancement of Science, the National Research Council (where he completed *Franz Boas*'s term after Boas was censured in 1919, as well as being elected on his own), the American Antiquarian Society, the American Ethnological Society, the Society for American Archeology, the Western Museums Conference, and many others. He was awarded an honorary Sc.D. by Pomona College in 1933, an LL.D. by the University of New Mexico in 1934, and a Litt.D. by the University of Southern California in 1943. Hodge was listed in the faculty of anthropology at USC, but characteristically objected to being addressed as "professor" or "doctor." He was also active as an advisor and a trustee for the Heard Museum and the School of American Research, among others.

Hodge was remembered by many for his gentle good nature, his hard work, and his attention to detail, which was masked by his casual appearance. He was also a practical joker and a fine storyteller. He was married a second time, to Zarah H. Preble, who died in 1934. In 1936 he married author and artist Gene Meany. At the time of his death, on 28 September 1956, he had one daughter and several grandchildren and great-grandchildren. Hodge's obituary in *American Antiquity* (Judd, Harrington and Lothrop 1957) was accompanied by a poem written by his widow. Inspired by a Navajo prayer, it reads in part:

> After a happy day in the mountains,
> Fred quickly slipped away.

> "It is finished in Beauty,"
> Says a Navaho prayer, and
> All who love Téluli know

"Beauty is before him as he goes,
Beauty is behind him,
He walked in Beauty,
In Beauty . . . it is finished."

Hodge was known affectionately to friends as Téluli; the name means "Dig Your Cellar" in Zuni and was given to him in 1886 by the three Zunis who accompanied the Hemenway Expedition.

FREDERIC W. GLEACH

Alfred L. Kroeber
1917–1918

Alfred Louis Kroeber was born on 11 June 1876 in Hoboken,
New Jersey. He was the oldest child of Florence Kroeber, a
prosperous importer of clocks whose immigrant father fought
in the American Civil War, and Johanna Muller ("Mimi") Kroeber, an
American of German descent. Although the family was Protestant, Alfred
grew up in an upper-middle-class German-Jewish neighborhood in
Manhattan, roaming Central Park and nearby farms. His fascination
with grammar came not from German, his first language, but from his
childhood study of Greek and Latin. He was first taught by a tutor, Dr.
Hans Bamberger, who emphasized natural history. He then attended
the Ethical Culture School (founded in 1876 by agnostic rabbi Felix
Adler and integrating post-Darwinian natural science and humanism)
and Dr. Sachs's Collegiate Institute.

Kroeber entered Columbia College in 1892 at age 16, receiving an

A.B. in 1896 and an M.A. in 1897 in English. With a few friends, including Carl Alsberg (later director of the Food and Drug Administration and a lifelong friend), he founded a literary magazine *The Morningside* in which he foregrounded culture history. When *Franz Boas* arrived at Columbia in 1896, Kroeber and two others enrolled in his first American Indian languages course, which met weekly at Boas's home. The next semester he added statistics and physical anthropology. After a fellowship in anthropology in 1898 at the American Museum of Natural History, Kroeber spent the summer in Wyoming with the Arapahos, researching material for his dissertation on their decorative symbolism.

In 1900 Kroeber became a curator at the California Academy of Sciences in San Francisco and began his lifelong fieldwork with the Yuroks and Mohaves. After a year, local philanthropist Phoebe Apperson Hearst agreed with University of California president Benjamin Ide Wheeler to pay Kroeber's salary for five years to curate her archaeological collections and teach anthropology at Berkeley. *Frederic Ward Putnam* was chair in absentia for several years, and linguist Pliny Earl Goddard also taught. Kroeber became an assistant professor in 1906, an associate professor in 1911, and a professor in 1919. After Putnam's retirement, ornithologist Edward Winslow Gifford became curator. Popular lecturer T. T. Waterman filled out the early faculty. The department's first Ph.D., on Pomo basketry, went to Samuel A. Barrett in 1908. Archaeologist Duncan Strong followed in 1926. In 1918 Kroeber hired fellow Boasian *Robert H. Lowie*. Physical anthropology and archaeology came much later. The permanent museum did not open until 1959.

Kroeber's early San Francisco years included several traumas. His wife, Henrietta Rothschild, whom he had married in 1906, died of tuberculosis in 1913. An infection resulted in loss of hearing in one ear. Kroeber became close to Ishi, the "wild" last survivor of the Yahi tribe, who lived at the museum for several years before dying of tuberculosis in 1916. In 1915–16, during a sabbatical in Vienna, Kroeber began to explore psychoanalysis, spending the next year in analysis in New York. After two years as a lay analyst in Berkeley, Kroeber chose to continue his career only in anthropology, and his ideas in the two fields remained separate. Culture, for Kroeber, was "superorganic," having little to do with psychology or the individual. In 1917 he moved from San Francisco to the Faculty Club in Berkeley.

Kroeber's mandate in California was to map the diverse cultures and languages of the state; linguistic classification provided the organizing principle. Kroeber was not primarily a linguist, but he collected data for others to synthesize. With *Roland B. Dixon* of Harvard he mapped the languages of the state, gradually coming to see them as genetically related. His almost daily consultation with *Edward Sapir* from 1911 to 1913 culminated in Sapir's six linguistic stocks for all of North America. Linguistics remained part of Kroeber's definition of anthropology, although his own contributions came only at the beginning and end of his career (Hymes 1961). His 1909 "Classificatory Systems of Relationship" pioneered the search for universal semantic features of kinship terms. The *Handbook of California Indians* appeared in 1925.

At Zuni in 1915 Kroeber studied child language acquisition and developed seriation for archaeological surveys. In 1924 he pursued interests in Mexican and Peruvian archaeology. His textbook *Anthropology* (1923), more than any other work, codified Boasian anthropology and marked the discipline's coming of age.

In 1926 Kroeber married Theodora Krakaw Brown, a widow with two sons, whom he adopted. They bought a redwood house in Berkeley and had two more children: Karl, later an English professor who drew American Indian literature into the canon, and Ursula (LeGuin), a writer of anthropologically sophisticated science fiction.

In the early 1930s Kroeber's research team collected culture element lists. *Cultural and Natural Areas of Native North America* (1939) generalized his ecological and taxonomic efforts. Kroeber's work and personality evinced remarkable continuity. His widow and biographer, Theodora, spoke of a consistent "personal configuration." Cultural relativism, for him, was part of a methodology of cross-cultural comparison that focused on style and pattern, holistic and unique to each culture. Kroeber's *Configurations of Culture Growth* (1944), despite the failure of his hoped-for correlations, culminated his interests in diverse human civilizations as well as so-called primitive cultures; *Style and Civilization* (1957), in which he demonstrated correlation between women's hemlines and periods of political upheaval, provided a more accessible version of his argument. *The Nature of Culture* (1952) collected his early theoretical essays, including "The Superorganic" (1917). His humanistically inclined essays appeared posthumously in *An Anthropologist Looks at History* (1963).

Kroeber appreciated analytic distance. He avoided political questions and applied anthropology, seeing these as separate from the work of a scientist. He sided with the conservatives in opposing the 1946 reorganization of the American Anthropological Association, preferring a loose aggregation of scholars sharing a journal (Steward 1973:21–22), and rarely entered into Indian land claims cases.

During World War II, Kroeber postponed retirement to direct the Army Specialized Training Program. He recovered from a serious heart attack and retired in 1946 in time to receive the Huxley Medal in England. After retirement Kroeber taught at Columbia, Harvard, Yale, Chicago, and Brandeis; he was twice a fellow at the Stanford Institute for Advanced Studies in the Behavioral Sciences. He also revised his textbook *Anthropology* (1948) and attended myriad conferences, becoming a spokesperson for the discipline of anthropology. Kroeber suffered a fatal heart attack in Paris while vacationing after a Wenner-Gren conference in the fall of 1960.

REGNA DARNELL

Clark Wissler
1919–1920

C larkson Davis Wissler was born on 18 September 1870 on a farm near Cambridge City, Indiana. He was the oldest of seven children of Benjamin Wissler, whose family came to Pennsylvania from Swabia, and Sylvania Needler, whose English ancestors settled in Indiana after the American Revolution. Benjamin Wissler was a farmer and sometime school superintendent and county newspaper editor.

After finishing high school Wissler taught in local rural schools for four years and was principal of Hagerstown High, his alma mater, for one year. He attended summer classes at nearby Purdue University while saving money to enroll at Indiana University in 1893. He received an A.B. in 1897 and an M.A. two years later, both in experimental psychology. He worked one summer for G. Stanley Hall at Clark University, serving concurrently as an instructor in psychology and in education at Ohio State University from 1897 to 1899.

Wissler became an assistant in psychology at Columbia University in 1899 and a university fellow in psychology the following year, receiving his Ph.D. in psychology under James McKeen Cattell in 1901. He continued researching individual differences in Cattell's laboratory while he was an instructor in pedagogy at New York University in 1901–02. From 1903 to 1909 he was an assistant, then a lecturer, in anthropology at Columbia. He then suffered a serious illness.

Wissler's ambivalence toward Boasian anthropology dates to his graduate years. Cattell and *Franz Boas* had adjacent offices and were professionally cordial. Cattell had chaired the Department of Anthropology and Psychology from 1896 until anthropology became independent in 1902. In Wissler's last term, he took three courses in anthropology, one each with Livingston Farrand and Boas, the third jointly taught by them. Nonetheless, Wissler remained an experimental psychologist like his supervisor, Cattell.

His decision to pursue a career in anthropology probably arose from the expedient spate of "expeditionary activity" at the American Museum of Natural History (Kroeber 1948:1); more jobs were available in a young discipline. Founded in 1869, the museum established a department of anthropology in 1873. In 1902 Wissler became an assistant in ethnology under Boas; *Marshall H. Saville* headed the archaeology division. Wissler became assistant curator of ethnology in 1904, and acting curator of ethnology a year later when Boas precipitously resigned amidst a vitriolic dispute with the museum administration over Boas's failure to present a final report for his ambitious Jesup North Pacific Expedition. The ethnographic results were eventually published, but Boas never wrote the planned synthetic volume on American Indian origins.

Wissler was caught in the middle; although he protested his innocence, Boas considered him disloyal. Wissler was also teaching part-time at Columbia, where Boas attempted to force his choice between the two institutions, insinuating that Wissler would regret his choice. Due to Farrand's intervention, Wissler continued at Columbia until his health broke down in 1909, the same year Pliny Earl Goddard was appointed associate curator at the museum.

Increasingly, Wissler's vocation lay with the museum. Archaeology and ethnology merged in 1907, and Wissler became curator of the Department of Anthropology, a position he held until his retirement in 1942. He was more successful than Boas at reconciling the museum's emphasis on popular education with scientific research, perhaps because Wissler was "quiet, reserved, a compromiser, not a charismatic figure" (Freed and Freed 1983:801).

Boas's own power base in New York had been constructed on the joint resources of university and museum (Darnell 1998); when he retreated to the academy, his enthusiasm for museum collaboration declined dramatically. Boas apparently carried the grudge for years; communication between the two institutions proceeded largely by terse, albeit civil, correspondence. Although Wissler's anthropology was in many respects Boasian, he was never part of the inner circle and "apparently was not at ease with Boas" (Freed and Freed 1983:806). Wissler was, however, among Boas's supporters when the American Anthropological Association Council censured Boas in 1919 for his letter to *The Nation* accusing anthropologists of acting as spies in Mexico.

From 1924 to 1940 Wissler sought teaching opportunities at Yale University that were unavailable at the museum. Initially, he was a researcher in Yale's new interdisciplinary Institute of Psychology, and later he worked in the Institute of Human Relations. When *Edward Sapir* established an independent department of anthropology in 1931 Wissler became professor of anthropology. He commuted to New Haven by train, lecturing and meeting students on Saturdays to avoid interference with his museum obligations. David Mandelbaum was among the Yale graduate students for whom Wissler funded fieldwork through the museum.

Wissler's Plains research program aspired to a coherent theory of culture change. His personal fieldwork with the Dakotas, the Gros Ventres, and the Blackfoot from 1902 to 1905 resulted in eleven monographs, seven of them on the Blackfoot. Leslie Spier's theoretical paper on the Plains sun dance in 1921 exemplifies the comparative project.

Although Wissler has not been remembered as a theoretician, he contributed two textbooks to the codification of Boasian anthropology (Darnell 1998): *The American Indian* (1917) and *Man and Culture* (1923). Freed and Freed (1983:800) suggest that he offered a "nomothetic alternative" to historical particularism, developing ideas that were implicit in the anthropology of the period, clarifying the concepts, and applying them to a large body of data.

Wissler's definition of culture went beyond the descriptive to include normative, learned complexes of ideas. For Wissler, environmental adaptation became social habit. The culture area explained culture change by diffusion; the equilibrium of trait-complexes could be disrupted by environmental change, population pressure, or external influences. Culture pattern determined which traits would be adopted and incorporated. The material and economic generally outweighed the ceremonial and social in defining culture areas for Wissler, who distinguished between typical and marginal tribes by the number of defining trait-complexes; the age and area hypothesis, deriving the antiquity of elements from their distribution, was less widely accepted than the culture area or culture pattern. Wissler also proposed a "universal pattern of culture," the elements of which were found everywhere, differing little between primitive and civilized yet leaving room for individual creativity.

In 1899 Wissler married Etta Viola Gebhart. They had two children; their daughter, Mary Viola, was a librarian at the American Museum of Natural History. Wissler died on 25 August 1947 in New York City.

REGNA DARNELL

William Curtis Farabee
1921–1922

William Curtis Farabee was born on 7 February 1865 in Washington, Pennsylvania. He received his A.B. in 1894 from Waynesburg College in Pennsylvania and his M.A. in 1900 from Harvard. In between degrees he taught for two years in Pennsylvania public schools and was principal of an academy at Jackson Center for four years. In 1901 he was appointed Austin Teaching Fellow at Harvard and began work toward his Ph.D., which he received in 1903; his thesis on genetics has been called the first demonstration of Mendelian heredity in humans (Brew 1968:17).

After receiving his Ph.D., Farabee remained at Harvard for the next ten years. In 1905 he and Vilhjalmur Stefansson took a group of undergraduate students to Iceland, crossing the island from Reykjavik to Akureyi on ponies. Louis de Milhau, one of the students on the trip and later a patron of the Peabody Museum at Harvard, noted that

"Farabee, who in his school days had pitched on his school team, kept his pockets full of rocks, and by straight throwing discouraged a pony many a time from leaving its proper place with its comrades" (de Milhau 1940:63). From 1906 to 1909 Farabee led the de Milhau-Harvard expedition to the headwaters of the Amazon in eastern Peru.

In 1913 Farabee left Harvard to become the curator of American archaeology and ethnology at the University Museum, University of Pennsylvania. By the summer of 1914 he was already at work in the interior of southern British Guiana and northern Brazil, and in the region south of the Amazon. He also conducted archaeological excavations on the island of Marajo, uncovering a large collection of pottery. Out of this early research came two of his most important publications, *The Central Arawaks* and *The Central Caribs*. While in Barbados recuperating from the trip he met Theodore Roosevelt; they became lasting friends, sharing an interest in South America and naturalism.

Farabee returned to South America with trips to Colombia in 1920 and Chile and southern Peru in 1922. The hardships of his work regularly took a severe physical toll on him, as conveyed in his description toward the end of the 1914–15 trip:

> Physically we were all in a very bad condition. For two months we had had chills and fever continually. This, together with poor food or the lack of it, had reduced us to skeletons. I was forty-eight pounds lighter than when I started on the expedition. One of the Indians had dysentery and all were suffering from sore feet. Ogilvie had "Bush Yaws" which kept him in the doctor's care for many months, while I had beri-beri, according to the diagnosis of the natives. They pressed their fingers into my swollen feet and legs making deep dimples which would remain for a long time. They said I would get to Georgetown all right, but no one ever recovered. I was not alarmed, because I knew I was suffering from cold feet only. . . . Eight months afterwards I was able to lace my shoes again. (Farabee 1917:101)

On the 1922 trip he became quite ill, and he returned to Philadelphia in 1923. But the pernicious anemia had progressed too far to be controlled, and after a long decline he died on 24 June 1925, at his birthplace.

Many of Farabee's South American explorations constituted the first visit by a westerner to these areas, and his "discoveries" thus remain important, even though much of his work seems old-fashioned in the context of Boasian anthropology and the work of the Bureau of American Ethnology. In addition to his explorations, Farabee was involved in diplomatic work. In 1910 he served on a Peruvian commission to settle the border dispute between Peru and Ecuador (a dispute that has proved very difficult to settle), and in 1921 he represented the United States at Peru's Independence Centenary celebrations. After World War I, Farabee served as an expert on ethnic questions pertaining to the peace settlement for the U.S. Peace Commission, accompanying President Wilson to Paris for the talks.

Farabee was elected to the American Academy of Arts and Sciences, the American Association for the Advancement of Science, the American Philosophical Society, and the Royal Geographic Society of Great Britain, and became an honorary member of the American Geographical Society. He received the Elisha Kent Kane medal of the Philadelphia Geographical Society in 1917 and the Gold Medal of the Explorers Club of New York. He was an honorary member of the faculty of science at the University of San Marcos in Lima and belonged to the Ancient Order of El Sol there. During his time as American Anthropological Association president, the Central States section of the AAA was authorized and begun as "a Middle-western branch." Publication of the *American Anthropologist* was moved to a new printer in Menasha, Wisconsin, and the AAA pledged resources to "guarantee the continuance of the *American Journal of Physical Anthropology*" to the extent that they were available without sacrificing the *American Anthropologist*.

Farabee married Sylvia Manilla in 1897. They had no children. He was hailed after his death as friendly, warm-hearted, helpful, and a tireless worker. Despite his service to the AAA not long before his death, Farabee received only a one-sentence death notice in the *American Anthropologist*. His "monumental achievements in geographical explo-

ration and anthropological discovery" (Anon. 1925a:96) are mostly forgotten today. Years after Farabee's death, Harold Colton would remem-
ber that when people asked Farabee to tell of his adventures he would
reply, "I never have any. Adventures are caused by bad management"
(quoted in Colton 1961:2).

FREDERIC W. GLEACH

Walter Hough
1923–1924

Walter Hough was born in Morgantown, West Virginia, on 23 April 1859. He was the son of Lycurgus S. and Anna Fairchild Hough. After studying at the Morgantown Academy and at the Preparatory School of West Virginia Agricultural College, Hough enrolled in West Virginia University. He received his B.A. (Phi Beta Kappa) in 1883, his M.A. in 1884, and his Ph.D. in chemistry and geology in 1894. From childhood, Hough was fascinated by natural history. He collected fossils and local Indian artifacts in his spare time, and he became something of an expert on West Virginia's economic resources, particularly coal. Geology and paleontology succumbed, however, to "a deeper interest in primitive peoples and the rise of civilization in various parts of the world" (Judd 1936:472).

After teaching at a boy's school in Alton, Illinois, for a year, Hough was appointed in 1886 as a copyist in the Division of Ethnology of the U.S. National Museum. He was promoted to an aide in 1887 and an assistant curator in 1894. Head curator Otis T. Mason was impressed by his "ingrained studiousness" (Judd 1936:473). Hough was put to work cataloging the collections presented to the U.S. government at the Philadelphia Centennial Exposition of 1876. They had been placed in storage pending completion of the museum building, which was delayed until 1881. Hough produced a few short papers each year on the new accessions.

There were no academic programs in anthropology at the time, so apprenticeship on the job was the usual museum practice. Hough received most of his training in anthropology through his association with Mason and the coincidence of their interests in descriptive ethnology and museum display of material culture. Hough's interest in the relationship of culture and environment was perhaps a holdover from his initial training in geology. His "few interpretive efforts" were geared toward demonstrating "the generally progressive nature of man's inventive activities," according to his Bureau of American Ethnology colleague *Neil M. Judd* (Glenn 1991:306).

When Mason died in 1908, Hough became acting curator of the Division of Ethnology and acting head curator of the entire Department of Anthropology. Two years later he was appointed curator of ethnology. Although he was temporarily in charge of the Department of Anthropology from 1920 to 1923 after the retirement of *William Henry Holmes*, Hough did not receive the curatorship of the entire department until 1923; he continued to serve de facto as curator of ethnology. His position at the National Museum was twice extended for two-year periods beyond the customary government retirement age until 1932, when an executive order exempted him from compulsory retirement. He was only three months short of 50 years in public service when he died three years later, just before returning to work from "a fortnight's rest from the effects of a rather strenuous summer in Washington" (Judd 1936:473).

Most of Hough's museum career was spent in the laboratory, cataloging specimens and preparing data for copyists. "He joined the staff at the height of the exposition era, when nations, states, and cities were vying with each other in commemorating historical events of greater or lesser moment" (Judd 1936:473). Many of the exhibited materials ended up in the National Repository as a result of donations or museum collaborations. Between 1892 and 1926 the National Museum prepared exhibits for 16 expositions. Among the expositions Hough headed was the Columbian Historical Exposition in Madrid in 1892, for which he was made a knight of the Royal Order of Ysabel la Católica.

Hough carried out his first fieldwork in the summer of 1896 in New Mexico and Arizona, while he was on loan to the Bureau of American Ethnology as an assistant to *Jesse Walter Fewkes*; the fieldwork involved surveys of ruins on the Little Colorado and Gila Rivers. In 1899 he joined the ethnobotanical expedition of J. N. Rose to Mexico and helped to collect specimens. Between 1901 and 1905, with the support of Peter Goddard Gates, Hough continued archaeological surveys, particularly in the Holbrook region of Arizona, and initiated ethnological research among the Hopis (and other Pueblos), the Apaches, and the Navajos of New Mexico and Arizona. His own research in the Southwest thereafter focused alternately on archaeology and ethnology. The account of the Museum-Gates Expedition was published by the National Museum in 1901 and 1914 (Judd 1967:71).

Although Hough wrote briefly on many topics, he was best known for his explorations of the role of fire "as an agent of human culture" (Judd 1936:474). This and related articles about illumination and methods of cooking began appearing in 1888 in the first issue of the *American Anthropologist* (old series) and totaled 21 items in all. Because he answered public inquiries on a range of subjects in response to a variety of material objects in the collections of the Smithsonian Institution, Hough dealt with topics as diverse as dolls, weapons, musical instruments, and Chinese punishments. Like his mentor, Mason, Hough preferred to treat similar artifacts together regardless of their provenance, implicitly accepting an evolutionary typology quite at odds with *Franz Boas*'s insistence on arranging museum artifacts according to their cultural context and their everyday use.

The breadth of Hough's interests was not fully reflected in his 148 publications or in his professional practice. He was also an expert on English, French, and Italian china, Old English, old lace, violins and pianos, and the history of art. Woodcarving and painting were his hobbies.

Hough was one of the founding members of the American Anthropological Association, serving as president in 1924. He was vice president of Section H of the American Association for the Advancement of Science in 1904 and president of the Anthropological Society of Washington in 1908–09. He was also a member of the Sons of the American Revolution. Hough represented the Smithsonian Institution at the International Congress of Americanists in Huelva in 1892, in Québec in 1906, in Rio de Janeiro in 1922, and in New York City in 1928.

He married Myrtle Zuck of Holbrook, Arizona, on 29 December 1897. The couple had three children and seven grandchildren. Hough died at the age of 76 of a sudden heart attack at his home in Washington DC on 20 September 1935.

REGNA DARNELL

Aleš Hrdlička
1925–1926

Born on 29 March 1869 in the town of Humpolec in Bohemia, Aleš Hrdlička emigrated to New York with his family in 1881. Hrdlička's formal training was in medicine, but he developed an interest in the young science of physical anthropology while working at the New York Middletown State Homeopathic Hospital for the Insane. In 1896 he went to France to study anthropometrical methods with Léonce Manouvrier.

Manouvrier had inherited the mantle of French anthropology from Paul Broca, and he promoted a field that was more egalitarian and less quantitative than it had been in the 1860s. He distrusted statistics in anthropology as tools for hierarchical ranking (Hecht 1977). While much of Hrdlička's work on race does not hold up well in retrospect, it unequivocally breaks with the discredited polygenist "American school" of physical anthropology represented by Samuel George Morton, Josiah Nott, and George Gliddon in the mid-1800s. Hrdlička set out to professionalize physical anthropology and create a fundamental break with the past.

Hrdlička left medical practice in 1899 and worked on several anthropological projects under the aegis of the American Museum of Natural History and *Frederic Ward Putnam* of Harvard. In 1903 he was hired as an assistant curator by the Smithsonian Institution to found the Division of Physical Anthropology, which would be his base for the next 40 years.

In 1908 Hrdlička defined the scope of physical anthropology in the journal *Science*, identifying four main areas of inquiry for the emerging field. First, "the study of the normal white man living under average conditions . . . and the complete range of his variations." Second, "the structure, function, and chemical composition—with their variations—in the primates." Third, "development and variation in [human] structure . . . in relation to time." And fourth, "the human races and their subdivisions." This medical and typological orientation naturally reflected his training and interests.

Hrdlička's greatest talent was organizational. Building the Smithsonian's division into a world-class research facility in physical anthropology was but his first lasting contribution. Hrdlička also founded the *American Journal of Physical Anthropology* in 1918 (which he edited until his death in 1943), and the American Association of Physical Anthropologists, whose first meeting was convened in 1930.

His principal area of interest was the peopling of the New World. Hrdlička was a staunch defender of the view that the indigenous inhabitants of the Americas are descended from Asians and came across the Bering Strait fairly recently. While this is a mundane theoretical stance today, at the time it stood in opposition to the views of Daniel G. Brinton, who saw indigenous Americans as descended from Europeans, and of others who held that the peopling of the New World occurred in the more remote past than the terminal Pleistocene. Hrdlička conducted extensive fieldwork in Asia, Russia, Canada, and Alaska, throughout his career and was ever vigilant in debunking the claim for early entry of people into the Americas.

The common morphology of the central incisors ("shovel-shaped") among Neanderthals, Asians, and Native Americans led Hrdlička to place Neanderthals in the direct ancestry of the human species, a position he argued in the 1927 Huxley Memorial Lecture, "The Neanderthal Phase of Man." His significant full-length works include the manual *Anthropometry* (1920), and *The Skeletal Remains of Early Man* (1930). Somewhat paradoxically, his anthropometrical study published under the title *The Old Americans* is not about the indigenous inhabitants of the continent, but about the descendants of the first wave of European colonists.

Like many prominent scientists, Hrdlička was recruited by the American Eugenics Society, but unlike most, he expressed his displeasure early on at what it stood for. When the society promoted Nordic superiority, Hrdlička wrote to its president to complain as both a physical anthropologist and a proud Bohemian:

> I have only one country and that is the United States, though I am justly proud of Bohemia the country of my birth. But I know personally and quite well most of the peoples of Europe; I also know a good deal of their anthropological as well as their other history; and while I know well that some of these people are much poorer or much less educated than others, and while I cannot help but like some more than others, yet I am wholly unable to say that any one group has superior or inferior endowments mentally or even physically. Nor do I know of as yet any tests in 'psychology' that would show us, outside of pathological defects, more than superficialities that can be given but little weight in matters of this importance (Hrdlička to Irving Fisher, 27 November 1923, NAA).

Like many of his contemporaries, however, he believed that the structure of the brain might hold information relevant to understanding the behavioral differences among different cultures and races. Accordingly, in addition to skeletons he began to amass a collection of brains (Hrdlička, 1916), and nearly a century later it became newsworthy that he had ended up with the brain of Ishi, "the last wild Indian of California" (Kroeber 1961; Bower 2000) and Qisuk, a "New York Eskimo" (Hrdlička 1901; Harper 2000)

Hrdlička regarded the *American Journal of Physical Anthropology* almost literally as his baby. He saw little value in statistical analysis, experimental research, or genetics, a stance that younger colleagues found frustrating. "Statistics," he said at a meeting of the American Association of Physical Anthropologists, "will be the ruination of the science." His own methods were entirely descriptive, leading Ashley Montagu to characterize him as a scientific product of the 19th rather than the 20th century. He was also known as something of a misogynist and a prude, avowing that women have no place in science, and walking out of a paper on primate sex after declaring it an improper subject.

Hrdlička was supportive of his juniors, however, and he was widely acknowledged to be a generous and endearing man in private life. Believing that a medical education was vital to a physical anthropologist, he encouraged and even financed the medical education of some of his protégés. He was married twice, but had no children. He died on 5 September 1943 at the age of 74.

JONATHAN MARKS

Marshall H. Saville
1927–1928

Marshall Howard Saville was born in Rockport, Massachusetts, on 24 June 1867. After graduating from the Rockport high school, he studied anthropology from 1889 to 1994 at Harvard University as a special student; he was a fellow there and an assistant in the Peabody Museum from 1891 to 1993. As early as 1890 he had began to conduct fieldwork with the Peabody expeditions to the Yucatán Peninsula. In 1891–92 he returned to work at the Classic Maya site of Copan, Honduras—one of the first large-scale excavations in Mesoamerica. He spent much of 1893 excavating mound sites in southern Ohio, working under the direction of Peabody curator *Frederic Ward Putnam*. In 1893 Putnam placed him in charge of the Central American exhibit at the World's Columbian Exposition in Chicago. Also in 1893 he married Anne Lyons, of Salem, Massachusetts; they eventually had two sons.

Saville left Harvard for New York in 1894 to become assistant curator of anthropology at the American Museum of Natural History (AMNH); in 1905 he was appointed the museum's first curator of Mexican and Central American archaeology, having brought in collections from several parts of Mexico over the decade. In 1897–98 he excavated at Palenque, and from 1898 to 1904 he worked on the sites of Mitla and Oaxaca.

In 1903 Saville joined the faculty of Columbia University as professor of American archaeology, and in 1908 reduced his commitment to the AMNH to an honorary capacity, keeping the connection into 1910. In his early years at Columbia, Saville maintained a normal teaching load, but his real devotion was to research; over the years he spent increasingly more time in the field and correspondingly less in the classroom. Saville conducted excavations in Ecuador under Heye Foundation auspices in 1907, almost a decade before its Museum of the American Indian was founded. He joined the museum staff in 1918 and played an active part in its research program. He remained with the museum and Columbia until his retirement in 1932.

With these various connections providing a base in New York, Saville conducted numerous excavations from 1905 to 1921 in Peru, Ecuador, Colombia, Honduras, Guatemala, Costa Rica, and Mexico, producing extensive archaeological collections for the museums and many valuable publications. On his 22nd expedition to the tropics, Saville found in Ecuador human teeth with gold inlays that led him to reconsider other such examples in a review of pre-Columbian teeth decoration (1913). These expeditions were often made under difficult circumstances. Saville's 1915 expedition into the interior of Honduras was turned back by swarms of locusts. On a trip into Ecuador, after narrowly escaping death from a group of Indians, his men were jailed as spies by the government. Sometimes, truly, *plus ça change, plus c'est la même chose.*

During World War I, Saville served as a captain in the military intelligence division of the U.S. Army. After the war he produced his great synthetic works, all published by the Museum of the American Indian, Heye Foundation: *The Goldsmith's Art in Ancient Mexico* (1920), *Turquoise Mosiac Art in Ancient Mexico* (1922), and *The Woodcarver's Art in Ancient*

Mexico (1925); these works are largely descriptive and well illustrated, and they provided an accessible source for scholars and others to work from. Not coincidentally, the development of the great Mexican silver jewelry tradition by Fred Davis, William Spratling, and others inspired by pre-Columbian design, dates to the period after these publications; but this work was also foundational for the development of Latin American archaeology.

In addition to the volumes cited above, which drew on the extant literature in addition to his own research, Saville published more than a hundred articles and several other books, including field reports, descriptive syntheses, and compiled bibliographies. His first two volumes of the planned series Contributions to South American Archeology (1907–10) were lavishly published in a limited edition, but subsequent volumes were not completed. During the 1920s the Museum of the American Indian acquired several important chronicles of Spanish colonization in Mexico and Colombia, and Saville spent considerable time working on translations. By the mid-1920s he was severely ill and had several major operations; he was always impatient to get back to work. After he retired, Saville returned to the AMNH as an honorary curator.

In 1924–25 Saville was sent to Peru and Mexico as an official delegate of the United States to the Third Pan-American Scientific Conference; he was awarded an honorary doctorate in the Faculty of Sciences of the University of San Marcos in Lima in recognition of his archaeological contributions, and he was elected an honorary fellow of the Instituto Histórico del Peru and the Sociedad Geográfia de Lima. In 1933 he was also elected an honorary professor of the Museo Nacional in Mexico City. Saville was the founder of the Cortés Society, which published several important translations of documents on Latin America, and of the Sandy Bar Historical Society and Museum in Rockport, Massachusetts; he was also cofounder and vice president of the Explorers Club in New York. In addition to the American Anthropological Association, the American Antiquarian Society, and other American professional societies, Saville was an officer of the Académie Française, a corresponding member of the Royal Academy of Spain, and an honorary member of the Mexican Geographic Society.

Saville died on 7 May 1935 in New York after a long illness; "He went from his desk to the hospital bed, from which he did not arise" (Anon 1935:297). He was survived by his wife and sons; in addition to his publications and the museum collections, his professional legacy includes the gift of his library to the Huntington Free Library in New York.

FREDERIC W. GLEACH

Alfred M. Tozzer
1929–1930

A lfred Marston Tozzer was "born on the Fourth of July," 1877, in Lynn, Massachusetts. He was the older son of a pharmacist. Tozzer served during World War I as a captain in the Air Services, presiding over the Air Service examining boards in Denver and San Francisco. Upon discharge he was commissioned a major in the Reserve Corps and trained reserve officers at Harvard for ten years. During World War II he served as director of the Honolulu office of the OSS, where his responsibilities included the analysis of intercepted Japanese radio messages. Before, between, and after his military service, Tozzer built an exemplary scholarly career, making significant contributions to Mayan studies. When *Franz Boas* was censured in 1919, Tozzer was one of his few strong defenders.

After graduating from high school in Lynn, Tozzer entered Harvard, receiving his A.B. in 1900, his A.M. in 1901, and his Ph.D. in 1904. During this period he traveled extensively in Europe and participated

in linguistic, ethnographic, and archaeological fieldwork. His first fieldwork, on Native languages in California, was conducted in summer
and fall 1900 with *Roland B. Dixon.* The following summer he worked
with Navajos in New Mexico, taking part in the nine-day Night Chant
ceremony. In December 1901 he was appointed the first traveling fellow of the Archaeological Institute of America (AIA) and he left in early
1902 for the Yucatán. He spent four months learning Mayan and working with the hieroglyphic inscriptions at Chichén Itzá, where he wit-
nessed E. H. Thompson's fabled dredging of the Cenote of Sacrifice.
Although hampered by an insurrection in the eastern Yucatán peninsula, Tozzer stayed in the Yucatán for the next four years in the hope
that locating some hitherto unrecorded Mayan-speaking groups would
lead to deciphering the hieroglyphs. In 1903–04 he worked with the
Lacandones of Lake Pethá in southern Mexico, readily achieving rapport and intimacy with them and participating in a variety of ceremonial rites; they were linguistically similar to the Mayas he knew, but
they were among the least acculturated groups in the region. Although
Tozzer failed to decipher the hieroglyphs, his dissertation was drawn
from this work and later published by the AIA as *A Comparative Study of
the Maya and Lacandones* (1907).

After his degree in 1904 Tozzer worked in linguistics with Boas and
Adolphe Bandelier at Columbia University; his *A Grammar of the Maya
Language* was eventually published in 1921. He returned to southern
Mexico in 1905, and then settled in Cambridge. In that first term Tozzer
offered for the first time what became his most celebrated course, "Anthropology 9," a seminar on the Mayas," which probably propelled more
students into Maya archaeology than all other courses that have been
given before or since" (Phillips 1955:74). In the spring he made a lecture tour of the northeast for the AIA (repeating the experience in
1913), and spent the following summer doing archival research in Spain.
Tozzer first taught the introductory anthropology course for Harvard
in 1906–07 and continued to teach it for much of the next 40 years. He
was by most accounts a gifted and enthusiastic teacher who, without
proselytizing, convinced many students of the value of anthropology—
although Eleanor Leacock recalled his telling women students around

1940 that "if they wanted to be anthropologists, they better have independent means, because they would never get a job in anthropology" (Gailey 1989:216).

In summer 1907 an archaeological project in New Mexico crystallized Tozzer's long-standing interests in archaeology. His fieldwork from 1907 through 1914 focused on Mexican, and especially Mayan, archaeology, and he participated in the mapping of Tikal and Nakum and the discovery of Holmul, among other projects. In 1910–11, following a visit as representative of Harvard at the inauguration of the University of Mexico, he began offering his course on Mexico. For Tozzer, research, teaching, and leadership were always closely related; teaching the course on primitive society, which he first offered in 1911–12, resulted in the publication of *Social Origins and Social Continuities* (1925).

In 1913 Tozzer was appointed an assistant professor of anthropology for a five-year term and the curator of Middle American archaeology and ethnology at Harvard's Peabody Museum for an unlimited term. Also that spring he married Margaret Castle of Honolulu and from that time on made frequent trips to Hawaii. These visits inevitably generated in him an ethnographic interest that would later be applied in his service during World War II. In 1914 he succeeded Boas as the director of the International School of Archaeology and Ethnology in Mexico, arriving in Vera Cruz just in time to witness the shelling of the city by the U.S. Navy. This was to be his last working field trip to the area, although he made several later visits.

After the war Tozzer returned to Harvard and actively pursued teaching and administration. He quickly advanced through the professorial ranks, chaired the Division of Anthropology, and served in the administration of Radcliffe College and later Harvard, becoming a professor emeritus in 1948. He was elected president of the American Anthropological Association in 1928, the same year he joined the administrative board of Harvard, and served on the National Research Council and the Social Science Research Council; he was elected to the American Academy of Arts and Sciences, the American Philosophical Society, and the National Academy of Sciences. In 1950 he became the first recipient of the Alfred Vincent Kidder Award. The honor he was probably proudest of, however, was the book produced secretly by his students and colleagues and dedicated to him, *The Maya and Their Neighbors* (1940). For many years Tozzer devoted his spare time to the translation and annotation of *Landa's Relación de las Cosas de Yucatán* (1941). This work ultimately served as one of the keys to the translation of Mayan hieroglyphics that Tozzer had sought decades earlier.

Alfred Tozzer died on 5 October 1954. He was survived by his wife, one of their two daughters, and five grandchildren. Tozzer taught countless students in anthropology, and although he proclaimed a preference for the observable evidence of experience to abstract theory, his research contributed to the turn in Mayan studies from the descriptive to the analytical.

FREDERIC W. GLEACH

George G. MacCurdy
1931

George Grant MacCurdy was born in Warrensburg, Missouri, on 17 April 1863. His parents, Margaret J. and William Smith MacCurdy, were farmers who freed their slaves in Georgia and moved west until the Civil War caught up with them. MacCurdy worked in the fields as a child. At the age of 18 he began teaching school in Warrensburg to pay for his normal school training. Two years after graduation in 1887, he was already a school superintendent.

In 1891 MacCurdy matriculated with advanced standing at Harvard University on a scholarship. He studied biology and geology and spent a summer working in Alexander Agassiz's biological laboratory in Newport, Rhode Island. He received an A.B. in 1893 and an A.M. in 1894. Yale professor Edward Salisbury and his wife, a distant cousin of MacCurdy's, supported his further study. He went to Vienna in 1895, and in the following year he attended the International Zoological Congress in Leyden, where *Pithecanthropus erectus* remains were first exhibited. He went on to study paleoanthropology in Paris in 1896–97 and in Berlin in 1897–98.

MacCurdy returned to the United States as an instructor at Yale in 1898, where he remained until his retirement in 1931. He obtained a doctorate from Yale in 1905 while serving as curator of Old World prehistory at Yale's Peabody Museum; from 1910 to 1912 he also served as curator at the American Museum of Natural History in New York. In 1919 he married Glenn Bartlett, who shared his passion for prehistory and accompanied him in his travels and excavations thereafter.

In 1921 the couple joined Charles Peabody, the curator of European archaeology at the Peabody Museum of Harvard, in founding the American School in France for Prehistoric Studies, with MacCurdy as the first director. At the time, the two were "practically the only American scholars conversant with the field of European Prehistory and known and recognized by workers in that field" (Hooton 1950:513). Peabody served as director for the second year and *Aleš Hrdlička* the third, with MacCurdy resuming the office in 1924. After the first few years, MacCurdy carried most of the practical burden of organizing the summer excavations. His American colleagues and the American Anthropological Association (AAA), with the exception of *Nels C. Nelson* at the American Museum of Natural History and Aleš Hrdlička of the United States National Museum, did not play an active role.

After five years, the school was incorporated under a board of trustees with a view to training students through the excavation of prehistoric sites rather than classical Roman and Greek sites. Cooperative relations were rapidly established with the Archaeological Institute of America and the AAA. Until World War II excavations were carried out in the Dordogne each summer, often at a site leased by the Archaeological Society of Washington. Students were also encouraged to visit the major museums of Europe and establish contacts among European archaeologists.

A joint expedition with the British School of Archaeology in Jerusalem under Professor Dorothy Garrod in 1928 led to seven seasons at Mt. Carmel in Palestine, including the excavation of the well-known Neanderthal site there. The school never attained MacCurdy's dream of a separate physical home; its collections eventually went to Harvard's Peabody Museum. The school was also responsible for the central and southeastern European excavations of Vladimir Fewkes.

MacCurdy's curatorship at Yale's Peabody Museum necessarily involved him with Americanist archaeology, including studies of the art of Chiriqui and of skeletal material from Peru collected for Yale by Hiram Bingham. His two volumes on *Human Origins* (1924) included a gazetteer of sites that is of lasting value (McCown 1948:519). He helped organize an international symposium in Philadelphia on early humans and edited the proceedings, published as *Early Man* (1937).

For 40 years, MacCurdy reported regularly to his American colleagues on "significant discoveries abroad of ancient man and his culture" (McCown 1948:519), often in the *American Anthropologist*. These brief informative notes provided a professional service not otherwise available. From 1911 to 1918 and in 1925, MacCurdy wrote annual summaries of "Anthropology and Ethnology" for the *American Year Book*. He edited the *Bulletin of the American School of Prehistoric Research* from 1926 to 1939. This systematic dissemination of research results was crucial in linking prehistoric archaeology in Europe and America, and his own work on eoliths "is still worthy of perusal" (Hooton 1950:513). Alumni of the American School of Prehistoric Research began to teach European prehistory at many American universities that had not previously included this subject within anthropology.

In addition to his efforts to broaden the geographic range of academic and museum archaeology, MacCurdy also disseminated information about Old World prehistory to educated laypersons. His converts included Addison L. Greene, chair of the trustees of Holyoke College, and Gen. Charles G. Dawes. Each year MacCurdy invited "a few of these influential and cultured Americans" to join the summer excavations so he could "indoctrinate them with his own zeal for prehistoric studies" (Hooton 1950:514). He had a talent for explaining archaeological facts clearly and nontechnically; even more important, his enthusiasm for scientific archaeology was contagious. Although many of their elders remained skeptical, American graduate students were drawn to European prehistory through his efforts. MacCurdy worked to develop American graduate training in anthropology and documented the growth of programs (1902, 1919). He also "stimulated the actual fieldwork of European archaeologists" through the school's grants for their fieldwork so that his students could join these excavations (Hooton 1950:514). Both Europe and America reaped the benefits.

MacCurdy was a founding member of the AAA, serving as secretary from 1903 to 1916 and as president in 1931. He also served as secretary of Section H of the American Association for the Advancement of Science, of which he was a vice president in 1905. He was vice president of the Archaeological Institute of America in 1946 and of the International Congress of Prehistoric and Protohistoric Sciences in Oslo in 1936.

MacCurdy was a kind, modest, and unassuming man, "wholly incapable of self-promotion and congenitally non-political in his behavior" (Hooton 1950:514). The American School of Prehistoric Research remains the primary monument to his achievements. He was killed on 15 November 1947 by a passing automobile near Plainfield, New Jersey, while crossing the road to ask for directions.

REGNA DARNELL

John R. Swanton
1932

J ohn Reed Swanton was born in Gardiner, Maine, on 19 February
1873, four years after the poet Edward Arlington Robinson (1869–
1935), whose work he greatly appreciated. Walter Swanton had
died before John's birth, and the child was raised in straitened financial circumstances and stringent moralism by his mother, his mother's
mother, and her sister. He was brought up in the Swedenborgian faith,
with a deep devotion to truth and justice. Although early on he doubted
the psychic claims of Swedenborg, he changed his position toward the
end of his life.

Swanton earned an A.B. from Harvard in 1896, an A.M. in 1897, and
a Ph.D. in 1900. In addition to anthropology courses from *Frederic Ward
Putnam* and C. C. Willoughby, Swanton took courses with Harvard
philosophers William James and George Santayana and participated in
archaeological digs in New Jersey, Maine, Ohio, and at Pueblo Bonito
in Chaco Canyon, New Mexico. Along with *Roland B. Dixon*, Swanton

spent the last two years of his graduate work studying with *Franz Boas* and Livingston Farrand at Columbia, writing a dissertation on the morphology of the Chinook verb (published in the *American Anthropologist* in 1900). After finishing his degree, Swanton took up a position at the Bureau of American Ethnology (BAE) of the Smithsonian Institution and remained there through 1944. Swanton's manuscript on the working of the BAE formed the basis of Judd's history (1967).

Swanton's collection of Haida oral literatures in the Queen Charlotte Islands (Haida Gwaii) in 1900–01 exemplifies the Boasian textual tradition. Canadian poet Robert Bringhurst (1999) identifies these collections as virtually unique in North American anthropology, because the classic poets of Haida oral tradition emerge there as gifted individual wordsmiths. He also undertook fieldwork on Vancouver Island and in Alaska (primarily among the Haidas and Tlingits), including during his honeymoon in 1903 with the former Alice Barnard. They had a daughter and two sons before Alice's death in 1926.

Swanton focused primarily on migrations of Native Americans, particularly in the Southeast. He critically reviewed documents inscribed by explorers, travelers, and missionaries for information on the social structure and tribal distinctions in that area, and he championed ethnohistorical research at a time when other Boas students refused to consider data not gathered by professionally trained anthropologists. Swanton's work on social structure was taken as disproving 19th century evolutionist claims on the order of structuration (Swanton showed that hunter-gatherers had recognizable families and that patrilineal descent occurred without regard to the level of technological development). In addition to critically sorting through historical documents for ethnological data, Swanton collected basic lexicons from the last speakers of Atakapa, Chitimacha, Natchez, and Tunica. Although his extreme shyness made him uncomfortable studying cultures through personal contact (as Lonergay [1998:192; see Kroeber 1940:3] suggests), Swanton did fieldwork with Native Americans in Oklahoma and Texas as well as on the northwest coast of North America. Swanton may serve as a prototypical example of Boasian particularism: he was devoted to gathering information, letting the folklore and linguistic texts he elicited and the historical chronicles he excavated "speak for themselves" without much (or any) interpretation.

William (Bill) Fenton (1959:664) detailed Swanton's accomplishments in five major areas of anthropology. Swanton traced the historical and presumptive prehistorical movements of North American aboriginal groups, while simultaneously de-emphasizing the importance of the present and/or historical locations of a people as the explanation of cultural traits. He also developed and refined methods for ethnohistory, providing several early exemplars of that emerging field. The lexicons he compiled of Dakota, Haida, Tlingit, Muskogean, and Tunica provided a basis for the classification of language history and kinship systems. This work in turn contributed to his disproving late-19th-century evolutionary claims about aboriginal American social organizations, thereby opening the way for more particularist historical research. Finally, he accumulated major collections of folk tales in the original languages from two areas, southeastern and northwestern North America. Fenton added that "Swanton was attracted to Andean civilization ... an extension of [his] method of using historical sources to solve an intriguing problem of how society kept its historical records and manipulated ideas" (Fenton 1959:666–667). In particular, Swanton wrote on *quipu*, the Andean system of record keeping, and cautiously took up questions of Viking voyages to America (*A Note on the Quipu* 1943; *The Wineland Voyages* 1947).

Swanton was an associate editor of the *American Anthropologist* for ten years, and then its editor from 1920 to 1924. He also served on the Social Science Research Council and the National Research Council. He was elected to the National Academy of Science in 1932, and appointed an Official of the Ordén Nacional de Mérito de Manuel de Céspedes in Cuba. His honors included the Loubat Prize in History in 1913 and the Viking Medal in Anthropology in 1948. In addition to serving as president of the American Anthropological Association, Swanton was also president of the American Folklore Society and the Anthropological Society of Washington. As chair of the commission celebrating the four hundredth anniversary of the explorations of Hernando De Soto, Swanton was primarily responsible for the commission's massive 1939 report.

Diffident and elfin, "Swanton suffered all his adult life from digestive ailments, which he believed were nervous in origin" (Lonergay 1999:193; also see Steward 1960:336). His extreme shyness also made him modest. Bill Fenton remembers encountering Swanton, "an elf of a man seated with knees drawn up to his chin on a deep window ledge facing Speck's office door," when going to meet Frank Speck for the first time. Swanton was also waiting to see Speck, and only after extolling Speck's virtues as an ethnologist did Swanton admit that "he also was an ethnologist" (1991:10). Swanton spent his retirement years doting on his five grandchildren and writing tentative defenses of spiritualism, bolstered by his enthusiasm for the parapsychological work of J. B. Rhine. He died in Newton, Massachusetts, on 2 May 1958.

STEPHEN O. MURRAY

Fay-Cooper Cole
1933–1934

F ay-Cooper Cole was born on 8 August 1881 in Plainwell, Michigan, but grew up in California. He attended the University of Southern California before entering Northwestern University, where he graduated in 1903. Cole once said he intended to sell bonds for a living after graduation, but the economic climate was not conducive to this line of work. After beginning postgraduate studies at the University of Chicago he joined the Field Museum, working as an ethnologist under George Dorsey.

Cole chose the northern Philippines for his first field expedition. In preparation Dorsey sent him to Columbia for a semester with *Franz Boas* and then to Berlin for training with Felix von Luschan. He left for the Philippines in 1907 with his new wife, Mabel Cook, who assisted him in his research; they later collaborated on several publications, and she wrote on her own as well. The couple settled in the village of Patok, where they proceeded to take anthropomorphic measurements and record language, folklore, and other aspects of Tinguian culture; they also made collections for the Field Museum, returning there in 1908. From 1910 to 1912 they made another expedition, this time to Mindanao, but they had to cut the research off when both were badly infected with malaria.

On their return Cole was promoted to assistant curator of Malayan ethnology and physical anthropology and prepared his first monograph, *The Wild Tribes of the Davao District, Mindanao* (1913). He decided he would like to teach and began to prepare for it. In 1915 he presented his dissertation to Columbia, based on his and Mabel's original work with the Tinguian people; a version was published the same year as *Traditions of the Tinguian*. The work later served as the basis for *The Tinguian: Social, Religious and Economic Life of a Philippine Tribe* (1922). Mabel also published on Tinguian folk tales, illustrated from photographs by Fay-Cooper.

In 1922 the Coles returned to Indonesia. While there in 1923 Fay-Cooper Cole received offers from both Northwestern University and the University of Chicago to develop programs in anthropology. He was appointed lecturer at Northwestern and taught briefly at both institutions, before deciding to take the position at Chicago in 1924, joining *Ralph Linton* to replace the charismatic Frederick Starr. Starr had taught mostly undergraduates, but Cole was interested in developing a research-oriented department devoted to graduate-student training. In 1929 anthropology became a separate department. Linton and Cole had been joined by *Edward Sapir* in 1925 and *Robert Redfield* in 1926. When Sapir left for Yale University in 1931 he was replaced by A. R. Radcliffe-Brown.

Fay-Cooper Cole took an active interest in public affairs and education as well as academics. In 1925 he helped organize and prepare the case for evolution in the Scopes trial in Tennessee. When he returned the university president told him that he had received numerous requests for Cole to be fired. He was promoted instead. During the 1930s Cole was among the anthropologists who took a prominent place in combating the problems of race. He spoke out publicly and published popular accounts to counter racism, including a coauthored volume with Mabel Cook Cole. Fay-Cooper Cole also headed the social science division of the 1933 Century of Progress Exposition in Chicago, but his efforts there highlight the difficulties of countering racism with such projects; the emphasis on progress and the nature of some of the exhibits actually reinforced prejudices. "Social science in the service of corporate visionaries, it seemed, could only perpetuate a racist morality by converting victims of American progress into sources of popular entertainment" (Rydell 1993:104).

Cole's appointment at the University of Chicago began a second career centered on teaching and program development. He continued to do research, but it shifted from Southeast Asia to the American Midwest and from cultural anthropology to archaeology—in part because he saw archaeology as a way to gain support for the new department. By 1927 Chicago students were surveying and excavating prehistoric sites in Illinois. Cole was a strong advocate of careful and precise excavation and recording at these sites; he also raised funds for the work. *Rediscovering Illinois* (1937, coauthored with Thorne Deuel) described the Midwestern culture sequence for the first time and was one of the first major works to shift from descriptive study of artifacts to a more analytical approach based on the functions represented by artifacts; the number of students involved in this research fostered the adoption of the approach. Cole treated graduate students as junior colleagues, giving them responsibility for their own projects and credit for their contributions. This trust was reciprocated. After his 1948 retirement to Santa Barbara a group of former students organized *Archeology of Eastern United States* (James B. Griffin, ed., 1952) as a tribute. The volume is still widely cited. He was also coauthor with several of his students on a final archaeological report, *Kincaid: A Prehistoric Illinois Metropolis* (1951).

During World War II Cole's experience in Southeast Asia was put to use training army and navy officers in the Civil Affairs Training School for the Far East; he also wrote *The Peoples of Malaysia* (1945) during this period. After his retirement he continued to teach (at Southern California, Northwestern, Indiana, Syracuse, Washington, Cornell, and

Harvard) and to write. He died on 3 September 1961, survived by his wife, his son, LaMont Cole, who was a professor of zoology at Cornell, and two grandchildren.

Cole had received honorary doctorates from Northwestern, Beloit, and Chicago, served on the National Research Council, and helped found the Social Science Research Council. He had been a member of the American Philosophical Society, and he had received a Gold Medal for Malayan research from the Chicago Geographical Society, of which he was president in 1931–32. Fred Eggan noted that Cole "did not consider himself a great scholar but he was a warm human being who brought out the best in everybody" (1963:644).

FREDERIC W. GLEACH

Robert H. Lowie
1935

Robert Harry Lowie, foremost student of social structure and religion among the first generation of Boasians, was born on 12 June 1883 into a middle-class German-assimilated Jewish family that espoused the ideals of the Revolution of 1848. His father, Samuel Lowie, was a Budapest-born businessman; his mother, Ernestine Kuhn Lowie, was the daughter of a Viennese physician with an avocation for classics and German literature. Lowie was particularly close to his mother and his sister Risa, who later taught high school English in New York City and wrote poetry. The family emigrated to New York when Lowie was ten. He attended public school on the Upper East Side, then City College of New York, receiving a B.A. in classics in 1901 at age 18.

After teaching briefly in the New York school system, fascination with science led him to enroll at Columbia University. Chemistry proved uncongenial, and he was drawn to *Franz Boas* as a scientist who embodied their shared admiration for the materialism of Ernest Haeckel and Ernst Mach. He entered Columbia's doctoral program in anthropology in 1904, reporting considerable resentment of Boas's sink-or-swim pedagogy; statistics and American Indian linguistics were equally alien. Lowie considered his anthropological education deficient. Livingston Farrand and *Clark Wissler* rather than Boas were his mentors. He minored in psychology with James McKeen Cattell and Robert S. Woodworth. His dissertation, "The Test-Theme in North American Mythology," earned him a Ph.D. in 1908.

Wissler invited Lowie to the American Museum of Natural History (AMNH) and in 1906 arranged his first fieldwork at the Lemhi (Northern Shoshone) Reservation in Idaho. Wissler orchestrated Lowie's early fieldwork to circumscribe his own on the Blackfoot (Murphy 1972:15). When Lowie began his work, the Shoshones spoke little English, and Lowie had to learn to ride a horse to locate them. The ethnology of the day emphasized basic survey mapping of cultures and languages (Darnell 1998). Lowie and his contemporaries took for granted that Indian cultures were moribund.

After Boas resigned from the AMNH in 1906, Lowie became Wissler's second-in-command, as an assistant in 1907, an assistant curator in 1909, and an associate curator in 1912. Most of his ethnographic fieldwork was done during these years. Lowie worked with Assiniboines, Northern Blackfoot, Chipewyans, Hidatsas, Southern Utes, Southern Paiutes, Northern Paiutes or Paviotsos, Washos, and Hopis. His Plains specialization, however, dominated his Southwest and Great Basin research. His personal identification was greatest with the Crows, whom he studied in 1907, every summer from 1910 to 1916, and again in 1931. Until Bronislaw Malinowski, this was "one of the most intensive" fieldwork commitments "ever undertaken by a professional ethnographer" (Murphy 1972:27). Lowie became reasonably fluent in the language, although he continued to use interpreters and set high standards of linguistic competence. He became attuned to intracultural variability and wrote about individual Crows (e.g., his life histories in Parsons 1922 and Casagrande 1960).

In 1917 Lowie was called to Berkeley as an associate professor of anthropology; he was promoted to professor in 1925. Lowie was the quintessential European gentleman of his generation. His formality and emphasis on decorum lightly masked the shy and sensitive personality of a perpetual foreigner. His teaching style emphasized ethnographic facts, for which he had a prodigious memory. He was a committed teacher but avoided disciples.

His collaboration with independent scholar Curt Nimuendaju involved Lowie in an ethnographic survey of the Ge-speaking peoples of Brazil and with South American ethnology more generally. He actively supported a handbook of South American Indians, eventually edited by Julian Steward for the Smithsonian Institution.

Through his books *Culture and Ethnology* (1917), *Primitive Society* (1920), and *Primitive Religion* (1924), Lowie contributed greatly to the textbook codification and popularization of Americanist anthropology by about 1925. Although he has been characterized as a pedestrian or orthodox Boasian, Lowie differed from his former teacher on multiple grounds.

Lowie's version of the critique of evolution focused on Lewis Henry Morgan's use of kinship data in his unilinear theory. Lowie retained some vestiges of evolutionary thinking about technology and overall complexity, however, and deemed comparative projects worthwhile. He coined the term "multilinear evolution," a method later developed by his student Julian Steward. Lowie objected primarily to careless methodology. Diffusion produced counterexamples to unilinear sequences, matrilineality was found at middle rather than lower ranges of complexity, kinship terms were not automatic evidence for social behavior, and not all Native Americans had clans ("sibs"). Lowie was fascinated by Plains military societies ("sodalities"). Despite the individualism of the vision quest, the coercive power of these societies in the annual buffalo hunt suggested that state-level societies were not the only ones with government.

Lowie's analytical method was deconstructive and functionalist. His oft quoted remark that culture is "a thing of shreds and patches" emphasized that cultural traits from diverse historical sources were integrated uniquely in each culture. Lowie pioneered the method of controlled comparison, for example, of Crow and Omaha kinship systems, which differed in lineality within the same language family. Within the historical particularist framework, his study of religion emphasized the psychological integration of meaning for the individual member of a culture.

Lowie also applied his fieldwork skills to his own culture and profession. *The History of Ethnological Theory* (1937) illustrates his internationalist breadth. Toward the end of his life he shared recollections of the colleagues from his younger years (1956), assembled for publication his correspondence with *Edward Sapir* whose intellect he regarded more highly than his own, wrote an autobiography (1959), and undertook fieldwork on the society from which his family had emigrated. Throughout, he chose the position of witness, observing more than participating and de-emphasizing his personal achievements. A pacifist during World War I, he was passionately opposed to Nazism. Unlike Boas, however, he avoided political writing. *Toward Understanding Germany* (1954) was criticized for its nuanced failure to lambaste Germany with national character stereotypes.

In 1933, at the age of 50, Lowie married Louella Cole, a psychologist, who survived him and saw many of his manuscripts to publication. Lowie was editor of the *American Anthropologist* from 1924 to 1933; president of the American Folklore Society in 1916, the American Ethnological Society in 1920, and the American Anthropological Association in 1935; and winner of both the Huxley and Viking medals in 1948. He died of cancer on 21 September 1957. In 1960 the University of California, Berkeley, dedicated the Robert H. Lowie Museum of Anthropology.

REGNA DARNELL

Herbert J. Spinden
1936

Herbert Joseph "Joe" Spinden was born in Huron, South Dakota, on 16 August 1879. His father was a teacher and one of the pioneer newspapermen in Dakota Territory. After high school Spinden worked with railroad survey parties in Washington, Idaho, and Montana, and in 1900 he joined the gold rush to Alaska. He entered Harvard in 1902, receiving an A.B. in 1906, an A.M. in 1908, and a Ph.D. in 1909. In 1905, with the help and guidance of *Roland B. Dixon*, Spinden went with three other students to North Dakota to excavate a prehistoric Mandan village, the first such work. Spinden and George F. Will (who also went on to a career in anthropology) produced an extensive and comprehensive report, published before they graduated, that included historical, cultural, and linguistic sketches in addition to the archaeological findings; Spinden produced the maps and artifact drawings and some of the photographs.

While pursuing his graduate studies in 1907–09 Spinden was Austin

Teaching Fellow in anthropology at Harvard. It was virtually the only formal teaching experience of his career. In 1909 he joined the American Museum of Natural History (AMNH) as an assistant curator of anthropology in charge of Mexico and Central America. He also began fieldwork in the Southwest, mostly in New Mexico with Tewa Indians, and continued this work over four years; *Songs of the Tewa* (1933) was drawn from this experience. Spinden also made extended explorations in Mexico and Central America, especially the Yucatán Peninsula.

In 1921 Spinden left New York for the Peabody Museum at Harvard, where he was curator of Mexican archaeology and ethnology until 1929. In 1926 he added duties as curator of anthropology at the Buffalo Museum of Arts and Sciences, also keeping that affiliation until 1929. That year he took the position of curator of American Indian art and primitive cultures at the Brooklyn Museum, where he remained until his retirement in 1951. He was also director of education there in the early 1930s and headed the Brooklyn Museum School Service department, an educational experiment supported by the Carnegie Foundation for the Advancement of Teaching that collected a large series of images for visual instruction in New York City.

Spinden made several significant contributions to the development of American archaeology. *A Study of Maya Art* (1913), a beautifully produced volume illustrated with Spinden's own drawings and developed from his dissertation (in turn inspired by *Alfred M. Tozzer's* "Anthropology 9" course), still offers provocative hypotheses in Mayan studies. In 1917 Spinden published what became known as the Archaic Hypothesis—"the first serious American hemispheric cultural-historical scheme devised for explicating the story of Precolumbian America" (Willey 1981). It was eventually demonstrated that the situation was far more complex than Spinden had described; similar frameworks had long been employed in the Old World, but the idea stimulated much research in the Americas.

Spinden became best known, however, for his correlation of the Maya calendar to our own, most fully developed in *The Reduction of Maya Dates* (1924), which enabled the study of Mayan astronomy as well as the precise dating of sites and events. The Spinden correlation quickly became a subject of controversy and was dismissed by some even as it was being employed by others. Today better correlations exist, and Spinden's is not much used; but no correlation (to date) fits all the evidence from archaeology, astronomy, and ethnohistory, and the possibility that different Mayan groups counted from different bases should be considered.

In addition to his direct anthropological work, Spinden worked for the federal government in Central and South America in 1917–18 and served in 1920 as an attaché to the American Legation in Havana to observe the Cuban elections. He organized a show of industrial art at the AMNH in 1919, and served with *Frederick Webb Hodge* in 1930–31 on the editorial board of the Exposition of Indian Tribal Arts, the first exhibit of Native American art as fine art. The latter appointment was probably related to his involvement with the Eastern Association on Indian Affairs, a progressive non-Native group that fought for Indian rights in the areas of education, industry, health and sanitation, land tenure, irrigation, religion, and autonomy; they argued, for example, that "the best education of our Indian wards would be achieved by developing instead of destroying their pride of race and by calling into active service, instead of suppressing, their group loyalties and communal responsibilities" (Weeren 1997). Spinden not only considered the art of Native America "rich in decorative quality and especially rich in symbolism," but he also recognized Native American poetics: "Americans of the future will surely realize an epic grandeur in the song sequences and word stories of the first Americans" (Anon. 1967). Today these words seem naive and perhaps romanticized, but they mark an early step in the development of a more sophisticated appreciation of Native American cultures. Spinden was a participant in Kidder's first Pecos conference, where he "had a leak in his air mattress and swore at it every night" (Martin 1974:5).

Spinden was a delegate to the Congress of Americanists in 1922, 1924, and 1930. He also served on the National Research Council and lectured at universities in Argentina, Chile, and Peru as a Federal Good

Neighbor Activity in 1941. He was married twice, to Ellen Sewell in 1928, and to Ailes Gilmour in 1948; with his second wife he had one son. The *New York Times* described Spinden as "a large, heavy-set man with blue eyes and white hair who managed to combine scholarly work with an active life and a warm sense of humor." He died on 23 October 1967.

FREDERIC W. GLEACH

Nels C. Nelson
1937

N els Christian Nelson was born on a farm near Fredericia, Denmark, on 9 April 1875. His early education was largely in the off-season from chores on the family farm. In 1892 he came to the United States, landing in New York and moving to Minnesota, where he could work on his uncle's farm to repay the cost of his steerage passage. After a few years there he was able to hire himself out to another farmer and continue his education; he completed high school in 1901 in Marshall, Minnesota. Nelson then worked his way to California, tending livestock for a family returning there. He drove a six-mule team and butchered hogs to earn enough money to enroll in Stanford University, where he began his studies in philosophy in 1901. In 1903 he transferred to Berkeley, working his way through school by doing office and janitorial work in a bank. In 1906 Nelson visited an archaeological excavation near Ukiah, California, with a friend and immediately converted from philosophy to anthropology; he received a B.L. in 1907 and an M.L. in 1908, working with Pliny Goddard and *Alfred L. Kroeber*. After graduation Nelson joined the U.S. Geological Survey as a field assistant; from 1909 to 1912 he was an assistant curator at the Museum of Anthropology at Berkeley. Much of that time he was also an instructor in anthropology. He married Ethelyn G. Field on Christmas day, 1911.

In 1912 Nelson left Berkeley to become an assistant curator of prehistoric archaeology at the American Museum of Natural History (AMNH) in New York. He was brought by Goddard, who had left Berkeley in 1909. Nelson was made associate curator of North American archaeology in 1921, associate curator of archaeology in 1923, and curator of prehistoric archaeology in 1928, remaining in this position until his retirement in 1943. This base allowed him to pursue archaeological work not just in the United States—where he made most of his contributions, particularly on work in the Southwest—but also in Spain, France, Mongolia, and China.

In 1913, during the off-season from his excavations in the Southwest, Nelson traveled to France and Spain and visited the great stratigraphic excavations of Hugo Obermaier and the Abbé Henri Breuil. He participated in the excavations at El Castillo, the famous deeply stratified Paleolithic cave site in northern Spain. Nelson had worked as a student on the stratigraphic excavation of shell mounds in San Francisco with Max Uhle, but Kroeber's criticism of the sequence developed there had tempered Nelson's enthusiasm temporarily. The experience in Europe renewed his interest in stratigraphy. Returning to work in the Southwest in 1913, Nelson employed a stratigraphic approach at a number of sites in the Galisteo Basin of New Mexico, including San Pedro Viejo, Pueblo San Cristobal, and San Marcos. But where the cave sites Nelson had seen and worked on in Europe had clearly visible natural and cultural levels that could be kept distinct during excavation, many of the sites he worked on in the U.S. did not. To get around this, in addition to the stratigraphic methods employed in Europe, Nelson introduced the use of arbitrary levels in excavation, in order to maintain any chronological sequence that might be preserved in relatively un-

NELS C. NELSON, 1937 • 79

differentiated deposits. Many archaeologists, especially in Europe, considered this inappropriate, but it has proven to be quite useful in excavations throughout the United States and elsewhere.

Leslie Spier worked with Nelson in 1916 and then on a Zuni site where he successfully applied Nelson's stratigraphic approach and a technique developed by Kroeber that Spier called associational seriation. Nelson and many others began to employ seriation with stratigraphic excavation, and a new era in American archaeology began. Along with the excavations of Manuel Gamio in Mexico (where *Franz Boas* suggested a stratigraphic approach), Nelson's work resulted in the widespread adoption of stratigraphic techniques in the Americas, and thus in the development of meaningful chronological sequences in American prehistoric archaeology.

From 1925 to 1927 Nelson was the archaeologist on the Central Asiatic Expedition of the AMNH, which went into the Gobi Desert, in Mongolia, and to Szechuan and Yunan provinces in China; on one occasion he reportedly awed a group of Mongols by demonstrating his ability to remove and replace his (artificial) eye. During the winter off-season from excavations he sailed along the Yangtze River and its tributaries, exploring caves and looking for archaeological sites—a relatively fruitless effort, but one he greatly enjoyed in the company of his wife. From 1928 to 1943 he was responsible for all the archaeological exhibits at the AMNH and was less involved in large-scale excavations; his last fieldwork was in 1941 at cave sites on the Crow reservation in Montana.

Nelson was a member and served as vice president of the American Association for the Advancement of Science and the New York Academy of Sciences. He served as president of the Society for American Archaeology, the American Ethnological Society, and the American Anthropological Association. He was also a member of the American Geographic Society and the Explorers Club in New York. Walter Granger, one of his colleagues on the Central Asiatic Expedition in the 1920s, said of him (in Barton 1941:303), "If I were going out on a desert island where I would have to be satisfied with the company of only one man, I'd choose him. . . . The most wonderful thing about him, I think, is that he knows when to talk and when to keep quiet, and that is an art few people ever learn." Nelson died in a nursing home on 5 March 1964, just a few months after his wife; they had no children.

FREDERIC W. GLEACH

Edward Sapir
1938

Edward Sapir was born in Lauenberg, Pomerania, on 26 January 1884 to Lithuanian Jewish parents, Eva Seagal and Jacob David Sapir, a cantor. The family emigrated to the United States by way of England, settling in Richmond, Virginia, in 1890. The death of Sapir's younger brother precipitated a decline in family fortunes. Sapir grew up on New York City's Lower East Side, where his mother ran a small shop to support the family. At age 14 he won a citywide Pulitzer scholarship competition designed to identify the brightest of the immigrant children. It financed his education at Columbia University.

Sapir received a B.A. in 1904 after only three years of study and an M.A. in 1905, the same year he began fieldwork with Wishram Chinook; both of his degrees were in Germanics, although he also took several courses in music. Linguistics at Columbia was then taught in the various language departments. Sapir switched to anthropology after a course in American Indian linguistics from *Franz Boas* persuaded him of the urgent need for fieldwork on endangered languages; he received a Ph.D. in 1909 for a grammar of Takelma based on fieldwork in the summer of 1906.

In 1907–08 Sapir served as research fellow at the University of California, Berkeley, under the direction of *Alfred L. Kroeber*. He immediately began fieldwork on Yana, but his serious linguistic interests clashed with Kroeber's California survey mandate, and the position ended after one year. Sapir accepted a Harrison fellowship at the University of Pennsylvania, which he held from 1908 to 1910. During this period he did fieldwork with the Utes and studied Southern Paiute, based on collaboration with Tony Tillohash in Philadelphia.

In 1910, at the age of 26, Sapir became the first director of the Anthropological Division of the Geological Survey of Canada, with a mandate to build up his discipline on a national basis. Over the next 15 years he carried out a personal fieldwork program primarily on Nootka, branching out to Sarcee, Kutchin, and Ingalik in the early twenties. Simultaneously, he built a program at the Victoria Memorial Museum, bringing to his staff British-trained *Diamond Jenness* and Marius Barbeau, as well as fellow Boasians Paul Radin, Alexander Goldenweiser, and Harlan Smith.

Sapir married Florence Delson, a distant cousin, in 1910. The couple had three children. Florence's illness after 1916 and death in 1924 coincided with cutbacks in scientific research because of World War I. Sapir was a pacifist whose critique of North American society coalesced in this period. He also turned to psychoanalysis and the relationship of personality to culture. Much of Sapir's most significant work was done during his years in Ottawa. He aspired to complete a grammar, texts, and a dictionary for each language on which he had done fieldwork. In collaboration with Kroeber and others, Sapir consolidated the 55 linguistic stocks of North America (proposed by John Wesley Powell of the Bureau of American Ethnology in 1892) into six major families (Sapir 1921). His "Time Perspective in Aboriginal American Culture: A Study in Method" (1916) codified Boasian practice in the reconstruction of Amerindian culture history. His only book, *Language*, appeared in 1921.

Despite this productivity, Sapir increasingly longed for an academic position. In 1925 he received a call to the University of Chicago, where *Fay-Cooper Cole* was rebuilding the department in a Boasian image. Soon after his move to Chicago, he married Jean Victoria McClenaghan, with whom he had two more children. Sapir was the superstar around whom the department attained independence from sociology in 1929. He fell readily into the role of interdisciplinary maven, becoming the communicator who linked Chicago sociology to psychology and psychoanalysis, adding a cross-cultural dimension to both. He developed a theory of culture that emphasized its symbolic nature and its unique embodiment in individual members. Through Rockefeller Foundation-sponsored seminars, Sapir established productive collaborations with interactional psychologist Harry Stack Sullivan and political scientist Harold D. Lasswell. The life history, adapted from clinical practice, was to be the cross-cultural method. Fieldworkers from anthropology would undergo training analysis with psychiatrists as a prelude to cross-cultural research.

During the Chicago years, Sapir's own fieldwork continued in linguistics rather than in culture and personality. He worked with Navajo from 1926 on, collaborating with Father Berard Haile and "Chic" Sandoval. In 1927 he worked on Hupa in California. Sapir began to choose field languages to fit his historical interests in linking the Athabascan language family to Haida and Tlingit (Nadene) and perhaps even to Sino-Tibetan.

In the academic context Sapir could pursue his theoretical interests in linguistics. He formulated the concept of the phoneme in 1925, the year that the Linguistic Society of America, and its journal *Language*, was founded. In 1933 he elaborated the "psychological reality" of the phoneme for native speakers. After years of being the only sophisticated linguist among Boasian ethnologists, Sapir thrived in the company of linguists.

In 1931 Sapir was unable to resist a call to Yale University, where he was to spearhead a research and teaching program on "the impact of culture on personality" with a cohort of foreign fellows, who would study both their native cultures and North America from an outsider's standpoint. Sapir's program quickly clashed with the interdisciplinary tenor of Yale's Institute of Human Relations. Anti-Semitism at Yale, especially during the prelude to Nazi power, left Sapir depressed and debilitated. He retreated increasingly to the family cabin in New Hampshire. Sapir suffered a heart attack in 1937 while teaching at the Summer Institute of Linguistics in Ann Arbor, Michigan. A planned sabbatical in China for 1937–38 was canceled; he spent the year in New York City attempting to recover his health. Sapir was president of the American Anthropological Association in 1938; Franz Boas read Sapir's presidential address because of his deteriorating health. He returned to teaching in the fall of 1938 and died of a heart attack on 4 February 1939.

Among Sapir's distinguished linguistic students, many of whom followed him from Chicago to Yale, were *Harry Hoijer*, Fang-Kuei Li, Morris Swadesh, Stanley Newman, Mary Haas, George Trager, George Herzog, C. F. Voegelin, Charles Hockett, and Zellig Harris. Hymes and Fought (1975) have argued that this "First Yale School" shared much of the program of the Yale school that developed around Leonard Bloomfield after Sapir's death and anticipated many meaning-centered tenets of contemporary linguistic theory.

REGNA DARNELL

Diamond Jenness
1939

Diamond Jenness was born on 10 February 1886 in Wellington, New Zealand. After graduating from Victoria University College of the University of Wellington in 1908, he went to Balliol College, Oxford, to study classics. There, however, anthropology became his focus, through the influence of the Canadian folklorist Marius Barbeau (who as a fellow student was also turning to that field) and Wilson D. Wallis. He received a Diploma in Anthropology in 1911, and a Master of Arts in 1916.

In 1911–12 Jenness became a research student under the direction of R. R. Marett. His fieldwork on Goodenough Island off the New Guinea coast resulted in a monograph (1920) coauthored with his sister's husband, A. Ballantyne, a Methodist missionary stationed on the island, and in a substantial collection of material for the Pitt Rivers Museum at Oxford. While recovering from malaria after this sojourn, he was recommended by Barbeau, by then at the National Museum of Canada, to be one of two anthropologists on the Canadian Arctic Expedition (1913–16) led by Vilhjamur Stefansson.

This intensive research experience provided the base for a career largely focused on the arctic peoples of Canada; Jenness went on to produce over 40 articles and monographs on arctic anthropology, ranging widely across topics in Canadian Inuit culture, technology, language, archaeology, and governmental administration. From 1917 to 1919 his career was interrupted by service overseas in World War I. In 1919, however, he returned to Ottawa, Canada, to become an ethnologist at the National Museum. In that year he also married Frances Eileen Bleakney, whom he had met when she was *Edward Sapir's* secretary in the anthropology division of the Geological Survey of Canada; they had three sons.

In 1926 Jenness succeeded Edward Sapir as chief of the anthropological section of the National Museum, a position he held until 1947 with the exception of several years of government intelligence service during World War II. His ethnographic work in the 1920s consisted of visits to and sojourns among several Canadian Indian groups, including the Sarcees, Carriers, Sekanis, and the Ojibwas of Parry Island, Ontario. He also conducted archaeological investigations on Bering Strait, and on the basis of surface finds by Inuit collectors in Hudson Bay, he was the first to define the Dorset culture as a predecessor, and in places a contemporary, of the Thule culture that later became dominant (Jenness 1925).

Most of Jenness's major publications appeared in the 1920s and 1930s: *The Copper Eskimos* (1923), *The People of the Twilight* (1928), and *The Indians of Canada* (1932), which has been reprinted numerous times. He also published widely in Canadian and American scholarly and popular periodicals, becoming the best-known Canadian anthropologist of his era. His final large work was a five-volume study of Eskimo administration in Canada, Alaska, and Greenland (1962–68).

Professionally, Jenness held offices and membership in several scholarly organizations. In addition to the American Anthropological Association, he was president of the Society for American Archaeology in 1936–37 and vice president of the American Association for the Advancement of Science in 1938. He was awarded five honorary degrees, four in Canada and one from the University of New Zealand. In 1969 the Canadian government awarded him its highest honor, the Companion of the Order of Canada.

After his death in 1969 Jenness was warmly remembered by friends and colleagues. William E. Taylor, who became director of the National Museum of Man in Ottawa in 1967, recalled him as "a kind, quiet, and modest man" (1988:1108). In her obituary of Jenness, *Frederica de Laguna* remembered his helpful counsel and kindness to her in the 1930s, most notably when she became the first professor of anthropology at Bryn Mawr College: he "unsolicited and spontaneously, gave that institution his entire personal professional library, just to help a junior colleague up the first rung of a difficult ladder" (1971:251).

Diamond Jenness made his major contributions through field research and synthesis rather than theory. In research he is probably known best for his identification of the Dorset culture. The other major work that established his reputation was *The Indians of Canada*. As the first extensive survey of Aboriginal groups across the country, it had a far-reaching influence that still shapes—sometimes in problematic ways—publications such as *First Nations in Canada* (1997), published by Indian and Northern Affairs Canada.

In recent times his views of Native peoples and his relation to the Canadian state and its shaping of Indian policy in the 1950s and 1960s have been reviewed critically. Although he was an active critic of government policies and actions, or lack thereof, he also held, like many others of his time, that the priority for Eskimo and Indian peoples was "educating and training them for citizenship." He compared Indian reserves to internment or concentration camps that fostered psychological dependency in their inmates. In the 1940s he drafted his own "plan for liquidating our whole Indian reserve system within a definite time limit . . . [say] twenty-five years" and predicted that "the greatest opposition to abandoning the present reserve system will come from the Indians themselves" (Kulchyski 1993:28–29), as indeed it did when Canada proposed its White Paper of 1969 removing their special rights and status. Peter Kulchyski reads Jenness's 1913–16 diary (published in 1991 by his son, Stuart Jenness) as a patriarchal narrative revealing "imperial desires for mastery," and *The Indians of Canada* as "a deeply ideological, ethnocentric, often highly distorted description of Native cultures . . . which served the interests of the Canadian State very well" in assuming that many cultures were disappearing and that assimilation was the best course (1993:45, 46). The critique scores some points, but it also reminds us that the anthropologists of the past and their critics of following generations reflect their own times, ideologies, and concerns and may have trouble standing outside the milieu and climate of opinion in which they write.

JENNIFER S. H. BROWN

John M. Cooper
1940

John Montgomery Cooper was born on 28 October 1881 in Rockville, Maryland. He was the youngest of three sons. His father came from a Quaker family, and his mother came from a French Catholic family in Baltimore. At an early age Cooper was drawn to the priesthood. The family moved to Baltimore, where Cooper attended Calvert Hall, a Christian Brothers school. He was an active athlete and particularly enjoyed swimming and tennis. In 1897 Cooper entered a preparatory seminary, and in 1899 he began his formal studies for the priesthood at the North American College in Rome. He received a Ph.D. in 1902 and an S.T.D. in 1905; he also traveled, especially through Italy, became fluent in Italian, and studied art and archaeology. He was ordained on 17 June 1905 and returned to the United States, where he was placed as an assistant at St. Matthew's Church in Washington DC; he proved to be an excellent catechist.

Father Cooper soon began taking vacation camping trips to Canada, where he developed an interest in Indians through working with Native guides. In Washington he met many anthropologists, including *John R. Swanton* and *Frederick Webb Hodge*. In 1909 he began teaching part-time in the religious education department of the Catholic University of America while retaining his parish duties.

In 1916 Cooper conducted his first formal anthropological fieldwork, with the Têtes de Boule Indians in Quebéc. His first anthropological work, an authoritative bibliography of the peoples of Tierra del Fuego, was published in 1917. World War I soon interrupted his work. In 1918 Cooper was appointed to the National Catholic War Council (after the war it became the National Catholic Welfare Conference) as secretary of the National Committee on Women's Activities. His office was a center for information exchange and was involved in a number of programs to train and organize women; Father Cooper was also the chaplain to the National Service School for Women (later the National Catholic School of Social Service). In 1920 he rejoined Catholic University as a full-time instructor, and began introducing anthropological material into his courses on religion as well as teaching anthropology courses for the sociology department. In 1923 he became an associate professor, and in 1928 a professor of anthropology. A separate department was created in 1934 with Cooper as its head.

Father Cooper published extensively on hygiene, birth control, and youth work during the early 1920s, but his anthropological questioning did not generally extend to his conservative positions in these areas; the works are largely doctrinaire. In 1926 he turned to anthropological work as his main focus, and a somewhat more progressive stance became evident, although his work always remained grounded in Catholic morality. That year he helped found the Catholic Anthropological Conference and edited their publications, including *Primitive Man* (renamed *Anthropological Quarterly* in 1953, after his death); funding for these publications came largely out of his own pocket. Cooper always attributed this work—the development of an anthropological stream in Catholic education—to a series of meetings at the Hofbraü, a bar near

Yale, during a convention of Learned Societies there in 1925 (Tibesar 1950:36–37).

Perhaps because he came to anthropology relatively late in life, Father Cooper felt pressure to work as quickly as possible. He hated interruptions but was too genial to brush off visitors, and he once confessed that he had even selected his barber on the basis of how fast he cut his hair.

Father Cooper returned to the Têtes de Boule in 1925, 1926, and 1931 and worked with the Ojibwas in 1927–28, the James Bay Crees and Montagnais in 1927 and from 1932 to 1934, and the Gros Ventres in 1931 and from 1938 to 1940. He authored many of the pieces in *Primitive Man* during its early years, but he also published elsewhere and was a prolific reviewer of books. In the 1930s, like many other anthropologists, he published on race. He also considered the cross-cultural significance of mental illness, including an early piece on Cree *witiko* as psychosis. Cooper's *The Northern Algonquian Supreme Being* (1934) remains a useful synthesis in Algonquian studies up to that date. Prompted by his work with northern Algonquians, in 1940 he pressed for the consideration of land tenure for indigenous peoples at the First Inter-American Congress on Indian Life in Mexico, where he served as acting chair of the economic section.

Although he made plans for fieldwork in South America, Father Cooper never carried them out, but he actively pursued knowledge of South America through ethnological sources, as his first anthropological publication suggests. From 1932 to 1937 he chaired the National Research Council's Committee on the Survey of South American Indians, and his 1942 paper inspired the structure of the seven-volume *Handbook of South American Indians*, edited by Julian Steward; he also contributed ten articles to the set. He was secretary of the American Anthropological Association from 1931 to 1937 (as well as president in 1940) and served on both the Social Science Research Council and the American Council of Learned Societies. He was awarded the Mendel Medal in 1939 for his achievements as anthropologist and educator, he was elevated by the Pope in 1941 to the rank of Domestic Prelate, and in 1946 he was presented a life membership in the American Social Hygiene Association for his service to that field.

In 1941 Father Cooper suffered a coronary thrombosis and had to reduce his activities. In doing so he prioritized his anthropological work and retained his humor, dignity, and geniality. On the morning of 22 May 1949, after enjoying the previous afternoon and evening with friends, he suffered another coronary thrombosis and died while receiving the last sacraments. His friend and colleague Regina Flannery completed the editing of his final monograph, the second part of *The Gros Ventres of Montana*, and it was published posthumously in 1957.

FREDERIC W. GLEACH

Elsie Clews Parsons
1941

Outspoken philanthropist, scientist, and feminist Elsie
Worthington Clews Parsons, the first woman president of
the American Anthropological Association, was born on 27
November 1874. Her father, Henry Clews, was a prosperous Wall Street
financier; her mother, Lucy Madison Worthington, came from a prominent family bankrupted by the 1873 crash and rescued by her felicitous
marriage. From childhood Elsie resisted her mother's emphasis on man-
ners and social class; with maturity, she phrased her rebellion as political and feminist.

In 1892 she entered the newly established Barnard College, where
she was particularly influenced in philosophy by Nicholas Murray Butler.
She earned an M.A. in sociology from Columbia University in 1897
with a thesis on relief programs for New York's poor. Her Columbia
Ph.D. in sociology in 1899 focused on education and colonial admin-

istration. Parsons looked to sociology for scientific guides to social reform and modernization.

In 1900 she married Herbert Parsons, also from a prominent family. He was active in politics, serving three terms in Congress and chairing the Republican Party in New York from 1905 to 1910. The couple created a devoted family, albeit unconventional in its gender roles. Of their six children, two died in infancy. Herbert died suddenly in 1925.

Because Parsons was a woman, her teaching career was, unsurprisingly, attenuated. Franklin Giddings, sociology chair at Barnard, appointed her as a fellow from 1899 to 1902 and an instructor from 1902 to 1905. Her lectures, collected into a book on the family in 1906, were scandalous at the time; she even recommended trial marriage. Because of Herbert's public career, he was frequently embarrassed by her social positions and by her World War I pacifism. Parsons's only other teaching experience was in 1919 at the New School for Social Research, which she helped to found.

Parsons's early feminist positions are ultraconservative by contemporary standards. Drawing on Giddings's social Darwinism, she opposed women's suffrage on the grounds that women were unprepared for it, and she condemned voluntary childless marriage among the well to do as socially irresponsible. Nonetheless, she was a visible public intellectual, existing at the fringes of Greenwich Village's bohemia, writing for the *New Republic* and other literary magazines.

Empirical ethnography provided Parsons with a platform from which to critique North American society. Parsons was the first of many women attracted to the discipline by *Franz Boas*. She began intensive southwestern fieldwork around 1915, with frequent short trips arranged around family responsibilities. Boas joined her on three field trips, the first in 1919. Despite clandestine recording and publication of esoteric knowledge, she had good rapport in communities usually hostile to outsiders and took pride in her adoption into a Hopi family in 1920. Work at many different pueblos facilitated comparative treatment of social organization and religion, the latter summarized in two volumes of *Pueblo Indian Religion* (1939). Unlike many of her contemporaries, she sought out women in the field, collaborating extensively with Flora Zuñi.

At a time when most anthropologists reconstructed precontact American Indian cultures, Parsons focused on the mechanisms underlying the Spanish influence on aboriginal American societies. Fieldwork in Oaxaca, Mexico, allowed her to compare Spanish colonialism to the more Anglicized southwestern pueblos in *Mitla:Town of the Souls* (1936). *Peguche:A Study of Andean Indians* reported Parson's collaboration with Rosita Lema about an innovative woman's role in rapid culture change. Parsons and Lema shared a determination to create a future for the community through their actions.The research was incomplete when Parsons died but appeared posthumously in 1945.At the behest of Boas, Parsons also collected New World black folklore, culminating in three volumes on *Folk-Lore of the Antilles, French and English* (1943).

During the 1920s and 1930s, before university research funds or government grants, Boasian fieldwork was mainly supported by Parsons's targeted philanthropy. Her Southwest Society funded many women— including Ruth Bunzel, *Ruth Benedict*, Esther Goldfrank, Erna Gunther, Ruth Underhill, Gladys Reichard, and Zora Neale Hurston. She also supported *Leslie Spier, Leslie A.White*, and Melville Herskovits. She became militant when "disciplinary and sexual politics" excluded women from ordinary professional activities, for example at the all-male field school of the Laboratory of Anthropology in Santa Fe in 1929; *Edward Sapir* was her particular target (Deacon 1997:155–78).

Unseen behind the scenes, Parsons enabled many of Boas's administrative and organizational projects through personal labor and financial support. She was associate editor of the *Journal of American Folklore* from 1918 until her death in 1941. "Mrs. Parsons," as she was formally addressed by many younger Boasians who were intermittently dependent on her largesse, implemented many pet projects. She assembled the devotees of the American Museum of Natural History luncheon club to humanize the ponderous details of technical ethnographic monographs through individual life histories written by anthropologists who had worked in various American Indian cultures. Although

Parsons's primary motive was to popularize anthropology to the general American public, *American Indian Life* (1922) foreshadowed the culture-and-personality method within the discipline.

Parsons served as president of the American Folklore Society in 1919–20, the American Ethnological Society from 1923 to 1925, and the American Anthropological Association (AAA) in 1941. Just before she was to preside over the AAA annual meeting, she fell ill. She died on 19 December 1941 of complications from a long-standing kidney infection. She was 65 years old and had recently returned from a field trip to Ecuador. Her presidential address, "Anthropology and Prediction," read by Gladys Reichard and published in the *American Anthropologist* the following year, reflected her pervasive empiricism and her conviction that scientific generalization would better human society.

Only toward the end of Parson's life did her reputation begin to match her achievements. More recently, however, feminist scholars (e.g., Babcock and Parezo 1988, Deacon 1997, Falk 1999, Zumwalt 1992) have acknowledged her as an early public intellectual who brought anthropology to the attention of American society (a cudgel taken up by Margaret Mead). She died just days after Pearl Harbor rocked the world and America's role in it.

REGNA DARNELL

A. V. Kidder
1942

Alfred Vincent "Ted" Kidder was born in Marquette, Michigan, on 29 October 1885. He was the youngest of three sons. His father was a mining engineer who had moved from Boston to Marquette to work in the iron-mining region of the Upper Peninsula. His mother was also from an old New England family. When Kidder was a child the family returned to Cambridge, Massachusetts, where he attended private school until 1901. He studied in Switzerland for two years before returning for a final year in Boston. His father's library included many works in anthropology and exploration, and Kidder held the same interests from an early age. He entered Harvard in 1904 with plans to study medicine, but his nascent interest in anthropology was aroused by studies with *Roland B. Dixon*; Kidder received his A.B. in 1908, his A.M. in 1912, and his Ph.D. in 1914, working also with *William Curtis Farabee*, *Frederic Ward Putnam*, George Reisner, and *Alfred M. Tozzer*. His first field experience, in 1907, was archaeological work in the Four Corners area of the Southwest, which would dominate his career. The experience sealed his decision to change from medicine to anthropology. *Neil M. Judd*, who encountered Kidder in the field , writes of him, "Fresh from Harvard, erudite, and of magnificent physique, Kidder impressed all of us." In summer 1908 Kidder returned to the Southwest; again Judd describes Kidder, this time how he "cultivated a beard—the most luxuriant beard it is possible to imagine—a maganificient [sic] beard curly as a bull buffalo's shoulder and bronzed by the Utah sun." Kidder remained charismatic throughout his life.

In 1908–09 Kidder also traveled in the Mediterranean with his family, where he encountered Old World archaeological techniques and his wife-to-be, Madeleine Appleton, whose family traveled with Kidder's. Kidder recalled nothing particularly stimulating in the archaeological methods used in Greece and Egypt, but perhaps Madeleine's presence can account for that. They were married in 1910 and had five children over the next 12 years. Madeleine also collaborated with Kidder in his famous fieldwork at Pecos, New Mexico, and they coauthored an article in 1917. Despite this work with his wife, like many men of his time Kidder was not very supportive of women in anthropology (Zumwalt 1992:13–14).

Kidder's 1914 dissertation on southwestern ceramics was never published in full, but a chapter was published in 1915; the work involved a comparison of the details of ceramic decoration to assess the relationships between different groups. It stands as one of the first works of modern anthropological archaeology. After receiving his Ph.D. Kidder returned to northeastern Arizona, which generated another classic archaeological work (Kidder and Guernsey 1919) defining the three "culture periods" of the southwestern culture sequence (Basket Maker, Slabhouse, and Cliff House or Kiva), and including a definitive study of Basket Maker culture.

In the summer of 1915 Kidder began work at Pecos, New Mexico, under the auspices of the Phillips Academy of Andover, Massachusetts. Excavations continued there until 1929, with only a three-year break for World War I. The site was chosen because of indications of a long occupation including prehistoric and historic periods. It received a careful, detailed stratigraphic excavation on which many archaeologists were trained and from which several significant works were produced. Kidder's *An Introduction to the Study of Southwestern Archaeology, with a Preliminary Account of the Excavations at Pecos* (1924) was the first monograph drawn from this excavation. It included a masterful synthesis of the current knowledge of southwestern prehistory. During World War I Kidder served in France as lieutenant and captain in the infantry, where he was made Chevalier of the Légion d'Honneur, but he seldom spoke of his experiences there.

In addition to the ongoing work at Pecos, Kidder became increasingly involved in the 1920s in the Maya research projects of the Carnegie Institution of Washington DC; by 1929 he was named chair of the new Division of Historical Research. At Carnegie he fostered what he called a "pan-scientific" approach to Mayan culture, employing biological, medical, geological, and social science research. He considered archaeology to be necessarily both anthropological and historical, problem-oriented around questions of culture and cultural history, and operating in conjunction with the other fields of anthropology; he encouraged and cooperated with *Robert Redfield* on his well-known work in the region. Kidder was a pioneer in the use of aerial survey and photography in archaeology, flying with Charles Lindbergh over both Mayan and southwestern sites. Kidder headed the Division of Historical Research for two decades, writing and overseeing dozens of works, but he was never able to complete his intended pan-scientific synthesis of Mayan culture.

Kidder was chair of the board of the Laboratory of Anthropology at Santa Fe from 1927 to 1935, and on the faculty of the Peabody Museum at Harvard from 1939 to 1950; he was also one of the founders of the Institute of Andean Research, and in 1927 he was the founder and leader of the first Pecos conference, a development that reshaped understandings of southwestern archaeology. Kidder was well known by this time as "the Dean of Southwestern archaeology." He was president both of the American Anthropological Association (AAA) and the Society for American Archaeology, was elected to the National Academy of

Sciences and the American Academy of Arts and Sciences, and received the first Viking Fund Medal for Archaeology in 1946 and several honorary degrees. On the day of his retirement in 1950, the first Alfred Vincent Kidder Award, to be presented every three years by the AAA, was given to Alfred Tozzer. Kidder's work was not without critics, however; first *Clyde Kluckhohn's* "The Conceptual Structure in Middle American Studies" (1940) challenged his frameworks and commitment to broad cultural questions, and then Walter Taylor's *A Study of Archeology* (1948) continued the attack, arguing that Kidder's work was largely chronicle rather than truly historiographic. Taylor was later raised to the status of ancestor figure in American archaeology, but Kidder's contributions also retain their value.

Kidder taught for one semester at Berkeley in 1951 (his first formal teaching since graduate school), and he continued to publish for a decade after his "retirement." He died at home in Cambridge on 11 June 1963.

FREDERIC W. GLEACH

Leslie Spier
1943

One of four children, Leslie Spier was born in New York City on 13 December 1893, during one of the most exciting and dynamic times in the history of that great city. He received his B.S. degree in applied mathematics and engineering from the City College of New York in 1915. By that time he had already become interested in archaeology through his work as an assistant anthropologist for the New Jersey Archaeological and Geological Survey. An important early publication in the development of American archaeology was drawn from that work. Published in 1918, it demonstrated through statistical analysis that the posited New Jersey "argillite culture" did not exist. Spier's training in mathematics gave him the base to employ statistics and to be wary of their potential for abuse. After graduation Spier was drawn to work with *Franz Boas*, and in 1916 he began his graduate studies in anthropology at Columbia University. Spier shared Boas's interest in a holistic approach to anthropology. Like many other anthropologists he turned from his archaeological beginnings to work more broadly in the discipline, including research in language and physical anthropology.

While at Columbia Spier worked as an assistant anthropologist at the American Museum of Natural History. He also visited Zuni Pueblo, several Plains Indian groups, and the Havasupais, with whom he would do some of his most significant work. Also among the circle of Boas students was Erna Gunther; Spier married her in 1920, the same year that he received his Ph.D. and she her M.A., and together they moved to the University of Washington. During the 1920s they worked together with the Havasupais and the Coast Salish; later Spier was most closely associated with the Havasupais and Gunther with the Coast Salish. They had two sons, one of whom followed his parents into a career in anthropology. Spier and Gunther separated temporarily in 1927 when he took leave from Washington for a visiting appointment at the University of Oklahoma, beginning a four-year period of visiting appointments there and at the University of Chicago. In 1930 Spier resigned from Washington; he negotiated a permanent position for Gunther there, and they were divorced in 1931. Later that year Spier married Anna H. Gayton, another anthropologist, who studied with *Alfred L. Kroeber* and *Robert H. Lowie* at the University of California, Berkeley.

Spier enjoyed teaching, and by all accounts he was an excellent teacher, bringing to the classroom a broad knowledge of the discipline developed through his training, his research, and his experience editing a variety of anthropological publications. Deeply committed to the publication of research, he founded the *University of Washington Publications in Anthropology* series in 1925, the first of several periodicals that he established. When Spier first left Washington, he took a research position at Yale; it became a faculty position in 1933. While there he edited *Yale University Publications in Anthropology* from 1936 to 1938, and the *American Anthropologist* from 1934 to 1938. He also directed field studies at Chaco Canyon and other field training programs in both the Southwest and the Northwest. Spier left Yale in 1939 for the University of New Mexico, where he remained until he retired in 1955; while there he founded the *Southwestern Journal of Anthropology* (currently the *Journal of Anthropological Research*) and the *University of New Mexico Publications in Anthropology*, continuing with both until his death.

Spier conducted ethnographic fieldwork with a number of Native groups from the 1910s into the 1930s, including Zunis, Havasupais, Kiowas, Wichitas, Caddos, Dieguenos, Salish, Wishram, Klamaths, Maricopas, Okanagons, Mohaves and Modocs, and his publications set a recognized standard for thoroughness and meticulousness. He consistently went beyond description in his work—although his descriptions were excellent—to historical and comparative analysis, a strong characteristic of his work throughout his life; *Havasupai Ethnography* (1928), *Klamath Ethnography* (1930), *Wishram Ethnography* (1930, with *Edward Sapir*), and *Yuman Tribes of the Gila River* (1933) exemplify the quality of this work. Spier was remembered with respect and affection by the peoples he worked with, and respect for them was a cornerstone of his life and work.

Like Boas, Spier stressed a methodology in which theory was necessarily constrained and dominated by empirical data, the greatest possible objectivity, and extreme caution in interpretation; "theory," in fact, was virtually defined as the absence of such controls. From his beginning in archaeology Spier was interested in the distributions of cultures in space and time, and recognized the importance of specific contexts in studying culture. In his early work (e.g., *The Sun Dance of the Plains Indians* [1921], which was based on his dissertation) Spier used carefully documented trait distributions to reconstruct a history of the Plains Sun Dance, including considerations of its historical changes. This work was used by many other scholars, but Spier himself became increasingly critical of using distributional data for historical reconstruction. The more integrational focus of *The Prophet Dance of the Northwest and its Derivatives* (1935) exemplifies his later approach to historical reconstruction. He also had a strong interest in kinship studies.

Spier was not gregarious, and tended to avoid publicity and disciplinary politics whenever possible. He was nevertheless recognized for his contributions by election to the National Academy of Sciences, the American Philosophical Society, the American Academy of Arts and

Sciences, and the California Academy of Science. He received the Townsend Harris Medal in 1946 and the Viking Fund Medal in 1960. Spier was a meticulous and respectful worker. "Any well designed, scrupulously executed study evoked his enthusiastic admiration even if it were in a field remote from his own interests. A shoddy piece of work, particularly in anthropology, aroused his fierce, though usually well controlled, resentment" (Mandelbaum 1962:173). He died on 3 December 1961 in Albuquerque and was survived by both of his wives and his sons.

FREDERIC W. GLEACH

Robert Redfield
1944

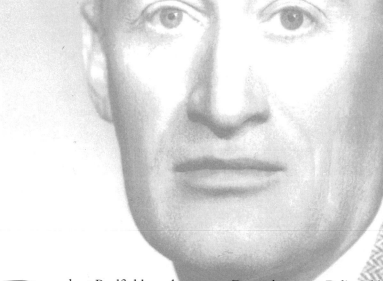

Robert Redfield was born on 4 December 1897. Believed by his overprotective (Danish) immigrant mother to be frail, Redfield was not sent to school until the ninth grade; he then attended the University of Chicago Laboratory School, founded by John Dewey. He read widely, and he carefully studied the local flora and fauna northwest of Chicago, where his father's family had owned property since 1833.

Horrifying his parents, Redfield became an ambulance driver in 1917 with the American Friends Field Service in France. Involved in only one battle, he received the Croix de Guerre. After the war he enrolled at Harvard University, where he was dismayed to find that students only worked on specimens preserved in formaldehyde. Redfield transferred to the University of Chicago after one term, graduating in 1920 with a philosophy major. In 1920 he married Margaret Park, the doted-upon daughter of Robert Park, the central figure in the Chicago School of Sociology at Chicago.

The senior Redfield pressed his son into law school (J.D., 1922). After clerking for a federal judge, Robert unhappily joined his father's firm. Dismayed, Park offered the couple a thousand dollars to undertake something else; they went to Mexico in 1923. There Redfield met and was inspired by Manuel Gamio. In 1924 Redfield began graduate studies in Chicago's sociology and anthropology department. He was a student of Boasians *Fay-Cooper Cole* and *Edward Sapir*, as well as of his father-in-law and Ernest Burgess, champions of urban ethnography. Under Burgess's supervision, Redfield worked half-time observing Mexicans in Chicago for a practicum in sociology (Godoy 1978:51–52).

Redfield applied in 1926 for a fellowship from the Committee on the Scientific Aspects of Human Migration of the Social Science Research Council to conduct fieldwork in Mexico. His research project was very much in the Thomas-Park tradition of Chicago sociology, which held that immigrants' slow and partial assimilation constituted a social problem.

Although Redfield proposed a nomothetic study of culture, he did not aim to inventory traits in the Boas-Kroeber manner, but rather to explore "attitudes" and the role of "communication" in cultural change within the Thomas-Park tradition, as well as ecological variation in culture and mentality in the Park-Burgess tradition. Following the spatial logic of Chicago sociology research, and foreshadowing the synchronic treatment of "modernization" in *Folk Culture of the Yucatán* (Redfield 1941), Redfield charted change across space (from the zocalo to barrios) rather than through time.

Accompanied by his wife, his mother-in-law, and two children under the age of three, on 4 December 1926 Redfield set up a household in Tepoztlán, Morelos, the village in central Mexico suggested by Gamio. Following a Cristero (Catholic counter-revolutionary) raid on 18 February 1927, Redfield evacuated his family to a suburb of Mexico City. He commuted to Tepoztlán until the end of June, when he left for Chicago. Although four to five months was a relatively long span of time for fieldwork in the mid-1920s, Redfield's was much better funded than most; he had support for a full year. Like *Margaret Mead* in Samoa, however, he left the field many months ahead of schedule. Despite the admitted sketchiness of its ethnography, *Tepoztlán* (1930) was reviewed positively. It established Redfield as the premier American anthropological authority on peasants and their acculturation.

Redfield consolidated his status by directing Carnegie-funded work on Yucatán communities. The work was conceptually organized along a folk-urban continuum, exemplified in space rather than time by its comparison of locales in the Yucatán. The relatively newly founded peasant community Chan Kom that Redfield studied was not at all a traditional village at the time of his first visit (1930–31) and was more socioeconomically stratified than Redfield claimed. The village, in particular its leader, had already "chosen progress" (Redfield 1950).

Redfield spent ten weeks visiting Chan Kom during the early 1930s. According to his co-researcher Alfonso Villa Rojas (1979:47–48) Redfield "had a facility for making friends with people; on the other hand, he did not really establish close ties with his informants. . . . He had a way of asking complex questions that informants found difficult to answer."

Redfield became an instructor in anthropology at Chicago in 1927; an assistant professor the next year, upon completion of his dissertation; an associate professor upon its publication in 1930; and a full professor upon publication of *Chan Kom* in 1934. Also in 1934 he began an 11-year tenure as dean of the Division of Social Sciences. Redfield was a favorite of University of Chicago president Robert Hutchins and, appropriately, became Hutchins Distinguished Professor in 1953.

In addition to pushing through educational changes at the University of Chicago, Redfield was active in organizations that defended civil liberties, particularly of racial-ethnic minorities. He was a director of the American Council on Race Relations and worked closely with the National Association for the Advancement of Colored People in its long-running desegregation campaign.

Redfield visited Guatemala periodically between 1937 and 1941. After resigning as dean in 1946 he returned to Chan Kom. The Chan Kom sequel was published in 1950, but by the late 1940s Redfield's

interests had shifted from Mesoamerica. In 1948 the Redfields undertook a world tour. Redfield had planned to teach for a year at Tsinghua
University in China, but the Chinese civil war prevented this. He fell
ill in southern China and left to recuperate in Sicily. During his conva-
lescence he outlined a new project that would compare civilizations'
(written) "grand traditions" with local ("folk") "little traditions" and
examine the transformation of local ways and values during "modernization" (Redfield 1953, 1955, 1956).

Robert Hutchins, by then an officer of the Ford Foundation, arranged support for Redfield's comparative program. Supplemented by
Carnegie Foundation funding, Redfield was galvanized into a new
burst of theorizing. China "having proved inaccessible, he turned to
India as the object of a study of an oriental civilization 'from the bot-
tom up,' through a village community. Although illness frustrated this
second attempt at a field study of civilization, from 1951 to 1958 Redfield
organized and chaired a continuing seminar on 'the comparison of
Cultures'" (Singer and J. Redfield 1999:253).

Redfield died of leukemia in Chicago on 16 October 1958, before
attempting to explicate the interrelations of great and small traditions
of India.

STEPHEN O. MURRAY

Neil M. Judd
1945

N eil Merton Judd was born in Cedar Rapids, Nebraska, on 19 December 1887. He studied Greek and Latin at the University of Utah with his uncle, Byron Cummings, who was the force behind the University Museum and had begun the teaching of archaeology in Salt Lake City. Judd began his practical apprenticeship in southeastern Utah archaeology as Cummings's field assistant from 1907 to 1909. After three summers, Judd transferred to work for Edgar L. Hewett, director of the School of American Research at Santa Fe.

In 1911 Judd began a 39-year affiliation with the United States National Museum in the Smithsonian Institution. Judd was hired as an aide in the Division of Ethnology, but his work was always in archaeology. He served directly under *William Henry Holmes*, head curator of anthropology; *Walter Hough* was curator of ethnology, and *Frederick Webb Hodge* headed the Bureau of American Ethnology (BAE). Judd's new colleagues included two brothers, Cosmo and Victor Mindeleff, and archaeological photographer W. H. Jackson. These were the men who had been defining "the foundation of southwestern archaeology for the preceding half century" (Brew 1978:352).

Judd received a B.A. from the University of Utah in 1911 and an M.A. from George Washington University in 1913. Deterred by the costs of attending Harvard, the only American university with a doctoral program in archaeology, and constrained to retain his employment in Washington DC, Judd elected to continue learning his archaeology informally through museum, fieldwork, and collegial interaction.

Judd became an assistant curator in the Division of Anthropology in 1918 and curator of American archaeology in 1919, a position he held until 1930. He served as curator of archaeology from 1930 until his retirement in 1949. He held an honorary position as an associate in anthropology until his death on 19 December 1976.

Judd was "the mainstay" of the National Museum in curating its collections (Brew 1978:353). His fieldwork specialization became archaeological survey in relatively unknown areas, particularly the Four Corners area of the Southwest. Through most of the 1920s, southwestern archaeology accumulated contradictory data without effort at synthesis; nonetheless, it was in the Southwest that "cohesiveness of research effort" in American archaeology coalesced (Emil Haury in Woodbury 1993:xvii).

In western and southern Utah Judd excavated the Kaiparowits Plateau, White Canyon, Payson, part of the old California Trail at Betatakin, and the north rim of the Grand Canyon. The preliminary results of his survey work from 1915 to 1920 were published by the BAE in 1926.

Judd's research was frequently seconded by other institutions. He discovered the Rainbow Bridge on a joint expedition of the U.S. General Land Office and the University of Utah, modestly giving credit to Paiute guide Nasja-Begay's prior knowledge of the location. The bureau assigned him to investigate the so-called Spanish diggings in Wyoming, which turned out to be Indian quartzite quarries. Hewett borrowed him to create reproductions of monumental Mayan sculptures from Guatemala for the San Diego International Exposition. Senator Carl Hayden, a major architect of the postwar Interagency River Basin Salvage Program, requested Gila-Salt River Basin studies of prehistoric irrigation canals as land was reclaimed for Pima Indians to grow cotton.

Judd's most extensive project was the excavation of Pueblo Bonito in Chaco Canyon, New Mexico, from 1921 to 1927 for the National Geographic Society. With 800 rooms, this was the largest excavation in Southwestern archaeology to the time. Not surprisingly, not all of Judd's interpretations have stood the test of time. Assuming that Chaco Canyon was isolated from outside influence, he thought that the roads out of Chaco Canyon were designed to transport logs for kiva and house roofs, whereas contemporary archaeologists believe they were external connections for trade networks and ceremonial exchange (Woodbury 1993:7). Judd's major site reports for Pueblo Bonito and for Chaco Canyon did not appear until 1954 and 1959 respectively.

At Pueblo Bonito, Judd established the precedent of inviting interdisciplinary experts to visit the Chaco Canyon field camp at the end of each summer's digging season. It was here that A. E. Douglass first tested his new method of dendrochronology on structural timbers from Pueblo Bonito in 1922. Judd was quick to realize that tree-ring dates held unique potential for establishing absolute dates. A master sequence back to A.D. 1400 was calibrated by 1927, and two years later an earlier floating tree-ring sequence was extended to A.D. 700.

The interdisciplinary openness of the camp during this long excavation was "the forerunner of the Pecos Conference" established in its final year (Brew 1978:353). Judd and A. V. Kidder were close friends, and so Judd did not object when Kidder took over in 1927. The focus of the conference changed, consequently, from interdisciplinary collaboration to a gathering of active archaeologists to exchange information on their ongoing excavations and interpretations (Woodbury 1993:15). The 45 attendees of the first Pecos conference had grown to more than three hundred after 60 years (Haury in Woodbury 1993:xvii).

After his retirement, Judd took it upon himself to record the history of the institutions he had been part of. *The Bureau of American Ethnol-*

ogy: A Partial History in 1967 and *Men Met along the Trail: Adventures in Archaeology* in 1968 matter-of-factly recorded the activities and publications of American archaeology. The former was written to mark the end of an era, the merger of the BAE with the Department of Anthropology of the National Museum to form the Smithsonian Institution's Office of Anthropology in 1964. Judd dedicated his work to the people who made the institution, all of them known to him from 1910 on; he "held most of them in high regard" and did not elaborate on the exceptions (Judd 1967:vii). During much of Judd's career, survey and descriptive archaeology were necessary preludes to more intensive and interpretive studies. His contributions were empirical and based on meticulous fieldwork, and he was of the last generation of archaeologists to make a distinguished career without formal academic credentials.

Judd served the American Anthropological Association as treasurer from 1916 to 1919 and was elected president in 1945. He was president of the Anthropological Society of Washington in 1928.

He is remembered for his responsiveness to inquirers at the National Museum and his behind-the-scenes mentoring of younger professionals. His stature in southwestern archaeology was recognized by the Kidder Award in 1965.

REGNA DARNELL

Ralph Linton
1946

Ralph Linton, christened Rolfe after a distant ancestor who married Pocahontas, was born in Philadelphia on 27 February 1893. His father, Isaiah W. Linton, came from a Devonshire Quaker family holding land grants from William Penn. His mother, Elizabeth Gillingham, was an old maid of thirty caring for her invalid mother when she married. Linton brooded for life over his unhappy childhood, dominated by his authoritarian father.

The family lived with Mrs. Linton's mother in Moorestown, New Jersey, until her death. At Moorestown Friends School, Ralph was "a fat, red-haired boy, disinterested and inept at sports and outstandingly bright . . . except in spelling and arithmetic" (A. Linton and Wagley 1971:6–7). Isaiah Linton ran a chain of restaurants in Philadelphia where Ralph worked—without access to the resulting savings account. Meat cutting skills, however, served Ralph well for woodcarving in the

Marquesas Islands, and an elderly Philadelphia jeweller inculcated his lifelong love of colorful gemstones.

Linton entered Swarthmore College in 1911, successfully battling his father's insistence on engineering rather than biology. He discovered archaeology digging at Mesa Verde (where he wrote a prizewinning poem about a night alone in a cliff house), in coastal lowland Guatemala (where he was intrigued by the Mayan workmen), and in New Jersey. He graduated Phi Beta Kappa in 1915 and married his classmate Josephine Foster.

Linton's M.A. in anthropology from the University of Pennsylvania in 1916 combined archaeology with ethnology under Frank Speck. Transferring to Columbia University to work with *Franz Boas*, he performed poorly in anthropological linguistics and reacted against Boas's perceived authoritarianism. At the outbreak of World War I he finished the year and the summer archaeology season and then enlisted. He was read out of the Moorestown Friends Meeting (although he was later reinstated and remained a member until after his mother died); his wife left him. He later wrote about totemism in a military unit (1924). Returning from the war in 1919, he visited Boas while still in uniform. Boas, who had opposed American involvement in the war, was unimpressed. Linton promptly enrolled at Harvard University, where, despite feeling socially inferior and unappreciated, he received a Ph.D. in 1925.

In 1920 Linton joined E. S. C. Handy's Marquesas Islands expedition for the Bishop Museum. His dissertation on material culture (1923) and his archaeological survey (1925) consolidated his shift from archaeology to ethnology. Linton learned Marquesan woodcarving from the "special occupational-priestly class" (A. Linton and Wagley 1971:21), described the polyandrous family, and discovered Paul Gauguin's grave.

In 1922 Linton became assistant curator at the Field Museum in Chicago. Despite his nominal American Indian position, he led an ethnographic survey and collecting expedition to Madagascar in 1925, producing a monograph on the Tanalas (1935). Linton contracted severe malaria (which ended his tropical fieldwork) and encountered considerable local resistance during his travels in the interior. He studied divining, providing a parlor trick until disturbingly accurate negative predictions proved uncomfortable to his friends.

Linton was remarried to Margaret McIntosh, a Swarthmore classmate, with whom he had a son; a year after their divorce in 1934, Linton married Adelin Hohlfeld, a widow and journalist.

Linton became an associate professor in 1928 and professor in 1929 at the University of Wisconsin, introducing anthropology in the sociology department and discovering a vocation for teaching. As the sole anthropologist (joined later by Charlotte Gower), Linton continued Midwestern archaeology and explored interdisciplinary contacts, encountering the functionalism of Radcliffe-Brown through his Chicago ties. Despite personal animosity, Linton and Radcliffe-Brown taught a joint seminar at Wisconsin in 1936. Linton's textbook *The Study of Man* appeared the same year. He emphasized historical process and the function of trait-complexes, differentiating form, meaning, use, and function. He distinguished status (positions within a society occupied by individuals, either ascribed at birth or achieved), and role (the dynamic aspect of status) as well as ideal and actual behavior.

When Boas retired in 1936, the Columbia University administration ignored his wishes regarding his replacement. Linton was appointed visiting professor in 1937 and professor and chair in 1938. Boas's obvious successor, *Ruth Benedict*, was passively hostile, and Linton's retaliation caused considerable tension within the program.

Linton edited *Acculturation in Seven American Indian Tribes* (1940) and worked to fund student fieldwork during the Depression. Through the Social Science Research Council Committee on Personality and Culture, he collaborated with *Robert Redfield* and Melville Herskovits in a "Memorandum for the Study of Acculturation" (1936). He sent *Charles Wagley* to central Brazil and Carl Withers to a midwestern town which he called Plainville U.S.A. in his published work.

At the New York Psychoanalytic Institute from 1935 to 1938, Abram Kardiner used anthropologists as informants to analyze cross-cultural data. Although leery of Kardiner's emphasis on socialization, Linton presented his Marquesan and Tanala data. In 1940 the Kardiner-Linton seminar moved to Columbia. *Cora Du Bois's* Alor work exemplifies this period. Linton's own ideas appeared in *The Cultural Background of Personality* (1945).

During World War II Linton taught at Yale University as well as at Columbia. Linton was active in Columbia's training program in military government and administration established for the U.S. Navy in 1942, which grew into the School of International Affairs and several area institutes. Linton edited *The Science of Man in the World Crisis* (1945) to educate Americans about cultural differences. His posthumous *The Tree of Culture* (1955) is pessimistic about human history, seeing totalitarian closures of "a rare period of freedom" already threatened by bigotries (A. Linton and Wagley 1971:74).

In 1946 Linton became Sterling Professor of Anthropology at Yale; despite heart problems, he refused to slow down or give up his New York contacts. In the early 1950s he enjoyed the University of Pennsylvania Museum's "What in the World" television program identifying ethnographic specimens, and he began to collect African art. At Yale's Institute of Human Relations he returned to psychiatry and culture questions (Linton 1956).

Ralph Linton "brought anthropology out of the museums and into the mainstream of the social sciences" (A. Linton and Wagley 1971:1), adding a dimension of process to Boasian historical particularism. He served as vice president of the American Association for the Advancement of Science in 1937, editor of the *American Anthropologist* from 1939 to 1944, and president of the American Anthropological Association in 1946. He received the Viking Fund Medal in 1951. He had been designated as the second American to receive the Huxley Medal when he died of a heart attack on 24 December 1953.

REGNA DARNELL

Ruth Benedict
January–May 1947

R uth Fulton Benedict was born on 5 June 1887. Her father, Frederick Fulton was a medical doctor who died soon after the birth of her sister, Margery, a year and a half later. Her mother, Beatrice Shattuck Fulton, never recovered from this shock. Ruth was indelibly imprinted with the image of peaceful death contrasted to the maternal hysteria of grief. In 1895 Ruth's partial deafness, as a result of childhood illness, was diagnosed. The Fulton sisters attended the elite St. Margaret's Academy in Buffalo where their mother worked in the public library. Ruth explored her feminine identity through writing. The sisters enrolled at Vassar College in 1905. After graduation in 1909 Margery married Robert Freeman, a minister, and Ruth traveled to Europe with friends.

Benedict worked as a social worker in Buffalo in 1910–11 and taught in Los Angeles from 1911–14 while living with her sister and brother-in-law. In 1914 she married Stanley Rossiter Benedict, a biochemist and friend of a college classmate; she expected her restlessness to be stemmed by marriage and children. Benedict contributed to the war effort by writing biographies of three feminists, beginning with Mary Wollstonecraft; the stories of Margaret Fuller and Olive Schreiner were left unfinished.

In 1919, after the war, Benedict enrolled at the New School for Social Research, hoping to comprehend this conflict of nations that had devastated the complacency of North America. At the New School she studied with Boasian anthropologists Alexander Goldenweiser and *Elsie Clews Parsons*. In 1921 Parsons introduced Benedict to *Franz Boas*, and she entered the Ph.D. program at Columbia University. Boas, *Edward Sapir*, and later, *Margaret Mead*, became her icons in the new discipline. During the 1920s Benedict published poetry under the pseudonym Anne Singleton, although Sapir in particular urged her to transfer her full energy to anthropology. Margaret Mead quickly went from being Benedict's student to friend and colleague (Mead ed. 1959, 1974, Lapsley 1999).

Benedict's 1923 dissertation on the guardian spirit quest in North America explored the problem of individual religious experience in relation to cultural context and mapped continental variations and unique integrations of visionary practice. Benedict's fieldwork focused on the relationship of culture and personality with the Serrano Indians in California in 1922 (supervised by *Alfred L. Kroeber*), with the Zunis in the Southwest in 1924 and 1925, at Zuni and Cochiti pueblos in 1927, and among the Pimas in 1927. In 1931 she led a student field party to the Apaches and in 1939 to the Blackfoot, expanding her Pueblo experience into the Plains.

The "Apollonian" Pueblo and "Dionysian" Plains Indians presented powerful contrasts in temperament and custom that Benedict elaborated on in *Patterns of Culture* (1934), her most famous work. To these cases she added contrasting portraits of the paranoid Melanesian Dobuans as described by Mead's then-husband Reo Fortune and the megalomaniacal Kwakiutl as reported by Boas. Together these three portraits of culture as "personality writ large" provided her with a template for the critique of North American society: "The portraits of a near-socialistic, a jealously possessive, and highly competitive society told a powerful lesson to a 1930s America facing the Great Depression" (Modell 1989:3). Her personal alienation from North American society led not only to a cultural reformulation of the notions of normal and abnormal psychology but also to *Race: Science and Politics* in 1940. She brought both psychology and humanism into the practice of Americanist anthropology.

During World War II Benedict reported on both allied and enemy nations for the Office of War Information in the Bureau of Overseas Intelligence. *The Chrysanthemum and the Sword* (1946) was intended to produce humane and effective postwar policy toward Japan. Social engineering could be based on cultural analysis of national character even without first-hand fieldwork. Benedict's work popularized the Boasian concept of cultural relativism. Anthropology was a tool to bring about cross-cultural tolerance, a method of moving away from American isolationism and prejudice. After her death, Mead and Rhoda Métraux continued the Columbia Research in Contemporary Cultures project that she founded.

Benedict edited the *Journal of American Folklore* from 1924 to 1939 and began teaching at Columbia University in 1923. Until Boas retired in 1936, Benedict was his closest associate. She received little public recognition of her work until after her marriage to Stanley Benedict disintegrated and she needed a salaried position. Columbia promoted her to professor only in 1948; she had been teaching there for 26 years, 12 of them as an associate professor.

Benedict was elected president of the American Anthropological Association in 1947 and died on 17 September 1948, just before she was to deliver her presidential address on anthropology and the humanities; the life history was her favored mode of analysis, allowing her to "test out a culture by showing its working in the life of a carrier of that culture" (1948:592).

Benedict's primary legacy resides in her style of writing, "a powerful expository style at once spare, assured, lapidary, and above all resolute" (Geertz 1988:108), rather than her fieldwork or theoretical acumen. Despite criticism of her purported cultural determinism and superficially impressionistic method of constructing the integrity of a cultural pattern and of individual personality configurations within it, she successfully problematized the taken-for-granted patterns of her own society for a wide audience. Although her "configurational, thematic, and value-oriented" approach (Mintz 1981:152) seemed to clash with the postwar turn to materialism, ecology, and renewed evolutionism, what Benedict called "multicultural awareness" was the unique contribution of anthropology. Individual choice was possible, both for societies described ethnographically and for anthropologically informed members of her own society. Her postwar work employed the concept of synergy to move "beyond cultural relativism" to cultural critique (Benedict 1970, Young MS).

Benedict the person remains somewhat elusive, despite considerable scholarship. Mead has written about her and about their friendship (1959 ed., 1974). Lapsley (1999) has explored their intellectual and sexual intimacies. Modell's biography (1983) emphasizes Benedict's alienation from the culture of her upbringing, resolved first through her poetry and later, more fully, through her anthropology, whereas Caffrey (1989) emphasizes Benedict's "cultural feminism," in which her poetry, anthropology, and modernism formed a single package of contemporary relevance.

REGNA DARNELL

Clyde Kluckhohn
May–December 1947

Clyde Kay Maben was born in Le Mars, Iowa, on 11 January 1905. His mother died shortly after his birth and he was adopted by his mother's brother, George Wesley Kluckhohn, and his wife Katherine. After spending his early years in Le Mars, Clyde attended Lawrenceville School in New Jersey and began his undergraduate studies at Princeton University. Ill health interrupted his studies, and he was sent to live with his adoptive mother's cousins Shirley and Evon Zartman Vogt Sr. in Ramah, New Mexico. From the Vogt Ranch, he took a number of horseback trips, the first when he was only 18 to the (then) nearly inaccessible Rainbow Bridge in Utah.

He wrote about these experiences in *To the Foot of the Rainbow* (1927) and *Beyond the Rainbow* (1933). During this period he was introduced to the Navajos, including those who lived in the Ramah area, and developed his life-long attachment to the Southwest. He once told David Aberle, as they sat with a Navajo family in front of a flickering fire watching the sun set gradually over red sandstone, "To me it's the most beautiful place in the whole world" (Aberle in Taylor, Fischer, and Vogt 1973:84).

Kluckhohn enrolled in the University of Wisconsin, where he majored in classics and received his B.A. in 1928. In 1931–32 he studied at the University of Vienna, where he underwent psychoanalysis, and he received a Rhodes scholarship to study anthropology at Oxford University with R. R. Marrett. In 1932 he married Florence Rockwood. Their only child, Richard, was born in 1934. Kluckhohn was an assistant professor at the University of New Mexico between 1932 and 1934. From 1934 to 1936 he worked on completing his Ph.D. at Harvard University, and in 1935 he was appointed as an instructor there; he remained at Harvard for the rest of his academic career.

In 1936 he returned to serious ethnographic work among the Ramah Navajos. His meticulous description and his concern for understanding cultural variability led him to stress the importance of long-term research by a team of anthropologists and students.

Kluckhohn worked closely with Lee C. Wyman to describe Navajo ceremonies and to understand how ceremonial knowledge was transmitted. He also planned a study of the socialization of Navajo children, an outgrowth of his interest in culture and personality and his contact with Dorothea and Alexander Leighton. After two summers he decided his initial description showed that "we had not yet mastered the basic patterns let alone the cultural dynamics" (quoted in Parsons and Vogt 1962:140–161). By 1939 he favored a long-term study, to overcome the "flat, one-dimensional quality" of most anthropological studies. He began the Ramah project to facilitate "multiple observations by different persons and multiple approaches by individuals who had received their training in various disciplines." The Leightons were his most important collaborators, but 15 graduate students from Harvard and other institutions also participated in summer fieldwork. This research contributed to *Children of the People* (1947, coauthored with Dorothea Leighton) and other publications in the Peabody Museum series. Kluckhohn's broadening knowledge of Navajo culture and language allowed him to craft *The Navaho* with Dorothea Leighton (1946), the standard text on the Navajos for over 35 years.

Although not a student of *Franz Boas*, Kluckhohn drew on the work of Boasians (e.g., *Ruth Benedict, Alfred L. Kroeber* and *Edward Sapir*), as well as clinical psychologists and other social scientists at Harvard, to forge his approach to culture. For Kluckhohn culture consisted of "designs for living" or "the set of habitual and traditional ways of thinking, feeling, and reacting that are characteristic of the ways a particular society meets its problems at a particular point in time" (Kluckhohn and Leighton 1946:xviii).

Following Benedict, Kluckhohn saw these designs for living as structured ways of thinking and doing, as "patterned." By pattern he meant an overt, conscious aspect of culture, a discrete interrelated set of facts that produces structural regularities in the realm of ideas (ideal patterns) or consistencies in social relationships and action (behavioral patterns). In contrast, patterning at the covert level was characterized as configuration, a generalization from behavior that was largely unconscious or unverbalized by the participants in a culture. The concepts of pattern and configuration helped Kluckhohn deal with variation in Navajo life both in examining topics of general ethnographic interest (e.g. ceremonialism, social organization) and in studying socialization and personality. In this period he was also influenced by functionalism. His well-known monograph *Navajo Witchcraft* (1944) is a blend of precise ethnographic recording and the analysis of Navajo witchcraft in terms of "functional dependencies." For Kluckhohn, Navajo witchcraft provided "culturally defined adaptive and adjustive responses," responses that adjust individuals to their larger social environment or contribute to the survival of either the individual or the society (Kluckhohn 1944:79).

After 1947 he launched the Comparative Study of Values in Five Cultures Project, funded by the Rockefeller Foundation. Over 35 fieldworkers from a variety of disciplines studied the five groups living in the Ramah area: the Mormons, the Texan homesteaders, the Spanish Americans, the Zunis, and the Navajos. At first Kluckhohn defined values as "orientations toward experience which influence choice," comparable to his notion of ideal patterns. Later he developed a framework for comparison of value emphases based on binary oppositions (Kluckhohn 1958). He outlined 13 value pairs (e.g., individual-group, unitary-pluralistic) to compare the values of different cultures; one cluster revolved around how a culture views relations between "Man and Nature," a second cluster centered on relations between "Man and Man," and a third around both "Nature and Man." Most of the results of the values project were published by other researchers on the project. A few were published after Kluckhohn's death (e.g., F. Kluckhohn and Strodbeck 1961).

Kluckhohn had considerable impact outside anthropology as an administrator and a public intellectual. During World War II he served as a staff member in the School for Overseas Administration (1943–44), the co-chief of the Joint Morale Survey in the Military Intelligence Service and the Office of War Information (1944–45), and a consultant to the secretary of war (attached to General MacArthur's headquarters, 1946–47). After the war he worked with the Department of Defense from 1948 to 1954 and the Department of State from 1956 to 1960, and he was the director of Harvard's Russian Institute from 1947 to 1954.

Kluckhohn died suddenly on 29 July 1960 in Santa Fe, New Mexico, after suffering a heart attack. He was 55 years old.

LOUISE LAMPHERE

Harry Shapiro
1948

Harry Lionel Shapiro was born on 19 March 1902 to a family of first-generation immigrant Polish Jews in Boston. He was the second of three sons. From a job peddling in the Lower East Side of New York City, his father had developed a successful business and moved to Boston before the children were born. Harry competed for and won a place in the prestigious Boston Latin School and was subsequently admitted to Harvard University, where he matriculated in 1919.

Shapiro was unsure of his choice of major until he took a class from Earnest Hooton, who inspired him to study physical anthropology seriously. Graduating magna cum laude in 1923, Shapiro remained at Harvard to become the first in a long line of Hooton's doctoral students in anthropology; in preparation for his doctoral research Shapiro also studied for a year at the Bussey Institute for Applied Biology at Harvard, working in statistics and human genetics. His doctoral thesis was on "race mixture," a subject he would continue to pursue throughout his career. The dissertation focused on the Polynesian-English population descended from the mutineers on the Bounty, after they had been transplanted from Pitcairn Island to Norfolk Island. Shapiro found that "race mixture" did *not* lead to degeneration, either physically or culturally, but rather to what he called "hybrid vigor." This study contrasted markedly from the only prior such study, on a colored-white community in South Africa, by the German geneticist and anthropologist Eugen Fischer.

Upon receiving his doctorate in 1926, Shapiro accepted an assistant curatorship at the American Museum of Natural History, where he remained for the rest of his career. He succeeded *Clark Wissler* as chair of the anthropology department in 1942, a post he held until his retirement in 1970.

Shapiro's work on "race mixture" permitted him to straddle the increasingly wide gap between the physical anthropology of his training with Hooton and the Boasian anthropology being taught in New York. In 1929 Charles Davenport and Morris Steggerda published *Race Crossing in Jamaica*, which argued along the lines of Eugen Fischer that interbreeding was harmful to human populations. Shapiro returned to the population of his doctoral project and published *The Heritage of the Bounty* in 1936, arguing in contrast that not only was "race crossing" not biologically harmful, but that it had been a positive cultural stimulus in the development of civilization.

His address on anthropology's contribution to interracial understanding, published in *Science* in 1944, derives its central arguments from Franz Boas's *The Mind of Primitive Man*, and cites no other source either in physical or cultural anthropology.

What is possibly Shapiro's most enduring work, that of immigrant studies and the developmental plasticity of the human body, lies within a field first plowed by Boas. Assisted by Frederick Hulse, Shapiro studied Japanese immigrants to Hawaii and contrasted them with their relatives who remained in Japan (sedentes) and their offspring born in Hawaii. The physical differences between the sedentes and immigrants replicated the results of Boas on the effect within a single generation of immigration upon the bodies of Italians and Jews. The same pattern of differences between the immigrants and their own children showed that the trend was real and multigenerational, and therefore not transient (or perhaps to be followed by a reversion to a racial norm).

Forensic anthropology was another of Shapiro's interests, and during World War II he worked on identifying the bodies of dead soldiers. After the war Shapiro grew into the role of a public anthropologist, writing many articles for mass consumption in *Natural History*, the magazine of the American Museum of Natural History. His popular book *Peking Man* also contributed to public anthropology, bringing together paleoanthropological insights and a lifetime of acquaintance with the material and its principal students.

Although bearing an obviously Jewish name, Shapiro moved freely in presumptively Gentile circles. After the American Eugenics Society was "reformed" by Frederick Osborn, Shapiro served as its president from 1955 to 1962; before its reformation, when much of its effort was devoted to promoting xenophobic legislation, its supporters had included Shapiro's advisor Hooton and his supervisor at the American Museum, Clark Wissler. Although much of his professional output was devoted to the "mixed race" populations of Polynesia, Shapiro also researched and wrote a monograph on his own ancestry, published by UNESCO in 1960 as *The Jewish People: A Biological History*.

Although known as a helpful colleague to his peers, Shapiro had a more ambivalently exploitative attitude toward his juniors. Neither William Lessa nor Frederick Hulse had been permitted to use in their own doctoral theses the data on Asian migrants they collected for Shapiro. Shapiro published on the data Hulse collected in *Migration and Environment*, but he never published on the data Lessa collected (Lasker 1999). Nor did he welcome *Sherwood Washburn*, a new Ph.D. teaching at Columbia Medical School, into his anthropological circle (Washburn, personal communication). In person, however, Shapiro affected a genteel and cordial air. He was an accomplished cellist and skilled gardener, and he was rarely seen without his pipe. Shapiro and his wife, Janice, had three sons during their 24-year marriage, which ended with her death in 1962. In addition to their home on the Upper East Side of

New York City the Shapiros had a home and gardens in upstate New York that Harry helped to build.

Elected to the National Academy of Sciences in 1949, Shapiro served on many committees for the academy and the National Research Council. The Theodore Roosevelt Distinguished Service Medal was bestowed on him in 1964, and he was subsequently honored by the New York Academy of Sciences and the American Academy of Forensic Sciences. In addition to serving as president of the American Anthropological Association, he was president of the American Ethnological Society in 1942–43.

Shapiro died in New York City on 7 January 1990.

JONATHAN MARKS

A. Irving Hallowell
1949

Alfred Irving "Pete" Hallowell was born in Philadelphia on 28 December 1892. He was an only child of Philadelphia natives. His father worked in the shipbuilding industry, and his mother taught school until she married. When Pete graduated in 1911 from a manual training school, she encouraged him to attend the Wharton School of Finance and Commerce at the University of Pennsylvania. There he became interested not in business, but in sociology, economics, and social reform. After his degree he spent eight years as a social worker. While taking further courses in sociology at the University of Pennsylvania, Hallowell became friends with Frank Speck, an Algonquianist trained by *Franz Boas*, and he moved to anthropology. He received his M.A. in 1920 and his Ph.D. in 1924. His dissertation, based on library research, focused on bear ceremonialism in the Northern Hemisphere.

Hallowell taught at the University of Pennsylvania from the early

1920s to 1962, with the exception of three years (1944 to 1947) at Northwestern University. Frank Speck had a formative influence, taking Hallowell on some of his field trips and inculcating in him many of his diverse interests, including social organization, ecology, folklore, religious beliefs, and ethnohistory (before it became defined as a field).

Many anthropologists settle on a domain of fieldwork while in graduate school. For Hallowell, that moment did not come until 1930, when he received Social Science Research Council funding to work among the Crees north of Lake Winnipeg. His project was to pursue research on Northern Algonquian cross-cousin marriage, a pattern for which he had assembled historical and linguistic data, and for which he found support in William Duncan Strong's ethnographic work with the Naskapis (Innus) of Labrador. The summer of 1930 was productive, but Hallowell never returned to the Crees because another opportunity arose for him; while traveling by steamer up Lake Winnipeg to the Crees, Hallowell met at Berens River the Ojibwa chief of that region, William Berens, an influential bilingual leader who informed him that non-Christian, traditional Ojibwa communities could be found up the Berens River, from Little Grand Rapids (Manitoba) into northwestern Ontario. Berens offered to take Hallowell to these communities, and in 1932 Hallowell was able to accept. His close collaboration with Berens extended through several more summer visits until his last field trip in 1940.

Hallowell's most well known ethnographic publications arose from this work. Amounting to close to forty articles (many of which are collected in Hallowell 1955, 1976), and two monographs (1942, 1992), they cover a remarkable range of topics related to Ojibwa religion, world view, spatial and temporal perception, myths, dreams, and psychology. The information he gathered provided, in turn, a base for analyses that offered new ways of thinking about the concepts of person and self, about the relations of myths and dreams, and about human behavioral environments as culturally constituted.

In the late 1930s and early 1940s, Hallowell turned increasingly to psychological studies, exploring the potentialities of the Rorschach test as a relatively culture-free mode of studying Ojibwa perception and assessing personality patterns. He was a pioneer in cross-cultural Rorschach analysis, and integrated psychological approaches into much of his work, for example in his tracing of an acculturational gradient from the remote Ojibwa communities of northwestern Ontario to the Ojibwes of Lac du Flambeau, Wisconsin, among whom he and a number of graduate students worked in the mid-1940s. More broadly, he sought through both evolutionary and ethnographic perspectives to explore, as Melford Spiro said, "the nature of man." Spiro has pointed out how Hallowell's work transcended the old dichotomy of the hedgehog who "knows one big thing" versus the fox who "knows many things." Keeping a focus upon larger questions about human nature, Hallowell drew connections between culture and personality, human and animal societies, kin terms and ecology, among others (Spiro 1976:609).

In the 1950s and 1960s, Hallowell shifted increasingly toward an emphasis on historical approaches. The first half of the text he wrote on the Berens River Ojibwas in the 1960s for the Case Studies in Cultural Anthropology series, for example, focused strongly on historical perspectives (it was published in 1992 when a draft of the previously lost manuscript surfaced in his papers). Doubtless this emphasis reflected, in part, the passage of time since his fieldwork three decades earlier; but his Ojibwa mentor, William Berens, received some credit too. As Hallowell wrote, "from the beginning of my association with him, I became historically oriented as a matter of course because we made constant reference to the "persons of past generations" (1992:11). It was also in this period that Hallowell undertook his pioneering work in the history of anthropology, most notably in his "The History of Anthropology as an Anthropological Problem" (1965, reprinted in Hallowell 1976).

Hallowell served the profession of anthropology in numerous ways. He was a highly respected scholar and teacher who was also regarded warmly by colleagues and students and by the Berens River Ojibwa people he knew in the 1930s. He was president of the American Anthropological Association in 1949 and chaired the National Research Council's Division of Anthropology and Psychology from 1946 to 1949.

From 1950 to 1956 he edited the Viking Fund Publications in Anthropology published by the Wenner-Gren Foundation. Among other honors, he received the Viking Fund Medal for outstanding achievement in 1956 and was elected to the National Academy of Sciences in 1961 (Wallace 1980:203).

Hallowell was twice married and had one adopted son, who predeceased him. He died in Wayne, Pennsylvania, on 10 October 1974, survived by his wife Maude Frame Hallowell.

JENNIFER S. H. BROWN

Ralph Beals
1950

Ralph Leon Beals was born in Pasadena, California, on 29
July 1901 to Leon and Elvina Blickensderfer Beals, populist
and socialist activists. The family moved to Berkeley in 1911
when Ralph's older brother, Carleton, matriculated there. Ralph interrupted his high school education to accompany his brother, who was
fleeing the draft, to Mexico in 1917. Returning to California after the
Armistice, Ralph spent a year as a cotton farmer before finishing high
school and beginning university work at Berkeley. In his sophomore
year he married Dorothy Manchester.

As a philosophy major, Beals undertook graduate study in anthropology with *Alfred L. Kroeber, Robert H. Lowie,* Edward Gifford, and
cultural geographer Carl Sauer. He did summer fieldwork with the
Nisenan (Southern Maidus) and wrote an ethnological dissertation based
on material on Northern Mexico in the Bancroft Library (Beals 1933,
1932).

After his Ph.D. in 1930, Beals received a two-year National Research

Council fellowship in biological sciences to study the Cahita peoples (Yaquis, Mayors, Opatas) of Sonora, a Mexican state that was under martial law with still-active Yaqui rebels inland. *Elsie Clews Parsons* visited Beals in the field and arranged for him to work with her among the Mixes in southern Mexico in 1932–33. "Essentially Boasian in outlook, Beals studied 'tribes' rather than communities" during the 1930s (Goldschmidt 1986:949).

Returning to Berkeley (where Dorothy had continued to teach in the private school run by her mother), Beals secured a job with the National Park Service that involved ethnohistorical publications on the aboriginal inhabitants of what became Glacier, Rocky Mountain, and Scots Bluff national parks, as well as on the Pimas, "Papagos" (Tohono O'odhams), and Western Apaches. On a leave of absence to teach a semester at Berkeley in 1935 and having accepted a job with the Federal Writers Project, he chose to go to the incipient University of California, Los Angeles (UCLA) in 1936. He taught anthropology within the psychology department until 1940, when university president Robert Sproul established the Department of Anthropology and Sociology and agreed to hire *Harry Hoijer*—with whom Beals later would write a widely used introductory textbook. The first UCLA anthropology doctorates went to Edward Dozier and George Spindler; separation of the sociology and anthropology departments occurred in 1962.

Beals returned to Mexican fieldwork for 15 months in 1940–41 with four students from the Instituto Nacional de Antropología e Historia. His community study of Cherán, a Tarascan town on a recently paved highway, was published in 1946 and marks a turn to applied interests (Beals was a founding member of the Society for Applied Anthropology) and to the phenomenon of urbanization that was the topic of his American Anthropological Association (AAA) presidential address (Beals 1951). In his 1973 introduction to anthropology, Beals noted that aside from some passing remarks on the inefficacies of planned cultural change, the Cherán research had "scientific" (descriptive) rather than practical aims.

A close friend of Julian Steward since graduate school, Beals supported the 1946 reorganization of the AAA, and claimed to have supervised "modernizing" its journal during his AAA presidency (Dillon 1977:104).

He was away from UCLA for another 15 months in 1948–49, traveling through South America and doing a community study of Nayón, a Quechuan village on the outskirts of Quito. In 1964–67 Beals returned to Oaxaca in a training program that, along with fieldwork on his own in 1972–73, resulted in his 1975 book on the peasant marketing system there. During the 1950s Beals conducted research on Mexican Americans (see Beals and Humphrey 1957). In the mid-1960s, called upon by the AAA to investigate anthropologists' involvement in the Defense Department counterinsurgency "Project Camelot," he produced an inconclusive 1969 book (also see Beals 1976). After his retirement from UCLA in 1969 and his completion of the Oaxaca market book, Beals worked on a history of Mexican Indians from the time of the conquest, seemingly to overlap and extend south Edward Spicer's (1962) *Cycles of Conquest*. Beals 1982b seems to be the only published part of this project; a comparison of the responses of Yaquis and Tarascans to Spanish colonization would have been especially interesting.

Beals was an active force in building up UCLA from a satellite of Berkeley into a major university. He championed the formation and growth of the School of Medicine, the Center for Latin American Studies, and the School of Social Welfare, as well as the anthropology department. Like his colleague Hoijer, Beals was regarded as remote. Goldschmidt (1986:952) remembered him as "always considerate, helpful, and sensitive to the legitimate interests of others, but not as affectionate" and his autobiographical statements (Beals 1976, 1979, 1982a; Dillon 1977) border on affectless. Two matters about which hints of passion appear are the injustices of racial segregation (Beals worked with NAACP lawyers in the landmark Brown v. Board of Education appeal to the U.S. Supreme Court) and fraudulent ethnography. It must have deeply pained him to criticize publicly the department he had founded and built and the University of California Press, on whose editorial board he had earlier served, in the matter of Carlos Castaneda (see Beals 1978 and letters to the *Los Angeles Times Book Review*, 17 July and 16 October 1977).

Although Beals's ethnographic research on native peoples of Oaxaca and Sonora during the 1930s and 1940s and his careful culling of earlier materials on those people is known to Mesoamericanists interested in them, there is no "Beals theory" about anything. He was a Boasian anti-theory descriptivist, though he took Kroeber as his model in encouraging students to follow their interests, whatever they were (even Freudian). As his long-time junior colleague (and fellow Berkeley alumnus) *Walter R. Goldschmidt* wrote, Beals's predilections were for cultural relativism and for viewing society as an orderly set of social interactions changing over time. Although he used the term *acculturation* in his first research application in 1930 and wrote the chapter of that name in the massive compilation of knowledge *Anthropology Today* edited by Kroeber in 1952, "his work on acculturation remained definitional; he never made a general theoretical statement on the nature of acculturation or [tried] to formulate a model of social change" (Goldschmidt 1986:952).

Beals died in Los Angeles on 24 February 1985.

STEPHEN O. MURRAY

William W. Howells
1951

William White Howells, "Bill" to his friends, was born in
New York City on 27 November 1908. He was the grand-
son of renowned belletrist William Dean Howells. After
secondary education at St. Paul's School in Concord, New Hampshire,
he attended Harvard University. Like many other students, he became
attracted by the charismatic lectures of Earnest Hooton. After receiving his bachelor's degree, Howells remained at Harvard for his doctorate, which he earned in 1934 with a thesis on craniometric studies of
Melanesians.

His first job was as an assistant to *Harry Shapiro* at the American
Museum of Natural History, where he remained for five years; George
Vaillant and *Wendell C. Bennett* were also colleagues there. Although
principally interested in Oceania, Howells published as well on the
skeletal remains of British and Native American populations. He took

a faculty post at the University of Wisconsin in 1939, where he remained until 1954 except for the war years. During that period he served as an intelligence officer in the U.S. Navy, holding the rank of lieutenant (j.g.). He was made an associate professor in 1946, and a professor in 1948; he chaired the department in 1953. That year he also helped to revive publication of *Human Biology*.

Howells matured in an intellectual generation of "generalist" anthropologists, but he surpassed most of his contemporaries in the breadth and scope of his writings. During the years he spent at the University of Wisconsin he published a triad of widely read and respected books, on human evolution (*Mankind So Far*, 1944), religion (*The Heathens*, 1948), and archaeology (*Back of History*, 1954); Howells was a meticulous and lucid writer. While at Wisconsin he served as treasurer of the American Association of Physical Anthropologists (AAPA), editor of the *American Journal of Physical Anthropology*, and president of the American Anthropological Association (AAA).

Upon Hooton's death in 1954 Howells succeeded him at Harvard. Lasker (1999:53–54) suggests that he always intended to return East, as he had neither bought a house nor engaged a dentist in Wisconsin, and as he had kept a great deal of furniture in storage over his midwestern sojourn. At Harvard his major output focused almost exclusively on the relationships among human populations, both past and present, that were discernible in the similarities of their skull patterns. Although Howells has retained a global interest, his primary geographical area has been Asia and Oceania. In the field of paleoanthropology, Howells used multivariate statistics to contrast the "Neanderthal phase" (later, "Candelabra") model of human origins with the "Noah's ark" theory. The Candelabra model emphasizes geographical continuity through deep time in human evolution, following the work of Franz Weidenreich; the Noah's ark model emphasizes migration and large-scale replacement of populations. More recently these have been recast as the "multiregional" and "out-of-Africa" models.

Like Hooton, Howells became one of the most well-known and popular professors at Harvard. One of his undergraduate advisees, science-fiction mogul Michael Crichton, recalled:

As a lecturer—which was the way most undergraduates experienced him—Howells was extraordinary. The famous lecturers at Harvard ... were all men who spoke well, moved well, and lectured with conviction and insight. They shared a common element of showmanship, and they conveyed a contagious enthusiasm for their field of study.

Even among this group, Howells was exceptional. His style was disarming: he lectured quietly, in a relaxed conversational manner, with occasional long pauses to look at his notes. The effect was one of complete spontaneity.... One never knew whether Howells was going to lecture for an hour behind the podium, or whether he was going to say five words and then run a film, or whether he would talk with slides, or what. He kept his audiences off balance, and they adored him. (in Giles et al. 1976:xxii–xxiii)

Crichton also noted that Howells "was a gifted performer, and his imitations of primate gaits were justly famous. But those imitations, like the jokes and puns and anecdotes and newspaper stories sprinkled through his lectures, all made a certain points and were all the more appreciated" (in Giles et al. 1976:xxiii).

Each of Hooton's students went in different directions from their mentor, with Carleton Coon and Howells remaining closest to the craniological methodological tradition that characterized so much of physical anthropology during the early decades of the 20th century. Even so, Howells introduced new levels of statistical rigor to the study of human skulls, specifically multivariate morphometric techniques, and he has generally interpreted his results from the more modern standpoint of patterns of similarity and difference among local populations than from the standpoint of essentialized global "races." Not only does Howells's work show skull variation to be principally local, but it also shows all modern populations to be very similar to one another craniometrically. In his own words, "attempts to fit even fairly recent prehistoric specimens into such a matrix were typically unsuccessful." And his data failed to support models of multiregionalism or regional continuity:"Neanderthal and earlier crania were far outside a modern range, with no credible relation to existing populations" (Howells 1992:3).

Howells was awarded the Viking Fund Medal in 1954 and the Distinguished Service Award from the AAA in 1978. He received a special Broca centennial prize from the Société d'Anthropologie in 1980, and the Charles Darwin Lifetime Achievement Award from the AAPA upon the institution of that award in 1992. Howells retired from Harvard in 1974, but he has remained active and productive, publishing the monograph *Skull Shapes and the Map* in 1989 and the textbook *Getting Here* in 1993. He has been married since 1929 to Muriel Gurdon Seabury and has two children, four grandchildren, and two great-grandchildren.

JONATHAN MARKS

Wendell C. Bennett
1952

W endell Clark Bennett was born in Marion, Indiana on 17 August 1905. His father, William Rainey Bennett, was a Protestant minister. "Wendy" attended the University of Chicago, where he received a B.A. in 1927, an M.A. in 1929, and a Ph.D. in 1930. In 1928 and 1929 he worked for the Bishop Museum on the archaeology of Kauai, Hawaii, producing one of the first reports on Polynesian prehistory. In 1930 and 1931 he carried out fieldwork among the Tarahumaras of northern Mexico with Robert Zingg. The University of Chicago published their joint monograph, one of the first to focus on remote areas of northern Mexico. Despite his archaeological interests, Bennett wrote the ethnological part of the report and "continued to collect ethnographic data whenever he had an opportunity" (Kidder 1954:270), believing that archaeology and ethnology were "so closely related as to make it advisable, wherever practicable, to do them together" (Rouse 1954:266).

Between 1931 and 1938 Bennett served as an assistant curator of South American archaeology at the American Museum of Natural History in New York. When his first Peruvian expedition for the museum began in 1932, Max Uhle and *Alfred L. Kroeber* had laid out the initial chronological sequence, but archaeologists urgently needed new Peruvian field studies in order to move beyond these preliminary results. At Tiahuanaco, Bolivia, Bennett established the stratigraphy of the type site in the Titicaca Basin and then linked this Tiahuanaco style to the Peruvian coastal sequence. His work identified the Early, Classic, and Decadent pottery sequence, which he related to two major building periods and to stone sculpture styles. At Tiahuanaco, Bennett applied the stratigraphic technique of digging refuse deposits by arbitrary levels, as developed in the Southwest by his American Museum colleague *Nels C. Nelson*. For the rest of his life, Bennett worked to document Tiahuanaco influence throughout the central Andes. His last fieldwork, at Ayacucho, Peru, in 1950 was published posthumously. On the same trip, Bennett stopped in Venezuela long enough to make "the first properly controlled excavation in that country" (Kidder 1954:279).

In 1934 Bennett identified Tiahuanaco influence in the lowlands of Bolivia as well as in the Titicaca Basin. He defined a post-Classic and pre-Decadent Tiahuanaco phase in the highlands that he named Chiripa. In 1947, however, he decided that Chiripa was actually much earlier.

Bennett married Hope Ranslow on 30 October 1935. They went together the following year to the Virú Valley on the north coast of Peru; this trip would later inspire the choice of Virú for intensive study in 1946. In 1938, the Bennetts worked at Chavín de Huantar in the highlands of northern Peru, clarifying the relatively obscure Recuay culture and discovering a new Tiahuanaco influence in the Callejón de

Huaylas. In 1941 he carried out pioneering fieldwork in Colombia.

This widespread Latin American experience led Bennett to administrative involvement with various committees, government agencies, and publications. From 1936 to 1940 he edited the section of the *Handbook of Latin American Studies* on South American archaeology. He was a charter member of the Institute of Andean Research, founded in 1937 serving as secretary treasurer from 1937 to 1942 and chair from 1942 to 1946; he remained on the steering committee from 1947 until his death.

In 1938 Bennett was appointed associate professor of anthropology at the University of Wisconsin. He moved to Yale University in 1940, where he was promoted to professor in 1945 and served as chair of the Department of Anthropology in 1949. At Yale he also served as a research associate of the Peabody Museum and a fellow of Pierson College. His teaching at Yale was primarily ethnological, emphasizing "the necessity for archaeologists to receive ethnological training" (Rouse 1964:267).

Bennett's administrative responsibilities continued to increase. From 1939 to 1942 he represented the American Anthropological Association (AAA) to the National Research Council's Division of Anthropology and Psychology; he chaired the division's committee on Latin American anthropology from 1941 to 1944. In 1942 he became executive secretary of the Joint Committee on Latin American Studies, which consolidated the wartime work of the National Research Council, the Social Science Research Council (SSRC), and the American Council of Learned Societies. During the war, from 1942 to 1945, he also served on the ethnogeographic board.

In 1946 Bennett was able to resume fieldwork with the Virú Valley Expedition of the Joint Committee; he returned to the Gallinazo site that he had first excavated a decade earlier. This work applied new functionalist models, "which were becoming popular in archaeology" (Rouse 1954:267). Simultaneously, he produced much of the second volume of the *Handbook of South American Indians* and coauthored *Andean Culture History* with Junius Bird for the American Museum of Natural History. Bennett edited a symposium entitled *A Reappraisal of Peruvian*

Archaeology and instigated a review of the archaeology of northwestern Argentina in 1948. He joined the board of directors of the SSRC in 1945, serving on its executive committee from 1946 until his death, in the role of chair from 1951 on.

Bennett's work was pivotal to maintaining the profile of anthropology within the postwar development of area training programs. He served on the SSRC's Committee on World Area Research for its total existence, from 1946–53. He analyzed the facilities of American universities for area studies in 1951 and lobbied both governments and universities to increase "the development of scientific knowledge of different areas of the world" (Kidder 1954:272). At Yale Bennett chaired the Area Studies Executive Committee and served as a consultant to the Human Relations Area Files.

Despite the specialized nature of his contributions to Andean archaeology, Bennett considered himself an anthropologist "in the broad sense" and applied "areal, cross-cultural and interdisciplinary" perspectives both to the problems of his own research and to the anthropology profession's broader contribution to public affairs and international development. Bennett's election as president of the AAA in 1952 constituted recognition within the discipline of his valuable efforts to broaden Americanist anthropology to meet the challenges of the postwar world.

Bennett suffered a fatal heart attack while swimming at Martha's Vineyard on 6 September 1953, at the age of 48. He was a man of modest demeanor, "proud of his record of prompt and thorough publication" (Rouse 1954:267).

REGNA DARNELL

Fred Eggan
1953

F rederick Russell Eggan was born in Seattle on 12 September
1906. His father, Alfred Junius Eggan, came from a working
class Norwegian-American community in Minnesota. Fred's
father had a restless streak and moved the family frequently during
Fred's childhood. His mother, Olive M. Smith, was a "well-disciplined
schoolteacher" of middle-class Yankee stock who instilled in her son a
love of books and learning (Vogt 1992:1).When Fred entered the University of Chicago in 1924, the family moved to an apartment near
campus for his undergraduate and graduate years.

Eggan shifted rapidly from business to psychology leavened by geography. A course on "Peoples and Races" with Boasian *Fay-Cooper
Cole* converted him to anthropology. As undergraduates, he and his
classmate Cornelius Osgood were invited to join Cole and *Edward
Sapir*'s graduate seminar on India; this sink-or-swim pedagogy produced a treatise on the Indian caste system. Although Eggan's M.A. in

psychology was supervised by psychometrician L. L. Thorndyke, the investigation of attitudes toward race and nationality was already anthropological.

Two years of junior college and private school teaching amassed enough money for Eggan to return to graduate work in anthropology in 1930. Cole (archaeology, physical anthropology) and Sapir (linguistics, ethnology, culture-and-personality) had been joined by *Robert Redfield*, who added the study of folk culture and peasant society to the department, which had become independent of sociology the previous year. Eggan, whose first love was archaeology, spent several summers digging in the Midwest with Cole. In the summers of 1929 and 1930 Eggan expanded into Hopi archaeology, a southwestern interest also encouraged by visiting professor *Leslie Spier*. He studied Navajo grammar with Sapir, within the four-square definition of Chicago anthropology.

In 1931 Sapir left Chicago for Yale University and was replaced by British social anthropologist A. R. Radcliffe-Brown. R-B, as he was called by his colleagues, was highly critical of the Americanist tradition, preferring to apply the methods of studying social structure developed in his Australian work (Vogt 1992:3). Eggan engaged with the new professor "rather reluctantly" at first (Eggan 1974:8). As R-B's research assistant, and through his own fieldwork, however, Eggan synthesized the British and American traditions, avoiding "both the narrowness and ahistoricity inherent in the British position and the fragmentary and diffuse problem focus of much American work" (Fogelson 1979:163).

In 1932 Eggan joined the summer field school directed by *Leslie White* at the Laboratory of Anthropology in Santa Fe, thereby making a commitment to sociocultural anthropology. His Hopi research produced a dissertation in 1933 on the matrilineal social organization of the Western Pueblos (Hopi, Zuni, Acoma, and Laguna) in contrast to the dual organization of the Eastern or Rio Grande Pueblos (Eggan 1950). The Keresan Pueblos formed a bridge, both structurally and geographically.

There were no jobs available in 1933, so Eggan stayed on at Chicago and expanded his fieldwork. He described the 1930s in retrospect (1974:17) as a period of growth in the size and complexity of anthropology, with increasing intellectual fragmentation accompanying the movement from museums to universities; "anthropology was a way of life that enabled its practitioners to escape the worst features of American culture."

In the summer of 1933 Eggan worked among the Mississippi Choctaws and the Oklahoma Cheyennes and Arapahos; supplementing the results by ethnohistoric research, he demonstrated that kinship systems changed in response to ecological shifts and historical experience (Eggan 1937). The Cheyennes, for example, adapted a settled agricultural lineage system to a generational social organization when they were forced into a more nomadic existence around the buffalo on the Great Plains.

Eggan planned to go to Australia in 1934, but devaluation of the U.S. dollar precluded his taking up an Australian National Research Council postdoctoral fellowship arranged by R–B. Instead, Cole sent him to the Philippines to restudy Tinguian social organization. Eggan described culture change among contiguous groups from the interior to the coast in the northern Philippines as "cultural drift" (adapted from Sapir's linguistic drift); change was understood to result from the definite internal direction of social structure, which had to be understood before the effects of European contact could be assessed. Sapir also taught him respect for long-range cultural process and "appreciation of the psychological dimensions of culture" (Fogelson 1979:163).

Eggan returned to the University of Chicago as an instructor in 1935 and was promoted in due course to assistant (1940), associate (1942), and full professor (1948). He served two terms as department chair. In 1953 he became chair of the Philippines Study Center at Chicago. The center was designed to prepare the country for independence. From 1963 until his retirement in 1974 Eggan was Harold H. Swift Distinguished Service Professor of Anthropology.

World War II, Eggan recalled (1974:16–17), "shook us up and provided new experiences." He worked for the Board of Economic Welfare, advised the Philippine government-in-exile, taught at the School for Military Government in Virginia, was a Philippines cultural relations officer in the Foreign Service, and developed a Civil Affairs Training School for the Far East at Chicago.

Eggan's middle range theory is exemplified in his 1953 presidential address to the American Anthropological Association, "Social Anthropology and the Method of Controlled Comparison" (1954). He proposed comparisons involving geographical or historical contiguity (e.g., within a culture area) or typologically related cases (e.g., dual organization). The method of controlled comparison was applied to many areas, especially in North America, by Eggan and his students, beginning with *Alexander Spoehr*. Theory and ethnography were inseparable (Eggan 1974:3). Eggan's interests in kinship and social structure were summarized in his Lewis Henry Morgan lectures at the University of Rochester, published as *The American Indian: Perspectives for the Study of Culture Change* (1966). A collection of his essays appeared in 1975.

Eggan married Dorothy Way, a researcher on Hopi dreams, in 1938. She died after a long illness in 1965. Four years later, Eggan married Joan Rosenfels, a photographer and psychotherapist who has applied Jungian analysis to Hopi dreams. Eggan retired to Santa Fe and continued his southwestern work as a consultant on land claims and on the "ancestral forms" of Hopi social organization in linguistically related areas of the Great Basin (Fogelson 1979:165). Eggan died in Santa Fe on 7 May 1991.

REGNA DARNELL

John O. Brew
1954

John Otis "Jo" Brew was born in Malden, Massachusetts, on 28 March 1906. From an early age he had an interest in classical archaeology, and although he would excavate mostly in the United States he never lost sight of the global context. He received a B.F.A. from Dartmouth College in 1928 and entered Harvard University with a Thaw Fellowship; he completed his requirements in three years and immediately joined the Peabody Museum's Claflin-Emerson Expedition to conduct an archaeological survey in Utah.

In 1931 Brew was made director of the museum's Southeastern Utah Expedition to Alkali Ridge. Although "snowed out" that winter, he led two long field seasons the following years; his 1946 report was an instant landmark in southwestern archaeology. The chapter "The Use and Abuse of Taxonomy" remains useful for teaching. In 1934 Brew excavated two early Christian sites with the Harvard Irish Expedition, and in 1935 he initiated the Peabody's Awatovi Expedition, which from

1936 to 1939 located almost 300 sites, and excavated 21, on Antelope Mesa and in the Jedditio Valley on the Hopi Indian Reservation. Local archaeologist and "bean farmer" Al Lancaster, who had worked with Paul Martin at Lowry and other sites before joining Brew at Alkali Ridge, was Brew's assistant at Awatovi and directed the Hopi workers employed on the project. During this period Brew also planned the Peabody's Upper Gila Expedition, studying Anasazi-Mogollon contacts, but the project was not undertaken until 1949 due to the war. Brew received his Ph.D. from Harvard in 1941 and became an assistant curator at the Peabody, continuing an association that began in 1930 and ended with his death. He became a curator in 1945 and director of the Peabody in 1948, an office he held until 1967; he was also the Peabody Professor of American Archaeology and Ethnology from 1949 to 1972.

Brew's archaeological projects employed a multidisciplinary research program and many consulting specialists. They also provided work opportunities for many Harvard students and volunteers interested in the archaeology of the Southwest. The excavated sites ranged from late Basket Maker through the historical period, including a Franciscan mission from the 17th century. World War II delayed the publication of most of the individual site reports, and the synthetic "final report," like many others from extensive field projects of this period, remained unwritten. Such projects were and are remarkable for the quantity and quality of the work accomplished, and the individual reports often remain valuable for specialists long afterward; nonetheless, the volume of information that makes them so valuable also makes synthesis very difficult to complete.

At Awatovi in 1939 Brew married Evelyn Ruth Nimmo, a member of the expedition staff. They had two sons; one became an archaeologist and the other a lawyer. Brew was widely noted for being generous, informal, and humorous. He also had an appreciation of good food, good wine, and good conversation. Many photographs show him smiling broadly around a pipe or cigar (at Awatovi he was teasingly called "the D-shaped Director, because of his figure's response" to the good food he considered essential to a productive crew [Adams 1994:38]). It was

Brew who polled colleagues in the Society for American Archaeology in 1949 "to determine whether or not we should retain the traditional spelling 'Archaeology' or adopt the bob-tailed version 'Archeology' in the official name of the society and all its works" (quoted in Woodbury 1990:453). In addition to his American Anthropological Association (AAA) presidency Brew was on the council of the Society for American Archaeology (SAA) from 1944 to 1946 and president in 1949–50; he was also active in many other professional societies as well as in the Harvard Faculty Club, the Cosmos Club of Washington DC, and the Club of Odd Volumes, a booklovers' society.

Brew's administrative and teaching work could alone have consti-tuted a career, as could his archaeological work, but he made further contributions in national and international advocacy for recognition of the significance of archaeological resources. In 1945 the AAA, SAA, and the American Council of Learned Societies appointed Brew to chair the new Committee for the Recovery of Archaeological Re-mains; the other members were Frederick Johnson, A. V. Kidder and William S. Webb. There was great concern that postwar construction of dams, particularly along the Missouri River, would cause the loss of countless sites, known and unknown. The government-sponsored River Basin Surveys, the well-known Tennessee Valley Authority develop-ment-related excavations, and many other projects were instigated by this committee. Brew also became an active member of the National Park Service Advisory Board, the National Trust for Historic Preserva-tion, and UNESCO's International Committee for Monuments, Artistic and Historical Sites and Archaeological Excavations, which he chaired for many years; he also chaired the U.S. National Committee for the Preservation of Nubian Monuments, which raised $22 million for the preservation of Abu Simbel and other Egyptian archaeological work in the 1960s.

In 1966, just before Brew stepped down as director, he organized the Peabody centennial celebration, which included a series of five lec-tures and a dinner for 450 graduates, friends, faculty, and staff in Me-morial Hall, at which cocktails were provided, cigar-smoking was al-lowed, and fifteen cases of good wine were consumed (Brew 1968:5).

Lecturers were *Gordon R. Willey*, Glyn Daniel, *Sherwood Washburn*, *Fred Eggan*, and Floyd Lounsbury, with each addressing a subfield of anthropology; the resulting volume remains a useful introduction to subfield histories. As director of the Peabody, Brew had responsibilities to all the branches of anthropology. He also made contributions beyond archaeology. For example, with *Clyde Kluckhohn* and Talcott Parsons he served from 1949 to 1955 on the advisory committee of the Comparative Study of Values in Five Cultures Project, helping graduate students as they worked in the many communities he knew in the Southwest.

Brew received the Viking Fund Medal for Archaeology in 1947 (he was the second recipient, after Kidder) and the AAA's Distinguished Service Award in 1979. In 1970 he received an honorary LL.D. in international relations from the University of Liberia in recognition of his work as trustee of Donations for Education in Liberia. After his retirement from the Peabody in 1972 Brew taught for four years as a distinguished visiting professor at Southern Methodist University, and then for a year as a visiting lecturer at the University of Calgary. He returned to Cambridge, where he died on 19 March 1988 of congestive heart failure.

FREDERIC W. GLEACH

George P. Murdock
1955

George Peter "Pete" Murdock was born on his parents' farm in Meriden, Connecticut, on 11 May 1897. His parents were New England Yankees of Scottish and English descent. They provided "a politically democratic, individualistic, and religiously agnostic" background that valued education, particularly at Yale (Goodenough 1979:554). Murdock served in the World War I as a first lieutenant in the field artillery.

An early interest in geography led him to study the social sciences at Yale University, where he received his B.A. in history in 1919. He went on to study law at Harvard University. After receiving a small inheritance, he dropped out of Harvard law school to travel through Europe and Asia. He returned determined to study anthropology. Murdock "interviewed *Franz Boas*" who dismissed him as a dilettante and rejected his graduate application (Whiting 1986:684). Murdock was unimpressed by Harvard and decided to return to Yale, where he had already worked with Albert G. Keller, protégé of William Graham Sumner, America's preeminent evolutionist. The graduate program in "Science and Society" spanned anthropology and sociology "with a strong cross-cultural orientation" (Goodenough 1988:2). Murdock received his Ph.D. in 1925 for a translation of Julius Lippert's work on the cultural history of mankind, published as *The Evolution of Culture* in 1931. In 1925 he married Carmen Swanson, a Yale graduate student in biochemistry.

After two years of teaching sociology and anthropology at the University of Maryland, Murdock returned to Yale in 1928 as an assistant professor, in what would become the department of sociology. Yale's response to the Boasian critique of evolution was to "define social evolutionists as sociologists and reserve the 'anthropologist' label for members of the historical school" (Whiting 1986:682). When *Edward Sapir* came to Yale to head a newly independent anthropology department, Murdock held a joint appointment; he moved fully to anthropology only in 1938 when he became chair; he was promoted to professor in 1939.

Although Murdock did not embrace the social evolution of the Sumner-Keller tradition, he shared their conviction that "a scientific study of society and culture required systematic comparative study" (Goodenough 1985:2). His passion for order manifested itself in increasingly sophisticated amassing of accumulated ethnographic data so that social science theories could be tested empirically.

In 1934 Murdock assembled *Our Primitive Contemporaries*, a collection of 18 ethnographic summaries in standardized format designed to allow students to compare societies representative of varying geographic areas and degrees of social complexity. This project provided a pilot for the Rockefeller Foundation-funded Cross-Cultural Survey established by Murdock at Yale's Institute of Human Relations (IHR) in the mid-1930s. The much more extensive *Outline of Cultural Materials* appeared in 1938. In 1935 younger members of the IHR established a "Monday Night Group" for interdisciplinary discussion; Murdock was the anthropologist in the group, which moved toward Clark Hull's learning theory to synthesize the social sciences.

Murdock was deeply committed to the anthropological enterprise of cross-cultural fieldwork; he believed that ethnographic data had value independently of theory and should be published. Although he was not primarily a fieldworker, Murdock studied the Haidas in 1932 and the Teninos in 1934–35. Only in Truk in 1947, however, did he study "a non-Western society with a fully functioning culture of its own" (Spoehr 1985:309).

Murdock's wartime work promoted ethnographic study in the Pacific. He was commissioned as lieutenant commander in the U.S. Navy Reserve in 1943. At Columbia University, with Clelland Ford and John Whiting, he authored a series of civil affairs handbooks on the Pacific islands. He was promoted to commander and served in the military government on Okinawa.

After the war he and Harold Coolidge organized the Pacific Science Board within the National Research Council. The Coordinated Investigation of Micronesian Anthropology was funded by the Office of Naval Research and the Wenner-Gren Foundation. Between 1947 and 1949, 42 anthropologists and linguists from 20 institutions worked in the U.S. Trust Territory; Murdock was overall field director and personally led the team that worked in Truk. Murdock chaired the Pacific Science Board from 1953 to 1957. From 1953 to 1964 the Tri-Institutional Pacific Program (Yale, the Bishop Museum, and the University of Hawaii) supported further work, including Isidore Dyen's Austronesian lexicostatistics in 1965.

After the war, the Cross-Cultural Survey was reorganized by a consortium of universities as the Human Relations Area Files (HRAF). Data remained incomparable and of uneven quality. Rising to the challenge, Murdock's students John and Beatrice Whiting developed "protocols for enhancing comparability of ethnographic data" for childrearing (Goodenough 1988:4).

Murdock sampled 250 cultures in *Social Structure* (1960), producing a typology for forms of social organization and a theory of how they changed. Gaps in data revealed new problems in social structure, including cognatic descent groups or double descent, bifurcate merging, the kindred, and "cognitive forms of social organization" (Spoehr

1985:309). Murdock applied his model to Southeast Asia in 1960 and to Africa in 1959. Successive editions of the *Ethnographic Bibliography of North America* appeared beginning in 1949, with a summary of North American social organization in 1955. His final comparative study was a world survey of "theories of illness" in 1980. The *Atlas of World Cultures* (1981) continued to extend the sample.

In 1960 Murdock accepted the call to initiate a department of anthropology at the University of Pittsburgh as Andrew Mellon Professor of Social Anthropology. He established the journal *Ethnology* in 1962, including an ethnographic atlas section, and served as its editor for 11 years. His editorial policy eschewed abstract theory in favor of its relation to "some body of substantive data," be it "descriptive, analytical, typological, distributional, historical, or comparative in subject matter and treatment" (1962, quoted in Spoehr 1985:311). From 1968 to 1972 Murdock directed the Cross-Cultural Cumulative Coding Center funded by the National Science Foundation. The project aspired to produce "stratified world and regional samples, amenable to statistical comparison and inference" (Spoehr 1985:311). At Pittsburgh he began a visiting foreign professor program, to avoid parochialism. He was a founder of the society of Cross-Cultural Research in Pittsburgh in 1972.

Murdock served as president of the Society for Applied Anthropology (1947), the American Ethnological Society (1952–53), and the American Anthropological Association (1955). From 1964 to 1968 he chaired the National Research Council's newly established Division of the Behavioral Sciences. He retired in 1973 at the age of 77 and moved to Philadelphia to be near his son. Murdock died in Devon, Pennsylvania, on 29 March 1985.

REGNA DARNELL

Emil W. Haury
1956

Emil Walter Haury was born on 2 May 1904 in the Mennonite community of Newton, Kansas, where his father was a professor at Bethel College. As a child Haury was fascinated by Indians; he read many adventure stories, and developed an interest in archaeology that was fueled by a black-on-white potsherd his parents brought back from Arizona in 1908. His first experience with a living Indian occurred when his parents housed a young Hopi woman, Polingaysi Qoyawayma (Elizabeth Q. White), who had been sent to Bethel College by Mennonite missionaries. She was a potter and school-teacher, and she and Haury remained in contact throughout her life.

Haury attended school in Newton and entered Bethel College in 1923. He probably would have become a teacher, but during his second year archaeologist Byron Cummings visited to lecture. Haury asked to join him in his work in Arizona; a year later he received an invitation to participate in excavations at Cuicuilco, in Mexico. After working there he transferred to the University of Arizona, where he completed his bachelor's and master's degrees in 1927 and 1928 respectively; he also attended *A. V. Kidder*'s first Pecos Conference in 1927.

In June 1928 Haury married Hulda Esther Penner in Newton; they were married by her father, a distinguished minister and, like Haury's father, one of the five original faculty members of Bethel College. Both parents were liberal Mennonites, committed to education and progress as well as traditional values of industry, integrity, simplicity, and helpfulness. Hulda accompanied Emil in much of his fieldwork, and they had two sons in the 1930s.

In 1928–29 Haury was an instructor at the University of Arizona. He then worked with astronomer Andrew Douglass, who was using tree-ring data to document climatic change. Haury was one of the people who found HH-39, the famous charred beam from the Show Low site that bridged the gap between two dendrochronological sequences Douglass had established, allowing the accurate dating of archaeological materials. Haury often spoke of that discovery as the most memorable experience of his career. He was the first person to learn Douglass's method of dating, and he assisted Douglass in teaching the first course on tree-ring dating in 1930. He went on to make many contributions to the theory and applications of the method, and he was cofounder in 1937 of the Laboratory of Tree-Ring Research at the University of Arizona.

In 1930 Haury joined Harold Sterling Gladwin's Gila Pueblo Archaeological Foundation as assistant director; in addition to other benefits, Gladwin was willing to help underwrite two years of doctoral studies. Haury studied at Harvard University from 1931 to 1933, working with *Alfred M. Tozzer* and *Roland B. Dixon*. He received his Ph.D. in 1934; his dissertation, published in 1945, remains a basic reference in Hohokam studies. After his doctoral studies, Haury returned to Gila Pueblo, where he conducted surveys and excavations over a large part of the Southwest. In 1937 Byron Cummings retired from Arizona, and Haury took his place, first as head of the Department of Archaeology and then, in 1938, as director of the Arizona State Museum.

Arizona in 1937 was a small land-grant university with a budget that had been slashed by the legislature. Haury took advantage of his status as a newcomer and immediately began working to increase the department's budget, faculty, library, and student support (interestingly, years later he advised a student, "Don't try to change anything your first year in a new job, or you will wound some egos" [Crown 1993:263]). He also renamed it the Department of Anthropology, and began working to establish a doctoral program, which he accomplished in 1948. "Doc" Haury was deeply committed to the integration of classroom and fieldwork experience for students, and his Point of Pines field school set a high standard for training. He took a similar course with the state museum, increasing budget and staff and pushing for more survey work to better protect archaeological resources; in 1959 he convinced the Arizona Highway Department to create the Arizona Highway Salvage Program, and in 1960 he gained passage for a revised Arizona Antiquities Act.

Haury was professionally active beyond the campus as well. He served on the boards of many museums in the Southwest, helped develop the social sciences in the National Science Foundation, and worked with many other organizations, including the Committee for the Recovery of Archaeological Remains and the National Council on the Humanities. He received many awards, including the Viking Fund Medal for Archaeology in 1950 and the Alfred Vincent Kidder Award in 1977; he was also the first holder of the first endowed chair at the University of Arizona, in 1970, and he was elected to the American Academy of Arts and Sciences, the National Academy of Sciences, and the American Philosophical Society. Haury retired from teaching in 1980, but he remained active in research and writing. After Hulda died in 1987 his spirits and vitality ebbed. But an old friend and former student, Agnese Nelms Lindley, helped him recover, and they were married in 1990 by Navajo Chief Tribal Judge Robert Yazzie. They traveled throughout the Southwest for two years before Haury died peacefully at home on 5 December 1992.

Haury made many specific contributions to archaeological knowledge and trained many students. But his main legacy is his holistic regional vision for southwestern archaeology, and his recognition of the dual nature of archaeology (and anthropology in general): "While supporting the premise that we must continually strive to improve our analytical procedures, to establish a higher level of credibility in what we do, and to be more 'scientific', I cannot lose sight of the fact that archaeology is and always will be a humanistic study, that much of its infinite content can never be recovered, and that the fraction available to us must be treated with a mixture of skills of the artist and the scientist in order to extract its essence." (Haury 1986:457)

FREDERIC W. GLEACH

E. Adamson Hoebel
1957

E dward Adamson "Ad" Hoebel was born on 6 November 1906 in Madison, Wisconsin; his father was a traveling salesman for the family harness-manufacturing company, and his mother was the state civil service commissioner for Wisconsin. After attending local schools he studied sociology at the University of Wisconsin, where fellow students included *John P. Gillin*, *Clyde Kluckhohn*, Lauriston Sharp, and *Sol Tax*; he received his B.A. in 1928 and initiated an interest in law and social control through work with Edward A. Ross. He studied in Cologne, Germany, for a year before entering New York University, where he was an instructor in sociology during his graduate studies. He received his M.A. in 1931. He then entered the doctoral program at Columbia University, where he worked with *Franz Boas* and *Ruth Benedict*.

When Hoebel indicated an interest in doing a dissertation on a Plains Indian legal system, Boas and Benedict expressed doubts and disinterest in the project, but Boas arranged for Columbia law professor Karl Llewellyn to serve as Hoebel's thesis advisor. Hoebel produced a dissertation on the Comanche Indians (published in 1940 as *The Political Organization and Law-ways of the Comanche Indians*) and received his Ph.D. in 1934. The next year he was promoted to assistant professor at NYU, and he became associate professor in 1941.

Many of Hoebel's ideas were developed in collaboration with Llewellyn, a leading figure in the "legal realism" school of jurisprudence. Most anthropologists at the time did not believe tribal peoples had anything that could properly be called "law," but Llewellyn's reading of Malinowski's *Crime and Custom in Savage Society* (1926) suggested that collaboration could be fruitful. Their work together demonstrated it. Llewellyn advised Hoebel on his early studies with the Shoshones, and they collaborated in *The Cheyenne Way: Conflict and Case Law in Primitive Jurisprudence* (1941). The basis of the collaboration was the consideration of law within its cultural context, a perspective common to anthropology and legal realism. Also coming from these shared precepts was the "trouble case method," which focused on disputes as the key to understanding the legal system and its procedures. Hoebel and Llewellyn then used a functional framework to consider how law worked to resolve disputes and maintain order. Their final collaboration was with the Keresan Pueblos in the 1940s, but Llewellyn died (in 1962) before that analysis was completed.

In 1948 Hoebel left New York to head the anthropology department at the University of Utah. In 1953–54 he was dean of arts and sciences there. In 1954 he moved to the University of Minnesota, where he remained until his retirement in 1972; even after retirement he was an adjunct professor of law there for nine more years. Over the course of his career Hoebel held a number of fellowships and visiting appointments, including to Oxford University, England, and Katholijke Universiteit, the Netherlands, and he was elected to the American Academy of Arts and Sciences and the American Philosophical Society. He also served as an officer for the American Council of Learned Societies, the Social Science Research Council, the American Ethnological

Society, and the Association of American Indian Affairs, as well as the American Anthropological Association.

In *The Law of Primitive Man: A Study in Comparative Legal Dynamics* (1954), Hoebel went beyond the descriptive case study of his previous two books to undertake a comparative study with the goal of defining "law" cross-culturally. He proceeds by clearly contextualized specific studies to derive "jural postulates"—"broadly generalized propositions held by the members of a society as to the nature of things and as to what is qualitatively desirable and undesirable"—and "law ways," the processes of keeping order. The work remains fundamental in anthropological studies of law, although it has been criticized for recognizing only physical sanctions.

Hoebel is best known for his ethnographic work with Plains Indians, but his fieldwork in the Keresan Pueblos, already mentioned, and in Pakistan in the early 1960s was also significant, as was his commitment to more general human rights issues and East-West relations. In 1943 he worked as a community analyst at Granada Relocation Camp, a Japanese-American internment camp in eastern Colorado. In 1964–65 he was a senior specialist in the Institute for Advanced Projects of the Center for Cultural and Technical Interchange between East and West in Honolulu, and he was a special officer for the Arms Control and Disarmament Agency of the U.S. Department of State from 1968 to 1973; he also participated in the UNESCO East-West Cultural Conference in Calcutta in 1961.

Hoebel prepared several books specifically for use in the classroom (of course, *The Cheyenne Way* and *The Law of Primitive Man* are also widely used). In 1949, recognizing the growing interest in anthropology following World War II, he prepared a textbook for undergraduate students, *Man in the Primitive World: An Introduction to Anthropology*; it went through five editions, with two title changes and additions by Thomas Weaver in the last (1979) edition. In 1955 he collaborated with Jesse Jennings to produce *Readings in Anthropology*, a reader that went through three editions (the last in 1972). He also wrote *The Cheyennes: Indians of the Great Plains* (1960, with later editions), one of the first volumes in the long-lived series of short ethnographies edited by George and Louise Spindler, and added commentary for the publication of *A Cheyenne Sketchbook* (1964). His writing was always clear and realistic, conveying well not just the concepts he was developing but also the feel of the ethnographic context.

Hoebel was married twice. In 1930, while working on his master's at NYU, he married Frances Elizabeth Gore; they had one son, Bartley, who became a psychology professor at Princeton. Frances died in 1962. In 1963 Hoebel married Irene Holth; she traveled with him during much of his later work. Hoebel died on 23 July 1993, survived by Irene, Bartley, and five grandchildren.

FREDERIC W. GLEACH

Harry Hoijer
1958

Harry Hoijer followed his teacher *Edward Sapir* in the comparative study of Athabaskan languages and in institutionalizing linguistics in North American universities. He was born on 6 September 1904 in Chicago to immigrant Swedish parents; his father was a skilled cabinetmaker. In 1927 he earned a B.A. in engineering and mathematics at the University of Chicago. In his senior year he roomed with Cornelius Osgood, who convinced him to continue at Chicago as a graduate anthropology student working with Sapir. Also in 1937 Hoijer married Dorothy Jared, who became a biochemist; they had three children.

Hoijer completed his Ph.D. in 1931, the year Sapir and most of his students moved to Yale. Hoijer remained at Chicago and took over teaching Sapir's linguistic courses; he was an instructor there through 1940. From then until his death he was a member of the anthropology faculty at the University of California at Los Angeles, retiring to emeritus status in 1970. During World War II he also taught in the Army Specialized Training Program. With his colleague *Ralph Beals*, Hoijer co-authored a widely used introductory anthropology textbook (Beals and Hoijer 1953). Hoijer was instrumental in forming a linguistics program at UCLA, chairing it from 1959 to 1963, as he had the anthropology department there in 1942–43 and from 1948 to 1952. He was also active in the American Anthropological Association and the Linguistic Society of America, serving as the president of each organization in 1958 and 1959, respectively. For many years Hoijer edited the Notes and Reviews section of the *International Journal of American Linguistics*, as well as being an associate editor of that journal and the *American Anthropologist*.

Concerned about the "relevance" of anthropology and linguistics from an early date, Hoijer worked beyond the academy. He was a consultant to the UNESCO Commission on Language and Mentality and served on the Committee on Research in American Indian Languages. He famously testified for the defense in the Sleepy Lagoon murder case (in the supercharged atmosphere of the "zoot-suit riots" of the 1940s), against prosecution claims of an irresistible blood lust that Mexican Americans were purported to have inherited from their Aztec ancestors. Hoijer also stepped outside the cloistered calm of his research to fight against the University of California loyalty oath and other challenges to academic freedom, and like many others, he was subpoenaed by the California Committee on Un-American Activities during the McCarthy era.

Hoijer worked with some of the last speakers of Tonkawa, producing a dissertation grammar that was published in 1933 (and summarized in Hoijer ed. 1946:289–311). Most of his subsequent publications dealt with Athabaskan languages, for which he attempted to standardize a comparative grammatical format. He began fieldwork with the Sapirian psychological anthropologist *Morris E. Opler* among Apaches in 1930. After Sapir's death in 1939, Hoijer prepared for publication the Navajo texts and lexicons amassed by Sapir between 1926 and 1936; these materials were explicitly consigned to Hoijer by Sapir on his deathbed. As Hoijer's longtime colleague Ralph Beals (1977:107) noted, "had he been less conscientious about Sapir's data, his own originality might have had greater scope."

Also as the intellectual heir of Sapir, at least by a system of primogeniture, it fell to Hoijer to edit a collection of grammatical sketches in memory of Sapir by his former students (Hoijer ed. 1946). This was the first effort to synthesize the typologies of Native North American languages since Franz Boas's *Handbook of American Indian Languages* in 1911 and 1922. These sketches exemplified dramatic changes in linguistic description from Boas's largely self-taught phonetic recording to Sapir's phonemic approach and process model of grammar, with its concern for "psychological reality" to native speakers. This shift also signaled the increasing separation of linguistics from the mainstream of anthropology.

As a custodian of his conception of a Sapir tradition, Hoijer criticized offshoots of later Sapir students that received considerable attention during the 1950s: the lexicostatistics of Morris Swadesh (Hoijer 1956), and the linguistic determinism attributed to Benjamin Lee Whorf (Hoijer ed. 1954). The latter publication reports on an interdisciplinary conference that attempted to test the so-called Sapir-Whorf hypothesis empirically. The inconclusiveness of the results initiated a long hiatus in the study of the relationships of language, thought, and reality, revived only with cognitive linguistics (e.g., Gumperz and Levinson 1996, Lucy 1992). Hoijer (1951) stressed the conception, which Sapir had already posed, of living in different linguistic worlds. Hoijer's approach to historical inference and to the links between linguistic morphology and cognition were more cautious than those of other Sapir students, Swadesh and Whorf in particular, although he shared their interest in such phenomena. Mostly, Hoijer persevered in what had been Sapir's major project during his Chicago years: reconstructing the proto-Athabaskan language. In addition to reporting results from recurrent linguistic fieldwork among Navajo and Apache (Chiricahua, Jicarilla, and Mescalero) speakers, Hoijer published on Hare and Galice.

Although he was admired and appreciated by some students, Hoijer seemed remote and extremely reticent to many. Rudolph Troike recalls that he was "a good, systematic, and enjoyable lecturer, who punctuated his lectures with occasional humorous anecdotes, some poking fun at himself. I think his own physical size may have contributed to his remoteness from most students. He probably was something of a workaholic, since my most enduring image of him is bent over his desk intensely working on something. When a student knocked, he would say 'come in' without looking up from his work, and continue to work, saying nothing, while the student stood there. Some took this to be intimidating" (cf. Fromkin 1977:171–172).

Hoijer died in Santa Monica, California, on 4 March 1976, after several years of declining health. As he wished, his body was cremated without ceremony and the ashes were strewn over the Pacific Ocean.

STEPHEN O. MURRAY

Sol Tax
1959

Sol Tax was born in Chicago, Illinois, on 30 October 1907. He was the older of two sons of Russian Jewish immigrants. Shortly after his birth the family moved to Milwaukee, Wisconsin, which was then one of the centers for progressive thought in the United States. Sol and his younger brother, Ervin, grew up dreaming of "saving the troubled world" (quoted in Blanchard 1979), and at the age of 12 Sol joined the "Newsboys' Republic," an organization of paper-carriers; he eventually became editor of their magazine and chief justice of their supreme court—but lost a closely contested election for president.

After high school Tax worked in Miami, Florida, as an assistant circulation manager for the *Daily News*. He then spent one quarter at the University of Chicago before entering the University of Wisconsin in 1926, where he continued to be active in political and organizational causes. Tax changed to anthropology from political science and economics after starting *Ralph Linton's* class in 1927. In 1930 he accompanied Beloit's Logan Museum Expedition to North Africa; the project was chiefly archaeological, but Tax spent Passover with a group of Algerian Jews and wrote about the experience in his first anthropology publication (Tax 1931). His Ph.B. thesis in 1931 attempted to integrate cultural and biological aspects of anthropology. He participated in the Summer Ethnology Program at the Mescalero Indian Reservation with *Ruth Benedict* before entering the University of Chicago to study with A. R. Radcliffe-Brown and *Robert Redfield*.

Tax's undergraduate thesis had already explored the relationship between "pure science" and application (called "therapeutic" science), but his experience also highlighted the informant/collaborator/patient, whose concerns seemed absent from anthropological science. Radcliffe-Brown directed Tax's fieldwork with Central Algonquian groups in 1932 and 1933, the latter year with his new wife, Gertrude Jospe Katz Tax. From this research Tax developed the "egoless" kinship diagram, using a color-printing technique developed by his brother. After a month in 1934 with the Fox Indians, Tax wrote and defended his dissertation. A few days later the Taxes left for Guatemala, beginning an eight-year project working with Redfield. In 1940 Tax became a research associate in anthropology at Chicago and continued to work in Guatemala; in 1942 he began teaching anthropologists at the National School of Anthropology in Mexico. The program included a six-week field-training project in Chiapas. In response to his students, who included not only the first large group of Mexican anthropologists but also liberal students who were exiled from Spain by the Franco government, Tax again confronted the relationships of anthropological science and society. His daughters, Susan and Marianna, were born during this period—and both entered the field with their parents at the age of four months.

In 1944 Tax was appointed associate professor at the University of Chicago. He was promoted to professor in 1948, and he chaired the department from 1955 to 1958. Early in 1948 he began plans to train graduate students on the Fox reservation in Iowa, where he had worked previously; the focus was on fieldwork training and working with the community to define social problems and possible solutions.This work developed into "The Fox Project" and continued for more than a decade.The theory and techniques of the project developed into "action anthropology": "an activity in which an anthropologist has two coordinate goals, to neither one of which he will delegate an inferior position. He wants to help a group of people to solve a problem, *and* he wants to learn something in the process" (Tax 1952:103).The approach openly recognized the inevitability of conflict—within the community being studied, between the community and others, and within the individual scholar.

During this period Tax published extensively on action anthropology, on his Guatemalan research, and on Native North America. He was also heavily involved in editorial projects, many stemming from his organizational work. He was associate editor (1947–52) and editor (1953–55) of the *American Anthropologist*, and editor of *Heritage of Conquest* (1952); he also edited three volumes of selected papers from the 29th International Congress of Americanists, *An Appraisal of Anthropology Today* (1953) from a Wenner-Gren symposium, and *Evolution After Darwin* (1960) from the Darwin Centennial. *Penny Capitalism* (1953), a study in economic anthropology drawn from his Guatemalan research, was influential beyond anthropology although largely forgotten within the discipline. In 1958, supported by the Wenner-Gren Foundation, Tax founded *Current Anthropology* to serve as an international journal with a holistic vision of anthropology, and he served as its editor until 1974. He also edited the Viking Fund Publications in Anthropology series from 1960 to 1968.

In 1960 Tax was invited to develop a conference of Native Americans to discuss the issues and problems of their communities; with support from the National Congress of American Indians and the American Anthropological Association, he organized in 1961 the American Indian Chicago Conference, "the opening call for the Indian activism that grew later in the 1960s and 1970s" (Johansen and Grinde 1997:382). Typically, Tax made the arrangements, coordinated invitations, brought people together, and then faded into the background as much as possible with the offer, "Anytime you need anything, here we are" (Rubinstein 1991:179).

Beyond Native American concerns, in the 1960s Tax attacked more general issues of social conflict in the United States, participating in and editing publications from conferences on urban conflict and the draft. He was a member of the executive committee of the U.S. National Commission for UNESCO from 1963 to 1965, was elected to the American Association for the Advancement of Science and the Illinois Academy of Science, served on the National Research Council, was awarded the Viking Fund Medal for Anthropology in 1962, and received several honorary degrees in the United States and Guatemala. He directed the Center for the Study of Man at the Smithsonian Institution from 1968 to 1976, and was president of the International Congress of Anthropological and Ethnological Sciences from 1968 to 1973, hosting the 1973 congress in Chicago, which produced more than ninety volumes of papers in *World Anthropology*.

Tax retired from teaching in 1976 but remained active for some time. His work had shifted from the problem solving of traditional scholarship to large-scale organization and promotion of an international and diverse vision of anthropology and the social sciences, but he continued to support students, and regularly attended anthropology defenses well into the 1990s. He died of a heart attack on 4 January 1995 after only a few months of illness, and was survived by his wife, Gertrude, and his daughters, Susan Tax Freeman, also an anthropologist, and Marianna Tax Choldin.

FREDERIC W. GLEACH

Margaret Mead
1960

Margaret Mead, quintessential public spokesperson for American anthropology, was born on 16 December 1901 in Philadelphia. Her father, Edward Sherwood Mead, was an economist at the University of Pennsylvania's Wharton School of Finance and Commerce. She accompanied her mother, Emily Fogg Mead, suffragist activist and sociologist, on her studies of Italian immigrants in Hammonton, New Jersey. The oldest of four children, she was largely home-schooled by her paternal grandmother, Martha Ramsay Mead, a retired schoolteacher and school principal. Mead attributed her feminism and ease in career socialization to this background of three generations of professional women.

After a disastrous first year at DePauw University, her father's alma mater and choice for her education, Mead emigrated to New York City, where she obtained a B.A. in psychology from Barnard College in 1923; she received her M.A. in the same discipline in 1924 and her

Ph.D. in anthropology in 1929 (with a library thesis on cultural stability in Polynesia), both from Columbia University. In 1923 she married her high school sweetheart Luther Cressman, a theological student later turned anthropologist. When they divorced five years later, Mead married New Zealand anthropologist Reo Fortune. From 1936 to 1950, after another divorce, Mead was married to British anthropologist Gregory Bateson. Their daughter, Mary Catherine Bateson Kassarjian, was born in 1939. Mead's only grandchild, Sevanne Margaret, was born in 1970.

Mead entered Boasian anthropology via *Ruth Benedict*, when *Franz Boas* himself was turning from problems of history to those of psychology and internal patterning of culture. Mead explicitly rebelled against American Indian research, frustrated by the cultural poverty of her single summer with the Omahas. She preferred the natural science orientation of British social anthropology, particularly in the person of A. R. Radcliffe-Brown. She determined to work comparatively in a series of Pacific cultures. The Pacific provided a laboratory within which to typologize human cultures. Her initial fieldwork in Samoa in 1925 was designed to demonstrate that the physiological stage of adolescence manifested itself in culture-specific terms. This was her only solo experience; as a woman, she encountered substantial resistance to the isolation of her field site. In five field trips over fourteen years, she studied eight cultures: Tau village, Samoa; Manus, Omaha, and three New Guinea cultures (Arapesh, Mundugumor and Tschambuli) with Fortune; and Iatmul of Tambunam (New Guinea) and Bali with Bateson. *Coming of Age in Samoa* (1928), quickly followed by *Growing up in New Guinea* (1930) and *Sex and Temperament in Three Primitive Societies* (1935), summarized the diversity of gendered socialization and sex roles.

Mead and Bateson's expedition to Bali (1936–39), which also included dancer Jane Belo and musician Colin McPhee, described trance, dance, and ritual as well as the relationship of socialization to adult personality (Bateson and Mead 1942). Although these studies pioneered the methodology of visual anthropology, Mead has been dismissed as "impressionistic" and Bateson as "philosophical" (Yans-McLaughlin 1989:255).

Mead entered government service during World War II as executive secretary of the National Research Council Division of Anthropology and Psychology's Committee on Food Habits, which helped ensure acceptance of rationing. Her optimistic analysis of American character, *And Keep Your Powder Dry*, appeared in 1942. Since fieldwork was impossible in wartime, Mead and her colleagues Rhoda Métraux and Ruth Benedict devised the "culture at a distance" method, developed under Mead's directorship of the Columbia Institute for Contemporary Cultures from 1948 to 1952 (Mead and Métraux 1953). After the war Mead eschewed government service, choosing to speak directly to the American public through lectures and popular writing. Her commentary column on American society, which consolidated her role as America's paramount public intellectual, ran in *Redbook* magazine for 17 years, beginning in 1961.

Mead did not hesitate to contradict herself. *Sex and Temperament* (1935) emphasizes cultural determination of sex roles. After the war, however, *Male and Female* acknowledged the inseparability of culture and biology. Once Hitler was defeated, she felt able to raise issues of biology again (Yans-McLaughlin 1989:256). Arguing that the war had irrevocably changed the world, she briefly but systematically revisited former ethnographic sites: six trips to Manus where Theodore Schwartz, Leona Foerstal, and Barbara Roll were updating her pioneering ethnography, and brief visits to Tambunam (with Métraux), Bali, Samoa (where Lowell Holmes re-studied Tau Village in 1954), and the Mountain Arapesh.

Mead's academic career was irregular. She was appointed at the American Museum of Natural History in 1926, retiring as emeritus curator of ethnology in 1969. Although her nonacademic employment precluded direct students, her office in the sixth-floor storage area of the southwest tower became a mecca for younger anthropologists from Columbia University and elsewhere. Only in 1954 did she become adjunct professor at Columbia. From 1968 to 1970 she taught at Fordham College. She became the third woman president of the American Anthropological Association (after Benedict and *Elsie Clews Parsons*) and was the first anthropological president of the American Association for the Advancement of Science after Boas. The Hall of the Peoples of the

Pacific opened in 1971; its current version bears her name. She died on 15 November 1978.

Shortly after Mead's death, Australian anthropologist Derek Freeman published a purported exposé of her Samoan fieldwork, critiquing Boasian cultural anthropology from a sociobiological standpoint (Freeman 1983). Although acknowledging that Mead's work was a product of its time and place, her American colleagues have largely defended the groundbreaking character of her work. A forum in the *American Anthropologist*, edited by Ivan Brady in 1983, assembled commentaries by Pacific specialists *Annette Weiner*, Theodore Schwartz, Lowell Holmes, Brad Shore, and Martin Silverman; it provided a context for reassessing Mead's work and decried the polemic, decontextualized character of Freeman's attack. The nuanced disciplinary response to Freeman's salvos has not, however, reached the larger public.

Mead carefully documented her participant version of the history of American anthropology. In addition to an autobiography of her early years (1972), she published her letters from the field (1977) and wrote extensively about Ruth Benedict (1959, 1974). Her daughter, Mary Catherine Bateson, wrote a memoir of her parents (1984).

REGNA DARNELL

Gordon R. Willey
1961

Gordon Randolph Willey was born in Chariton, Iowa, on 7 March 1913, to Agnes Wilson and Frank Willey, a pharmacist. He grew up in Long Beach, California, and was recruited by the University of Arizona as a high school track star. At Arizona Willey was steered toward archaeology by Byron Cummings.

He received his B.A. in anthropology from the University of Arizona in 1935 and remained for an additional year to obtain an M.A. in 1936. From 1936 to 1938, he was an archaeological assistant to Arthur R. Kelley for the National Park Service in Macon, Georgia, where he met and married Katherine W. Whaley in 1938 (the couple had two children). In 1938–39 he worked with James A. Ford on a synthesis of the prehistory of the eastern United States and taught archaeology at Lousiana State University. Willey's early work was "descriptive, historical and chronologically oriented" (Willey 1974:157); it focused on pottery and artifact typology based on stratigraphy and seriation.

After being turned down at Harvard University because of insufficient foreign language training, Willey entered Columbia University's doctoral program in 1939, where William Duncan Strong engaged him in South American prehistory. His dissertation research in the Chancay Valley built sequences based on ceramic typology, as did his 1941 and 1942 work on the Florida gulf coast. He earned his Ph.D. in 1942 and served as an instructor at Columbia in 1942–43.

From 1943–50 Willey worked at the Bureau of American Ethnology in Washington DC, under the direction of Julian Steward, who encouraged him to move from "potsherd chronicle" to settlement pattern (Willey 1974:157). Willey, Steward, and *Wendell C. Bennett* applied their new ideas in the Virú Valley program beginning in 1945. Archaeologists W. D. Strong, Clifford Evans, James Ford, Junius Bird, and Donald Collier, and geographer F.W. McBryde concentrated on traditional stratigraphic data collection, while Willey followed the lead of social anthropologist Alan Holmberg and carried out a settlement pattern survey, attempting "to say something about the forms, settings, and spatial relationships of the sites themselves and what all this might imply about the societies that constructed and lived in them" (Willey 1974:153). Site maps from aerial photographs were checked in the field and architectural forms were located on a master map. To Willey's surprise at the time, the settlement pattern data integrated everything known about the Virú Valley and set a standard for future archaeological research programs. With Charles R. McGimsey, Willey then turned to the Intermediate Area between the southern Mayas and Peru, discovering an early cultural sequence at Monagrillo, Panama.

Willey was appointed the first Bowditch Professor of Mexican and Central American Archaeology and Ethnology at Harvard in 1950, simultaneously becoming curator of Middle and South American Ethnology at Harvard's Peabody Museum. Through the Carnegie Institute, Willey brought such Mesoamerican scholars as Harry Pollock, Ledyard Smith, and Tatiana Proskouriakoff to Harvard. He also chaired the Pre-Columbian Committee at Dunbarton Oaks.

After completing his Monagrillo work in 1952, Willey began three decades of lowland Maya research with a settlement-pattern study in the Belize Valley of British Honduras. A valley bottomland fully cleared for agricultural activity revealed dense clusters of ancient mounds. In 1965 Willey and his colleagues summarized both the settlement-pattern methodology and its application to ancient Mayan civilization. Willey then moved to the western Maya lowlands, spending a decade excavating in the Río Pasión drainage, especially at Altar de Sacrificios and Seibal. Here, he combined settlement pattern studies with large-scale excavation in major centers. Mayan cultural history intersected with theoretical questions about urbanism, ceremonial center communities, peripheral zones, and settlement segments likely to represent class, kinship, political, or craft groups. Willey went on to work in Nicaragua in 1959 and 1961, in Guatemala in 1958, 1960, 1962, and from 1964 to 1968, and in the Copán Valley in Honduras.

Willey's work on settlement patterns was a significant forerunner of the New Archaeology in its move from gathering artifacts and presenting a narrow view of prehistoric societies toward a more systemic approach. Indeed, settlement-pattern archaeology has now become virtually synonymous with a holistic view of the past (Vogt and Levanthal 1983:xiv). A Wenner-Gren-sponsored symposium at Burg Wartenstein celebrated Willey's 70th birthday. The first of the two festschrift volumes, edited by Evon Z. Vogt and Richard M. Leventhal (1983), focused on settlement-pattern studies, building on Willey's seminal work and including his own responses to the papers. By this point in his career Willey had adopted a role as synthesizer or summarizer, enabling him to revise his own previous findings and keep up with new developments, including "the role of art styles in the development of civilization, the use of iconography for the archaeologist's understanding of prehistoric cultures, and the use of ethnographic and ethnohistoric data as models for understanding the past" (Vogt and Levanthal 1983:xiii). Willey collected his essays in a 1990 volume that showed the development of his work and his openness to revision as more data became available. Although an evolutionary theory was implicit in his work (e.g., Willey and Phillips 1958), Willey remained most interested in cultural history, a "space-time sorting" of the particular interlinked changes in subsistence, settlement, sociopolitical organization, and ideology or worldview. "Patterns in the data" necessarily preceded theory (1990:187).

Willey received the Viking Fund Medal in Archaeology in 1953, the gold medal of the Archaeological Institute of America in 1973, the Alfred V. Kidder Medal for Achievement in American Archaeology in 1974, the Huxley Medal of the Royal Anthropological Institute in 1979, the Golden Plate Award for American Academic Achievement in 1987, and the Order of the Quetzal from the government of Guatemala. Willey served as president of the American Anthropological Association in 1961 and of the Society for American Archaeology in 1968.

Since his retirement in 1987, Willey has continued as professor emeritus at Harvard University and the Peabody Museum.

REGNA DARNELL

Sherwood Washburn
1962

S herwood "Sherry" Washburn was born to privilege in Massachusetts in 1911, and as a young man he spent time during the
summers at the Museum of Comparative Zoology (MCZ) in Cambridge. He attended Harvard University and became inspired by the
courses given by *Alfred M. Tozzer* and Earnest Hooton. Upon graduation in 1935 he stayed on to do graduate work in physical anthropology under Hooton. While Hooton focused on human variation,
Washburn was more interested in primate evolution and spent much
of his time at the MCZ.

As a graduate student, Washburn participated in the Asiatic Primate
Expedition to Thailand led by Harold Coolidge, C. R. Carpenter, and
Adolph Schultz, and came to recognize the importance of nonhuman
primate biology for a comprehensive understanding of human behav-

ior in an evolutionary framework. He completed his doctorate in 1940 on langur and macaque skeletal material, shortly after being appointed to the anatomy faculty at Columbia University Medical School. The anthropological relevance of Washburn's experimental research on the growth of the skull in rats, however, was incomprehensible to the senior physical anthropologists in New York, such as *Harry Shapiro* and Franz Weidenreich. Washburn made what contacts he could in anthropology, but also made significant connections to the biologists at the American Museum of Natural History who were formalizing the "Synthetic Theory" of evolution. Washburn would later champion the idea of an intimate biological history and recent separation of humans and African apes, which had been the pet theory of paleontologist William King Gregory.

Washburn remained involved in anthropology through seminars sponsored by the Viking Fund in New York. In 1947 he moved to the University of Chicago on the promise of a joint appointment in anthropology and anatomy. At the last moment the anatomy department reneged on the offer, but through the intervention of *Robert Redfield* the anthropology department was able to pick up his full appointment; Redfield and *Sol Tax* were both strongly interested in bringing Washburn to Chicago. By moving to Chicago Washburn regained the holistic perspective of his anthropological training and had the opportunity, in turn, to train a number of graduate students, but because he no longer had the medical facilities to do experimental work on skulls, his primary research interests began to shift to primate behavior and its role in illuminating aspects of human evolution.

It was at about this time that Washburn crystallized a plan for the reformation of physical anthropology to bring it into harmony with contemporary developments in evolutionary biology. With the distinguished geneticist Theodosius Dobzhansky, he organized a Cold Spring Harbor symposium in 1950 that attempted to refocus the field around real populations instead of Platonic racial types. The following year he published his most famous and influential paper, "The New Physical Anthropology," in which he argued for the replacement of the static typological approach to human variation by a dynamic, evolutionary, adaptive approach; in 1952 he presented these ideas in the Wenner-Gren "Anthropology Today" symposium.

Washburn's first generation of students at Chicago included Irven DeVore, Phyllis Dolhinow, James Gavan, and Clark Howell. In 1957, while a fellow at the Institute for Advanced Study in the Behavioral Sciences, Washburn was recruited by the University of California at Berkeley to expand its biological anthropology program. Over the next two decades, until his retirement in 1978, he would build Berkeley's program into the premier biological anthropology training ground in the country.

Like his Harvard mentor Earnest Hooton, Washburn became a charismatic and inspiring teacher, whose introductory class might attract a thousand students in a given semester. His influence came through his teaching, his vision for the field, and also his organizational skills. Following the landmark Cold Spring Harbor Symposium, Washburn organized two major international conferences with the assistance of the Viking Fund: "The Social Life of Early Man," the proceedings of which were published in 1961, and "Classification and Human Evolution," (1963).

Under the postwar humanistic aegis of UNESCO, Washburn promoted the vision of a unified species that was evolving under the leadership of "Man the Hunter." A sponsor of many women students, Washburn would see that idea augmented by them in the 1960s and 1970s, as gender roles, which had been taken for granted as part of nature, became more keenly questioned (Haraway 1988).

Of all his works, Washburn was proudest of the published version of his American Anthropological Association presidential address, which appeared in 1963 as "The Study of Race." The address was written at the behest of *Joseph B. Casagrande* and the AAA executive committee, which was trying to cope with the scandal aroused by Carleton Coon's *The Origin of Races*, a book that was being invoked by segregationists for its argument that blacks had evolved into *Homo sapiens* 200,000 years later than whites. Washburn, who had once been a teaching assistant for Coon at Harvard, dismissed his former mentor's work as the last vestige of an archaic paradigm and repudiated the political evils for which it was being utilized. Washburn maintained that the published version of his speech was virtually identical to the podium presentation, but an oral lore has the podium version being more strident and more damning. His own recollection, obviously melodramatic, has it that silence followed the talk until his friend, the geneticist Dobzhansky, leaped up to congratulate him, and thunderous applause ensued.

Washburn's honors and awards were legion. The Viking Fund Medal was presented to him in 1960; the Huxley Medal in 1967, the Distinguished Service Award of the AAA in 1983, and the Charles Darwin Lifetime Achievement Award from the American Association of Physical Anthropologists.

He died in Berkeley, California, on 16 April 2000.

JOANATHAN MARKS

Morris E. Opler
1963

M orris Edward Opler was born on 16 May 1907, in Buffalo,
New York. He was the son of Fanny Hass and Arthur Opler,
a businessman. Opler received his B.A. summa cum laude
in 1929 and his M.A. in 1930 from the University of Buffalo, where he
was a student of *Leslie A. White*. He married Catherine Hawkins in
1930. A year after her death in 1956, he married Lucille Ritter.

Opler received a Ph.D. from the University of Chicago in 1933, remaining there as a research assistant and an associate in anthropology
from 1933 to 1935. He served as an assistant anthropologist at the Bureau of Indian Affairs in 1936–37, was a visiting lecturer in sociology at
Reed College in 1937–38, and became an assistant professor of anthropology at Claremont College from 1938 to 1942.

During World War II Opler served as social science analyst for the

War Relocation Authority in California, where he was assigned to two Japanese American internment camps (Poston, in Arizona, and Manzanar in California; see Gesensway and Roseman 1987). He then worked for the Office of War Information in Washington DC. By 1946 he was deputy chief and eventually chief of the Foreign Morale Analysis Division. During these years Opler was a strong advocate of Japanese American civil rights. Two of his three legal briefs were heard before the U.S. Supreme Court, and he received the formal thanks of the Japanese American Citizens League. He also worked for the American Civil Liberties Union. This work had strong emotional value for him.

From 1946 to 1948 Opler was an assistant professor of education and anthropology at Harvard University. From 1948 to 1969 he served as a professor of anthropology and Asian studies at Cornell University, becoming an emeritus professor in 1969. In the same year, Opler took up a position as professor of anthropology at the University of Oklahoma.

Most of Opler's publications have dealt with the Apaches of the southwestern United States. He collected the myths and tales of the Jicarillas in 1938, the Lipans in 1940, and the Chiricahuas in 1942 (all reissued by Kraus Reprints in 1977). As a result of his Chicago contacts, Opler contributed to Fred Eggan's 1937 collection of essays on the social anthropology of North American tribes, a project combining the Boasian commitment to American Indian ethnography with the social and functionalist anthropology of A. R. Radcliffe-Brown. He continued what would become a lifelong commitment to write about the Apaches; *Apache Odyssey: A Journey between Two Worlds* (1969) epitomized his approach in an accessible format. He compiled Grenville Goodwin's letters from the field among the Western Apaches in 1973.

Opler's ethnographic method emphasized careful recording of detailed information reflecting his informants' points of view and covering a broad range of cultural topics. Folklore and biography were two of his favored strategies for getting inside a culture as an outsider anthropologist. During the interwar years, he was much intrigued by culture-and-personality approaches to American Indian cultures. Following an individual through the life cycle allowed him to personalize the cultural preoccupations of warfare, raiding, and ritual.

After World War II his work turned increasingly to the dynamic forces of cultural themes. He sought a cross-cultural typology for characterizing the relationships of individuals to their diverse cultural backgrounds. He wrote on topics of interest to a broad public audience outside anthropology, including technological change, adult education, values in American culture, and the meaning of world affairs for ordinary people. He contributed to a number of collections on comparative religion, political institutions, and mental health (e.g., Opler 1959). Much of this work was applied, in the sense that it made recommendations based on a cross-cultural anthropological insight into issues of development and cultural change. Strategic intervention was the mandate and responsibility of the anthropologist as citizen and ethnographer.

Opler also wrote about the Third Reich, Japan, China, and American culture. At Cornell he directed the Cornell India Program from 1948 to 1966. This long-term multidisciplinary study of village life in India established Cornell as a major center of South Asian study in North America.

Opler was outspoken in his distaste for mono-causal explanations of cultural phenomena, which set him against his former mentor Leslie White, as did his tendency to privilege idealist rather than materialist phenomena. He argued that White exaggerated the evolutionary arguments of Lewis Henry Morgan and Edward Burnet Tylor, and that Karl Marx, not Leslie White, first recognized the relationship of technology, social organization, and ideology, attributing priority to the first of these. In the heyday of "un-American anthropological activities," Opler "apparently sought to damage the scientific status of the cultural-materialist position by emphasizing its incorporation into Communist dogma" (Harris 1968:637). Harris berated Opler for his knowledge of Marxist literature combined with a failure to acknowledge that dialectics as well as materialism were needed for a Marxist evolutionary position. Harris (1968:638) pleaded passionately for separating the value of Marxist thought from contemporary American ideology and for the freedom of intellectuals to pursue ideas independently of political pressure. George W. Stocking Jr. (1968) took up the debates between Opler and White (abetted by Betty Meggers) during the 1960s as an exemplar of presentism or Whiggish history, chiding both parties for their lack of historicism.

Opler was much valued as a teacher by his former students. Mario D. Zamora and others edited a festschrift entitled *Themes in Culture* in 1971; another volume in honor of Opler was edited by Gerry Williams and Carolyn Peel in 1977.

Opler was president of the American Anthropological Association in 1962–63. He also served as a fellow of the Laboratory of Anthropology, Santa Fe (1931), and of the Center for Advanced Study in the Behavioral Sciences (1956–57). He was a visiting professor at the University of Wisconsin (1941), at Howard University (1945), and at Lucknow University (1953–54). He served on the Board of Trustees of the American Institute of Indian Studies from 1963 to 1966. He held fellowships from the Social Science Research Council (1932–33, 1946–47), the Guggenheim Foundation (1942–43), and the National Endowment for the Humanities (1968–69).

Opler died in Norman, Oklahoma, 13 May 1996.

REGNA DARNELL

Leslie A. White
1964

L eslie Alvin White was born in Salida, Colorado, on 19 January
1900. His father, Alvin Lincoln White, was a civil engineer and
sometime tenant farmer. After a divorce when Leslie was five,
his father obtained custody of the three children. The family lived in
rural Kansas and Louisiana. White enlisted in the U.S. Army in 1918, an
experience that moved him to reevaluate the accepted patriotic plati-
tudes of his upbringing. He returned to Louisiana to attend the state
university for two years, switching from physics to history and political
science. After transferring to Columbia University, White turned to
psychology, sociology, and philosophy. He received his B.A. from Columbia in 1923 and his M.A. a year later, both in psychology. He took
no anthropology courses at Columbia, but studied anthropology un-

der Boasian Alexander Goldenweiser at the New School for Social Research.

In 1924 White moved to the University of Chicago to study sociology, which then included anthropology. His initial Keresan Pueblo fieldwork was sponsored and funded by *Elsie Clews Parsons* and resulted in a dissertation on Southwestern medicine societies. According to White, accusations that the topic was insufficiently theoretical "helped to precipitate the formation of the separate department of anthropology" in 1927, under the leadership of Boasian *Fay-Cooper Cole*. White was successful in obtaining information from the secretive Pueblo communities. Despite what are today considered serious ethical problems, White believed that he had treated his informants fairly and that they wanted their reminiscences recorded (in Carneiro 1981:226).

In 1927 White became an instructor in anthropology at the University of Buffalo. His training had been conventionally Boasian, not directly but through Goldenweiser, Cole, and *Edward Sapir*. Gradually, however, White came to distrust the Boasian critique of evolution. In Buffalo, he read Louis Henry Morgan on the Seneca (Iroquois) of the nearby Tonawanda Reservation and began a lifetime campaign to rehabilitate Morgan's version of cultural evolution; he edited Morgan's letters and journals, and prepared a definitive edition of *Ancient Society*. His philosopher colleague at Buffalo, Marvin Farber, encouraged this interest. White's visit to Russia in the summer of 1929 brought into focus Morgan's influence on Karl Marx and Friedrich Engels and convinced him that socialism would prevail in the West. His 1930 paper to the American Association for the Advancement of Science predicting the collapse of capitalism received media attention around the world.

This was the first of White's many confrontations with the academic establishment at the University of Michigan, where White had moved in 1930 to succeed Julian Stewart and where he remained until his retirement in 1970. His overtly political writings, however, were published under the pseudonym John Steele. In 1931 White married his former Buffalo student Mary Pattison. He remained an associate professor from 1932 to 1943; until 1944, his title was "acting" chair. He held the position until 1957. White's outspoken socialist politics antagonized the Michigan administration, while his anti-Boasian insistence on reviving evolutionary theory isolated him within the profession. Nonetheless, White was a remarkably popular undergraduate lecturer, teaching a large lecture course in "culturology" (the science of culture approached in a nonreductive materialist framework) under the rubric "The Mind of Primitive Man." The course "described the slow and reluctant progress of humanity" toward recognizing the self-containment of culture "rooted in the human faculty for creating and manipulating symbols" (Beardsley 1976:617). The Ann Arbor Catholic Church attacked his rejection of both free will and deism. "His mordant lectures, his radical-populist political attitudes, and the assertive style of some of his critical essays" (Service 1976:613) contrasted sharply with a quiet, friendly, scholarly demeanor and a self-deprecating wit.

White rejected the term "neo-"evolution, contending that he was reviving 19th-century evolutionism. He considered his own major contribution to be *The Science of Culture* (1949) rather than evolution as such. Even he recognized that *The Evolution of Culture* (1959) was something of an anticlimax, emphasizing function as much as evolution. After this publication, White replaced his course in the evolution of culture with "Ancient and Modern Civilization," in which he explored continuing cultural evolution in terms of technological harnessing of more energy per capita. Culturology, he concluded, was incompatible with utilitarianism because individuals were virtually irrelevant to the integrated structure of culture itself. His posthumous *The Concept of Cultural Systems* (1975) elaborated these final insights. White was a determinist who believed that material factors dominated in the specification of culture (Carneiro 1981:240).

White's career contains apparent contradictions (Barrett 1989). His Pueblo ethnographic work emphasized religion, whereas the theoretical work focused on economics and technology. White believed that salvage ethnography was descriptive and that religion persisted longest under conditions of rapid cultural change because it was hidden from public view. In this, he considered himself Boasian (Service 1976:616). White published four monographs on the Pueblo Indians and the consequences of their contact with mainstream American society. His presi-

192 • PRESIDENTIAL PORTRAITS

dential address to the American Anthropological Association (AAA) in 1964 challenged his colleagues to analyze modern capitalism and the problems of "whole modern national cultures" (Service 1976:615).The analysis of culture would explain the behavior of nations.

His course in the history of anthropology was required for all graduate students at Michigan. His "disdain of bandwagons" (Carneiro 1981:225) was legendary.White insisted that he was not interested in establishing a school of thought, at Michigan or within the general profession. He critiqued the Boas and Radcliffe-Brown schools because they seemed to him to limit intellectual progress. His later contributions to the history of Americanist anthropology are vitriolic (1963, 1966).

In 1947 White represented social scientists in a Sunday afternoon radio series "The Scientists Speak." His lecture "Energy and the Development of Civilization" was widely publicized. White received the Viking Fund Medal of the Wenner-Gren Foundation for Anthropological Research in 1959 and served as vice president of the American Association for the Advancement of Science in 1958, in addition to his AAA presidency.

Mary White died in 1959 after a long battle with cancer.White remarried hastily and divorced soon after. He suffered a fatal heart attack on 31 March 1975, after several years of ill health.

White's work has invited passionate response, both positive and negative (e.g., Barrett 1989, Beardsley 1976, Carneiro 1981, Kroeber 1948). A conference honoring the centenary of his birth was held at the Bentley Historical Library of the University of Michigan in September 2000.

REGNA DARNELL

Alexander Spoehr
1965

Alexander "Alex" Spoehr was born on 23 August 1913 in Tucson, Arizona. His father was a biochemist with the Carnegie Insitute who identified the role of chlorophyll in photosynthesis and its application in toothpaste; his mother was a writer and a translator of Danish and German who later translated Alfred Tetens's (1958) *Among the Savages of the South Seas: Memoirs of Micronesia, 1862–1868*. In 1920 the family moved to Palo Alto, California, where Spoehr attended public schools. He studied at Stanford University for two-and-a-half years, and then transferred to the University of Chicago, where he earned his A.B. in economics in 1934. Coursework with *Fay-Cooper Cole* and A. R. Radcliffe-Brown had interested him in anthropology, and he pursued graduate work at Chicago. He spent three seasons doing archaeological fieldwork in Colorado (Martin, Lloyd, and Spoehr 1938) and at the Kincaid Mounds in Illinois, but his main interest was in social anthropology. In addition to Cole and Radcliffe-

Brown, Spoehr cited Manuel Andrade, *Robert Redfield*, and *Fred Eggan* as his most influential mentors. Eggan supervised his dissertation research, which focused on social change among southeastern Indians; Spoehr did ethnographic research with dispersed families in Oklahoma and with a community of Seminoles in Florida (Spoehr 1942, 1947).

Back in Chicago to complete his doctorate in 1940, Spoehr became an assistant curator of American archaeology and ethnology at the Field Museum, where he worked on the new "Indians before Columbus" halls. There he met talented exhibits designer Anne Harding, and they were married in August 1941, shortly after he received his Ph.D. When the United States entered the war Spoehr did short tours of duty in the Marine Corps Reserve and the Army Corps of Engineers. He was then commissioned as a lieutenant in the Naval Reserve, where he served as a navigator on MARS flying boats, locating downed Allied pilots in the South Pacific. He served in active duty from 1942 to 1945, but even after returning to the Field Museum, he was persuaded by the Navy to join a team working in the Pacific to convince holdout Japanese soldiers to surrender.

Military service shifted Spoehr's research interests to the Pacific, a focus he retained the rest of his life. At the Field Museum after the war he supervised the reorganization of the Oceania collections and exhibits; he also conducted ethnographic and archaeological fieldwork in the Marshall Islands, Marianas, and Palau, which resulted in a number of publications (including *Majuro: Village in the Marshall Islands*, 1949; *Saipan: The Ethnology of a War-Devastated Island*, 1954; and *Marianas Prehistory*, 1957). During this period he also taught sessions at Chicago and Harvard, and helped Fred Eggan develop a research program in the Philippines.

In January 1953 Spoehr left the Field Museum to become the director of the Bernice Pauhi Bishop Museum in Honolulu, filling the vacancy left by the death of Sir Peter Buck (Te Rangi Hiroa). He remained there until 1962, also holding an ex officio professorship at Yale, where he taught classes for one semester. He left the Bishop Museum to help establish the new East–West Center but resigned that position two years later due to internal power struggles; he then traveled with his wife through the South Pacific before returning to Honolulu to set a future course. He was offered several administrative positions but chose instead to teach, and in 1964 he was appointed professor of anthropology at the University of Pittsburgh, where he remained until his retirement in 1978; also during this period he coedited *Ethnology* with his friend and colleague *George P. Murdock*. Spoehr was respected by and responsive to students, supervising more dissertations than any other faculty member in the department.

Spoehr was strongly committed to the role of anthropology as a science. However, he also recognized the importance of more humanistic approaches; he authored the American Anthropological Association's contribution to the Report of the Commission on the Humanities, and as AAA president he testified before the Senate Special Subcommittee on Arts and Humanities, supporting the establishment of the National Endowment for the Humanities and the National Endowment for the Arts. He was elected to the American Association for the Advancement of Science and the National Academy of Sciences, served as chair of the National Research Council's Pacific Science Board from 1958 to 1961, and was president of the Hawaiian Academy of Sciences in 1961–62. He received an honorary doctorate from the University of Hawaii in 1952 and the Charles Reed Bishop Medal, the highest honor of the Bishop Museum, in 1991. He also served as the U.S. commissioner to the South Pacific Commission (now the Secretariat of the Pacific Community) from 1957 to 1960.

Spoehr's term as AAA president (1965) coincided with one of the greatest crises for the association and for the discipline. Concern over U.S. involvement in Vietnam was growing, and it was also disclosed that an anthropologist had been employed in Project Camelot, a clandestine CIA operation in Chile designed to study and affect political attitudes in order to combat what were represented as communist tendencies. Social scientists across the country were angered and concerned at what many considered violations of a moral responsibility, but others felt the AAA should not get involved in "political" issues. At the time the AAA had no code of ethics. A special session was convened at the AAA meeting to discuss the situation, with efforts being taken by the AAA council to keep the focus not on the individuals and institutions involved, but on "the issues of access to foreign areas, the integrity of the field worker, and the effects upon field work of mission-directed projects supported by the government" (AAA 1966:770). After considerable discussion Spoehr appointed *Ralph Beals* to investigate the matter and submit a report to the council, which eventuated in the adoption of a code of ethics by the AAA.

After his retirement in 1978 the Spoehrs returned to Honolulu, where Alex continued research and writing. In 1990 his wife Anne suffered a stroke that necessitated his constant attention. On 11 June 1992 Alex Spoehr suffered a fatal heart attack; Anne died two weeks later. They were survived by their son, Hardy, their daughter, Helene Spoehr-Clarke, and two grandchildren.

FREDERIC W. GLEACH

John P. Gillin
1966

John Philip Gillin was born on 1 August 1907 in Waterloo, Iowa. His father was distinguished sociologist John Lewis Gillin, noted for his work on poverty and criminology; together they later wrote an introductory textbook for sociology. In 1912 John Lewis left Iowa State University for the University of Wisconsin and the family moved to Madison. John Philip attended public schools there before entering the University of Wisconsin. He received his B.A. in sociology in 1927 and immediately set out on a trip around the world with his father to study prisons. In 1928, in preparation for graduate work, Gillin began studying German at the University of Berlin, and then attended the London School of Economics. But poor health forced his return to the States, and he began graduate studies at the University of Wisconsin, where his fellow students included *E. Adamson Hoebel*, *Clyde Kluckhohn*, Lauriston Sharp, and *Sol Tax*. Gillin had considered a career in journalism, but his first course with *Ralph Linton* persuaded him to focus on anthropology. He also continued studying sociology and psychology; as he noted later, "since it has become clear that culture is learned rather than inherited biologically, anthropologists have had to become familiar with the principles of learning as developed by psychology. Likewise, psychology has helped with the understanding of personality types in diverse cultures" (1969:xi).

In 1929 Gillin participated in a Beloit College archaeological expedition to Algiers (along with Sharp and Tax). In a piece he wrote about the experience for the *Milwaukee Journal*, he captured the transition of the end of a field season and his perspective on the discipline: "The Circus has moved on; the Show is over—and now comes the reckoning with Science" (1969:9). Gillin received his M.A. from the University of Wisconsin in 1930, and then went to Harvard University, where he received a second master's degree in 1931, and his Ph.D. in 1934. He also married Helen Norgord in 1934; four years later they had a son, John Christian, who later became a psychiatrist, continuing the family tradition in the social sciences. In 1932–33 Gillin did his dissertation fieldwork with Carib Indians in British Guiana, and in 1933–34 he was a full-time tutor at Sarah Lawrence College. After receiving his Ph.D. Gillin worked a year at the Peabody Museum at Harvard, where he was in charge of work in Peru and Ecuador. In 1935 he left the Peabody to teach at the University of Utah, where he was promoted to associate professor and curator of the university museum the next year.

In the summers of 1936 and 1937 Gillin directed archaeological excavations at Nine Mile Canyon in Utah. Gillin was attracted to this area in part because it was known to have had a stable climate for 1500 years, providing an environmental baseline from which to consider cultural variation. Excavations identified three distinct types of settlements (Gillin 1938). In 1937 Gillin joined Ohio State University as an associate professor, and from there he worked with Wisconsin Chippewas in 1938–39; in 1940 he began research in Guatemala, but it was interrupted by the war. He was a fellow at the Institute of Human Relations at Yale in 1940–41 and then left Ohio State for Duke University. During World War II, Gillin was assigned to the U.S. Embassy in Lima, Peru, as a member of the Board of Economic Welfare. He then served as representative of the Smithsonian Institution there, engaging in field-work in the Pueblo of Moche. This work, following on the preliminary research he had begun with Ladinos and Mayas in Guatemala (which he would resume in 1946), led to the conceptualization of a Criollo culture in Latin America. Also in 1946 Gillin was appointed professor at the University of North Carolina, Chapel Hill, where he stayed until 1959. During the 1940s he led research on the contemporary cultures of the Southeast, working primarily with sociology students who were interested in employing ethnographic techniques. He also continued research in Latin America, along with evaluation projects, administration, and consulting with the National Research Council, UNESCO, and the federal government.

In 1949 Gillin testified before the U.S. Senate Labor and Public Welfare subcommittee on the need to study American children. He pointed out how little was known about cultural aspects of child development, arguing that the country "has devoted itself almost exclusively to economic development. It is time to go into the development of a race of healthy, happy people." Gillin's own health was beginning to weaken, and he did little extended fieldwork after this time, turning instead to more administrative work, with shorter trips to various parts of Europe and Latin America. He founded and directed the Ph.D. program at the University of North Carolina and helped organize its Institute for Research in Social Science. In 1959 Gillin went to the University of Pittsburgh as its first dean of social sciences and founded the anthropology department there. He stepped down as dean in 1962 and served as the National Institute of Mental Health research professor until his retirement in 1972.

Gillin was interested in developing anthropology as a holistic social science; although he worked mostly in social and cultural anthropology, he also did archaeological research and served as a member of the American Association of Physical Anthropologists. Gillin believed that anthropology was a practice rather than merely an academic discipline; in addition to the work mentioned above he was a member of the Society for Applied Anthropology, and its president from 1959 to 1960. His concern also led to his development of anthropological study of complex modern societies, which had often been considered the realm of sociology. He was elected to the American Association for the Advancement of Science and was a member of sociological as well as anthropological professional societies. As American Anthropological Association president in 1965, Gillin opened the meeting of the AAA council that was dominated by *Ralph Beals's* report on anthropological ethics following from the Project Camelot scandal debates of the previous year. By this time Gillin's respiratory problems had left him very weak, and after opening the meeting he turned the chair over to *Frederica de Laguna*, the president-elect; as Gillin slowly walked from the hall the council rose in appreciation of his dedicated work. Gillin continued at the University of Pittsburgh until he retired in 1972 and returned to Chapel Hill. He died peacefully at home on 4 August 1973, with his wife at his side.

FREDERIC W. GLEACH

Frederica de Laguna
1967

Frederica "Freddy" Annis Lopez de Leo de Laguna was born on 3 October 1906 in Ann Arbor, Michigan. She was the oldest child of two Bryn Mawr College philosophers, Grace Mead Andrus and Theodore Lopez de Leo de Laguna. Her cross-cultural experience began with parental sabbaticals in England and France. In 1927 she graduated from Bryn Mawr College summa cum laude with majors in economics and politics. She postponed Bryn Mawr's European Fellowship, awarded on graduation, for a year of graduate coursework in anthropology at Columbia University. De Laguna enjoyed *Franz Boas*'s "rather haphazard" linguistic seminar with Ella Deloria as Dakota informant. She avoided statistics, studying folklore with *Ruth Benedict* and social organization with Gladys Reichard (McClelland 1989b:768). Following Boas's advice, she joined *George G. MacCurdy*'s field school in the Dordogne and attended Bronislaw Malinowski's seminar in London. She did not appreciate the latter's anti-Americanism or pretentious claim that functionalism was new to anthropology; Grafton Elliot Smith was much more helpful. A visit to Arctic archaeologist Therkel Mathiassen in Copenhagen produced an invitation to join his excavation in Greenland, which was documenting previously unknown Eskimo-Norse contacts (de Laguna 1977 is a personal memoir). There were few opportunities for women in archaeology in North America at the time. European contacts made de Laguna's initial field trips possible.

Boas suggested a dissertation topic on the historic connection between Upper Paleolithic and Eskimo art, foreseeing pedagogical benefits in the negative conclusions of his "somewhat disgruntled student" (McClelland 1989b:770). When her Ph.D. was awarded in 1933, de Laguna had already completed three archaeological field seasons in Alaska, summarized in *The Archaeology of Cook Inlet* (1934). Danish archaeologist Kaj Birket-Smith joined her in the summer of 1933 in Prince William Sound; his *Chugach Eskimo* appeared in 1953 and her *Chugach Prehistory* in 1956. De Laguna's discovery of the continuing separate identity of the Eyaks in 1930 led to a joint monograph with Birket-Smith in 1938 and eventually to Michael Krauss's classification of Eyak as an independent branch of the Na-dene linguistic family. Her 1935 Yukon work, reported in *The Prehistory of Northern North America as Seen from the Yukon* (1947) produced myths and masks as well as the first archaeological survey of the Alaskan interior.

Her father died unexpectedly in 1930 while de Laguna was in the field. Grace de Laguna assumed the chair of Bryn Mawr's philosophy department and became a frequent companion on her daughter's field trips, sabbaticals, and holidays. Her younger brother Wallace, who later became a geologist, also shared some of her fieldwork. In addition to her scientific works, de Laguna wrote a youth book on Garibaldi in 1930, and two detective stories (1937, 1938).

De Laguna worked for the University of Pennsylvania Museum from 1931 to 1934. In 1938, as lecturer at Bryn Mawr, she introduced the teaching of anthropology and established a field school. She became assistant professor of anthropology in 1941, associate professor in 1949, and professor in 1955, chairing the joint Department of Sociology and

Anthropology from 1950 to 1966 and the newly independent Department of Anthropology from 1967 to 1972. She retired in 1975 as William R. Kenan Jr. Professor Emerita. That same year she and *Margaret
Mead* were the first women anthropologists to be elected to the National Academy of Sciences. De Laguna was devastated by the cancel-
lation of the anthropology graduate program at Bryn Mawr in 1987
due to financial exigency.

Alongside her academic career, de Laguna continued her fieldwork.
In 1936 she surveyed Pima social organization for the U.S. Soil Conservation Service. In 1938 she studied the Alaska collections from her
work with Birket-Smith, financing the Danish research by proceeds
from her first detective novel. During World War II she served in naval
intelligence at the Alaskan and later German desks, resigning in 1945 as
lieutenant commander. In 1947 she surveyed archaeological sites to be
flooded by the St. Lawrence Seaway.

Beginning in 1949, on the sixth of thirteen field trips to Alaska with
various student collaborators, she returned to the Tlingit villages of
Angoon and Yakutat. De Laguna aspired to trace the "distinctive culture growth of the coastal Tlingit" (McClelland 1989b). *The Story of a
Tlingit Village: A Problem in the Relationship between Archaeological, Ethnological, and Historical Methods* (1960) exemplified, through Angoon, archaeology as the ethnography of the past. She developed "a holistic
approach to cultural patterning through time" based on "a continuum
of native societies in coastal and interior northwestern America"
(McClelland 1989a:40). In 1954 de Laguna and Catherine McClelland
began studying the Athabascan-speaking Copper River Atnas and their
links to other Alaskan groups.

De Laguna's monumental synthesis of her Yakutat research, *Under
Mount Saint Elias* (1972) combined ethnography, ethnohistory, and archaeology in one of the most extensive compilations of available information on a single Native American community. She edited selected
papers from the *American Anthropologist* in 1960 and served as president
of the American Anthropological Association in 1967 during the political polarization of the Vietnam War. In her presidential address, De
Laguna maintained that personal political opinions were not the proper

business of a professional organization. She stressed "objectivity and subjectivity in fieldwork, values, the individual and culture, and the historic sweep of cultures" (McClelland 1989a:42). Anthropology, she concluded, was a way of life.

Retirement has not ended her fieldwork or writing. She returned to Greenland in 1979 and to Alaska in 1978 and 1985. In 1986, just after her 80th birthday, de Laguna was honored by a potlatch at Yakutat and rejoiced at the revitalization of the Tlingit; she also received the AAA's Distinguished Service Award that year. She edited a Tlingit manuscript by Lt. George T. Emmons (1991) with extensive synthetic commentary, and wrote about the Atnas in *Travels among the Dena* (2000); she also attended the first Eyak potlatch in 85 years in 1994.

Although she does not consider herself a theoretician, de Laguna has written on primitive mentality, Northwest Coast matrilineal kin groups, and "problems of objectivity in ethnology" (1957), in which she embraces the empathetic potentials of personal standpoint as compatible with scientific ethnography. Insisting on theory illustrated by data, "her insatiable holism and a vision of irrecoverable loss" (Ferzacca 1998:31) are characteristic of mid-century American anthropology. Post-Marxist Russian scholars have found her work invaluable (Grinev 2000).

REGNA DARNELL

Irving Rouse
1968

B enjamin Irving "Ben" Rouse Jr. was born in Rochester, New York, on 29 August 1913. His father was a nurseryman educated at Yale University. The son earned high grades in high school, received a fellowship to Yale, and began his studies in botany, entering the Sheffield Scientific School at Yale in 1930; he intended to pursue graduate studies in forestry. The little money his family had been able to give him after the stock market crash had been lost in a bank failure, and he needed a job. Cornelius Osgood, also just arrived at Yale, needed someone to catalog artifacts at the Peabody Museum, and Rouse was hired. Osgood felt Rouse should have some anthropological training for the job and enrolled him in his own course in the graduate school. By his junior year Rouse had decided not to go into forestry, and Osgood persuaded him to study anthropology. Rouse received his B.S. in 1934 (graduating at the top of his class), and his Ph.D. in 1938, with Osgood as his dissertation adviser.

Rouse remembers a contentious graduate program:

> I would say that my main recollection of graduate school was that the
> professors had diverse and conflicting points of view. That bothered me,
> because as an undergraduate I had been led to believe that there was a
> right way of doing things and all I had to do was learn what it was. I'd be
> told one thing by *[Edward] Sapir,* for example, and a contradictory thing
> by *[Leslie] Spier,* and others by *[George P.] Murdock* and Osgood. It
> bothered me a great deal at the time, but when I look back I think it was
> perhaps very good for me because it forced me to develop my own
> viewpoint, and it also forced me to be relatively open to other points of
> view, which I've tried to do throughout my career. (Siegel 1996:672)

Rouse elsewhere noted (1939:8) that he "derived whatever theoretical knowledge I may have of the nature of culture" from Sapir, who
died shortly after Rouse completed his Ph.D.

Rouse began teaching at Yale shortly after receiving his Ph.D., having continued to hold his museum appointment. He retained an affiliation with Yale's department of anthropology throughout his career.
He was an instructor from 1939 to 1943, an assistant professor from
1943 to 1948, an associate professor from 1948 to 1954, and a professor
from 1954 to 1970. In 1970 he was named Charles J. MacCurdy Professor of Anthropology. He directed undergraduate and graduate studies
in the department as well as the archaeology program, and also worked
extensively in the Peabody Museum. He retired as professor in 1984
and as curator in 1985.

Rouse's dissertation was on Haiti, based on fieldwork he conducted
in 1935 as part of an extensive and long-term archaeological research
program in the West Indies sponsored by the Peabody Museum. Osgood
had planned and directed this program from its inception. In addition
to Haiti, Rouse did fieldwork in Puerto Rico, Cuba, Florida, Trinidad,
Venezuela, and Antigua, collaborating with and training many local
archaeologists as well as students from Yale. He has published extensively from this work. He was awarded the Medalla Conmemorativa
del Vuelo Panamericano pro Faro de Colon by the Cuban government

for his *Archaeology of the Maniabón Hills, Cuba* (1942), and the A. Cressy Morrison Prize in Natural Science for his two-volume work on Puerto Rican prehistory, published by the New York Academy of Sciences in 1952.

In addition to the American Anthropological Association, Rouse was president of the Society for American Archaeology (1952–53) and the Eastern States Archaeological Federation (1946–50) and vice president of the American Ethnological Society (1957–58). He is a member of the National Academy of Sciences and the American Academy of Arts and Sciences. Rouse helped found the Archaeological Society of Connecticut and edited its *Bulletin* (1938–50); he also edited *American Antiquity* (1946–50) and the *Yale University Publications in Anthropology* (1950–63). In 1960 he received the Viking Fund Medal and Award in Anthropology.

Classification has long been a notable characteristic of Rouse's archaeological work. Attracted to taxonomy in botany before studying anthropology, he saw a need to improve classification in anthropology (especially archaeology); this was more interesting to him than fine-tuning the Linnaean classification of plants. His dissertation developed a conceptual scheme for classifying artifacts into types and modes and using these constructs as units of analysis rather than artifacts per se (see also Rouse 1939). His focus on analysis through classification has continued. He once noted, "We have to use classifications, and there's still room for a person like myself, who's interested in refining the established classifications" (in Siegel 1996:672).

This reflection came after a number of criticisms from younger archaeologists. First had come a postwar shift toward social archaeology, then the "New Archaeology" of the 1960s and 1970s, and more recently postprocessual archaeologies. Colin Renfrew reviewed *Introduction to Prehistory* (1972), noting the nine years from its inception to its publication and asserting: "Archaeology has moved far since the stasis of that time, to challenging new fields of enquiry. For a contemporary archaeologist to read this book is therefore a disappointment: it doesn't even reject the developments of the past decade ... in order to reassert older, supposedly truer, values. It simply ignores them altogether"

(Renfrew 1974:244–45). Renfrew also admitted that "it is painful to be critical of an author both liked and respected" (1974:245). More recently, some have criticized Rouse (among others) for neglecting ongoing political ramifications of Caribbean colonial relationships and for considering Caribbean history only in the context of broader American movements, and not in its own right (e.g., Sued Badillo 1992). Although these criticisms are legitimate, they also neglect the real value of work that has gone before, including Rouse's, on which later work is constructed.

Irving Rouse still lives in New Haven. Although retired he continues to write and do research in Caribbean archaeology. In his current research, he has found that prehistoric West Indians occupied water-centered "passage areas"—both sides of a passage between two islands—rather than the island-centered areas typical of modern settlements; the concept has also proven useful in other parts of the world.

FREDERIC W. GLEACH

Cora Du Bois
1969

Cora Du Bois was born in Brooklyn, New York, on 26 October 1903. Her father, Jean Jules Du Bois, was French Swiss; his family took American citizenship during World War I. Her mother, Mattie Schriber Du Bois, was a child of the 1848 German emigration to the United States. Both sides of the family stayed in close contact with their European relatives. Consequently, Du Bois spent five years of her youth in Western Europe.

She received her B.A. in history Phi Beta Kappa from Barnard College in 1927, continuing with an M.A. in medieval thought and culture from Columbia University in 1928. Having taken introductory anthropology at Barnard with *Franz Boas* and *Ruth Benedict*, she switched to anthropology for doctoral study. On Benedict's advice, she rejected Boas's proposed thesis topic of European contacts in East Africa. She moved to Berkeley, where she completed a library thesis in 1932 on New World female adolescent rites (Seymour 1989:73). Between 1919 and 1935, however, she carried out fieldwork with several California and Oregon tribes, beginning with the Wintus, partly in collaboration with Dorothy Demetrosopoulou Lee.

Du Bois spent 1935–36 as a National Research Council fellow in at Harvard's Harry A. Murray Psychological Clinic. At the invitation of Abram Kardiner, she joined his seminar on culture and personality at the New York Psychoanalytic Society. She remained in the seminar for a second year while teaching at Hunter College. From 1937 to 1939 she tested Kardiner's modal personality model in the field in Alor, Indonesia. She returned to teach at Sarah Lawrence College, where she wrote *The People of Alor* (1944). Du Bois (1980:2) considered herself fortunate to have "escaped the long and discouraging stultification of the depression in the 1930s."

Like most her contemporaries, Du Bois was caught up in "'the real world' of political power, of status-ridden bureaucracies and narrow self-interests" of government service during World War II. In 1942 she became chief of research and analysis for the Indonesia Section of the Office of Strategic Services. Until 1949 she headed the research division of the Southeast Asian branch for the Office of Intelligence and served as a consultant for the World Health Organization. She was director of research for the Institute of International Education from 1951 to 1954. Du Bois (1980:3) felt "trapped in what some called applied anthropology and others called 'relevance.'" Her sympathies did not lie with administration and management. Her expertise was often "unwelcome" in the State Department, where many researchers "were suspect during the anti-Communist witch-hunt of the McCarthy era" (Du Bois 1980:2). In 1949 she "quixotically" and publicly refused a tenured appointment at Berkeley because of McCarthy-inspired inquiries there (1980:3).

In 1954 Du Bois became Radcliffe's Zemurray Professor, a tenured position targeted for a woman and to be held in "association with relevant departments" (Seymour 1989:74). Du Bois was affiliated with the departments of anthropology and social relations, remaining the only tenured woman in either department until her retirement in 1969. On her return to academia from the State Department, Du Bois was startled by how much the discipline had changed in her 15-year absence: she highlighted the fragmentation of anthropology, the growth in numbers of graduate students, and the dissipation of personal involvement among colleagues. In her early years in anthropology, "we all knew each other": despite theoretical and personal conflicts, "we stood solidly in mutual support against outside attack;" at Harvard, however, "at best we were an aggregate of isolates, at worst of self-seeking careerists" (Du Bois 1980:3–4). She was also surprised by the hidden workload of teaching (1980:4).

These were years of honors and obligations. In 1968, she became president of the American Anthropological Association and the following year of the Association of Asian Studies. The increasing specialization and managerial organization of the AAA disturbed her because it was based "more on expediencies than on a community of scholars" (Du Bois 1980:6–7).

Fieldwork, for her, was the "determining polish of professionalism in anthropology" even though her initial fieldwork was salvage ethnography in which she could leave her own culture only "by an act of imagination" (Du Bois 1970:233, 221). She went on to carry out interdisciplinary psychological work in remote, isolated Alor. In Alor she sought—and believed she had found—a society relatively unchanged by colonial contact. She pioneered in demonstrating the cross-cultural applicability of psychological tests, studying Alorese childhood through autobiographies and children's drawings. *The People of Alor* was the critical test case for the collaboration of psychoanalysis with anthropology.

From 1961 to 1972, after her State Department years, Du Bois turned to the study of long-term cultural change in a complex society, "in an attempt to tackle, as an ethnographer, even a single community, in a culture far more sophisticated than mine" (Du Bois 1980:4). She concluded that conventional ethnographic methods were inadequate for the study of complex societies. Holism was "an unrealizable fantasy" (1980:4). From provisional acceptance of anthropology as a social science, Du Bois (1970:223) increasingly defined her discipline as "philosophical humanism . . . a science in the earlier sense of the word, as it was used in the past century: an attempt to understand." She did not, however, lose her conviction that anthropology promised "an under-standing of the growing variations and uncertainties of the moderniz-ing world" (1980:5). Her version of anthropological humanism retained its commitment to empiricism, the effort by the anthropologist as ob-server to be "as culture-free as possible" (1989:9). Despite the fuzziness and ambiguity of the integrating term *culture*, which oscillated between the panhuman and the culture-specific, Du Bois saw anthropology as exploring the intersection of the psychological, the social, and the symbolic.

With an interdisciplinary team of graduate students from India and the United States, Du Bois worked in the "double town" of Bhubaneswar, Orissa, a new state capital as well as an ancient temple center. Nine dissertations resulted from this collaboration. Although Du Bois did not publish her own results, she summarized the general insights of this work in *Social Forces in Southeast Asia* (1949), which approached acculturation in terms of its political and historical deter-minants and their policy implications.

Cora Du Bois died in 1991.

REGNA DARNELL

George M. Foster
1970

George McClelland Foster Jr. was born on 9 October 1913 in Sioux Falls, South Dakota. His father, a meat-packing plant executive trained in engineering, moved the family to Ottumwa, Iowa, in 1922, where Foster completed his primary and secondary education, graduating from Ottumwa High School in 1931. He entered Harvard College the same year, expecting to follow his father in engineering. When he found he would first have to complete a bachelor's degree at Harvard before studying engineering, and suffering from culture shock, he transferred to Northwestern University Engineering School in 1932. Realizing after failing five units of coursework that he did not have an engineer's mind, he stumbled upon Melville Herskovits's introductory anthropology course.

He found Herskovits to be a dynamic and inspiring teacher. Mary LeCron (born in Des Moines, Iowa, in 1914) was also a student in this course; Foster has often said, "I found my wife and my profession in the same class." Upon graduation in 1935 he immediately entered graduate school at the University of California, Berkeley, to study with *Alfred L. Kroeber* and *Robert H. Lowie*. He has described the program as factual and rigorous, emphasizing data rather than theory, and requiring predoctoral field experience but no training in methods of any sort (Foster 1976). The dozen or so graduate students in residence provided supportive interaction in which the older students, including Margaret Lantis, Homer Barnett, and Omar Stewart, served as informal mentors to the incoming ones, such as Foster, *Walter R. Goldschmidt*, Robert Heizer, and Dimitri Shimkin.

Kroeber decided on the most desperate needs for salvage anthropology of indigenous California memory cultures, and in 1937 he sent Foster off to elicit what he could from some elderly Yukis in Round Valley. Foster completely ignored their then-current situation, which, given his background of studying with Herskovits, he finds surprising.

In January 1938 he married Mary LeCron. They spent the following ten months in Europe, principally in Vienna and Paris, studying German and French and unintentionally becoming participant observers of the *Anschluss*, Hitler's takeover of Austria.

Foster had visited Mexico as a tourist in 1936 and, noting that in the late 1930s it was still, anthropologically speaking, nearly *terra incognita* for American social science, he decided upon doctoral research among the Sierra Popolucas of southern Veracruz State. Accompanied by Mary (who worked on analyzing the language) he gathered economic data in the winter of 1940–41. He completed his dissertation, *A Primitive Mexican Economy*, in the spring of 1941. A committee comprised of Kroeber, Lowie, and the cultural geographer Carl Sauer approved it.

Foster took up a teaching position at Syracuse University for a year. After being rejected by the military in 1943, he went to the University of California, Los Angeles as a lecturer. From there he was hired by Julian Steward, under the auspices of the Smithsonian Institution's Institute of Social Anthropology (ISA), to teach (in Spanish) one semester a year at the National School of Anthropology in Mexico City, and to take students to Michoacán (the home state of President Lázaro Cardenás) for collaborative fieldwork.

Foster undertook fieldwork in the mestizoized village of Tzintzuntzan in 1944. *Empire's Children* (1948) is a comprehensive monograph that carefully worked through extant records from earlier times and described myriad aspects of the culture and economy of what in the mid-1940s still approximated a closed corporate community.

Foster was director of the ISA in Washington DC, from 1946 until its closure in 1952 (see Foster 1979b), visiting a number of Central and South American countries. Impressed by the common elements he found in these countries, and reflecting Herskovits's teachings about acculturation, he spent the academic year 1949–50 in Spain searching for the origin of elements of Spanish-American culture, such as the grid-plan town, humoral medicine, and fishing and pottery techniques in the company of Julio Caro Baroja. The research resulted in *Culture and Conquest* (1960). He was the first North American to do major ethnographic research in Spain.

The Fosters returned to Tzintzuntzan in 1958 (Mary working predominantly with Tarascans, George with mestizos), and they made annual revisits into the 1990s. Long-running observation of behavior and attitudes of Tzintzuntzeños was the basis for Foster's theorizing about peasant worldviews and social organization. His 1967 book *Tzintzuntzan* focuses on the image of a limited good and dyadic contracts as organizing principles that explained much about the Tzintzuntzan peasants of the 1940s (the ethnographic present of the book, although supplemented by data from later times), particularly the lack of communal cooperation. In addition to research on changes in how Tzintzuntzeños lived and understood their lives, Foster organized comparisons of peasants around the world in a reader, *Peasant Society* (1967), which he coedited and for which he wrote an analytical introduction.

Foster's half-century of interest in medical anthropology began under duress; threatened with the loss of State Department funding for the ISA, he turned to the Institute of Inter-American Affairs, asking ISA personnel in Latin America to analyze aspects of U.S. Public Health programs in this first American government international technical aid program. The work of ISA anthropologists Isabel Kelly, Charles Erasmus, Ozzie Simmons, Kalervo Oberg, *Richard N. Adams* and Foster played a major role in the early development of medical anthropology. Foster's knowledge of U.S. government technical aid programs led to a series of consulting assignments in community development with the Agency for International Development in India, Pakistan, Nepal, the Philippines, Afghanistan, and Northern Rhodesia (now Zambia). Later he was a frequent World Health Organization consultant on health education and primary health care in India, Sri Lanka, Malaysia, and Indonesia, as well as at its headquarters in Geneva.

Best known as a theorist and observer of peasant societies and as a medical anthropologist, Foster has also written extensively on pottery techniques (the traditional mainstay of Tzintzuntzan's economy), on socioeconomic change, and on long-term community studies. His rich database on Tzintzuntzan continues to be supplemented by his former students' work, notably Robert Van Kemper's research on Tzintzuntzan migrants to Mexican cities and to the United States (e.g., 1977), and Stanley Brandes's publications on religious fiestas (e.g., 1988) and symbolic aspects of culture in general.

STEPHEN O. MURRAY

Charles Wagley
1971

Charles Wagley was born on 9 November 1913 in Clarksville, Texas. After beginning his college career at the University of Oklahoma, he attended Columbia University, where he received his B.A. in 1936, and his Ph.D. in 1941. A student of *Franz Boas* and *Ruth Benedict*, Wagley was also influenced by Alexander Lesser, Ruth Bunzel, and *Ralph Linton*. Shortly after his return from the field in 1941, Wagley attended the famous culture and personality seminar organized by Linton and Abram Kardiner.

Wagley is widely recognized in the United States as the founder of Brazilian anthropology. After receiving his doctorate he taught at Columbia for the next 30 years, becoming a full professor in 1949 and Franz Boas Professor in 1967. He did fieldwork among Brazilian Indians, first studying the Tapirapé Indians in 1939–1940. In 1940–41 he went to study the Tentehara Indians with his Brazilian-born wife, Cecilia Roxo Wagley. Accompanying the couple was Brazilian author Eduardo

Galvao (Wagley's first doctoral student and lifelong friend), and Galvao's wife. The work resulted in the publication of *The Tentehara Indians of Brazil* (Wagley 1949). Taken together, the studies of the Tapirapés and the Tenteharas demonstrate how social and behavioral factors contribute to different ways of life in groups living in similar environments.

During World War II Wagley participated in a joint project between the U.S. government and the Brazilian public health agency, producing slide programs and other educational materials. Wagley collaborated with novelist Dalvidio Jurandir to test the new materials in Gurupa, a small riverine community on the lower Amazon where Jurandir had once served in the municipal government. This was Wagley's first experience in the region; he returned in 1948 to study farmers and rubber collectors in research that became the basis for Wagley's best-known work, *Amazon Town: A Study of Man in the Tropics* (1953), which focused on inter- and intra-class relations. Wagley's contributions during the public health project were recognized by the Brazilian government, which named him to the National Order of the Southern Cross and awarded him the Medal of War.

From 1961 to 1969, as director of Columbia University's Institute of Latin American Studies, Wagley mentored anthropologists in both Brazil and the United States, creating a strong relationship between Brazilian and North American anthropology and anthropologists. As part of his enduring personal and professional relationship with Brazilian colleagues, Wagley set up the Bahia State-Columbia University Community Study Project in 1951–52, which he directed with Brazilian anthropologist Thales de Azevedo. This project resulted in the publication of *Race and Class in Rural Brazil* (1952). Similar interests were pursued in his collaboration with Columbia University colleague Marvin Harris on the publication of *Minorities in the New World: Six Case Studies* (1958), which, in its focus on race, class, and ethnicity, foreshadowed the interests of anthropology nearly fifty years later. Wagley's fluency in Portuguese, his work with Brazilian students and social scientists, his experiences as a visiting professor in Brazil, and his marriage into a Brazilian family, together gave him a profound grasp of Brazilian culture and identity that informed his *An Introduction to Brazil* (1963). This compilation of articles is considered an essential introduction for students pursuing Brazilian studies and continues to be widely used as a standard text.

In 1971 Wagley left Columbia University for the University of Florida, where he became a graduate research professor of anthropology and Latin American studies, a position he held until his retirement as professor emeritus in 1984. The publication of his edited volume *Man in the Amazon* (1974) evidenced Wagley's ongoing deep commitment to studies of the Amazon. As had been the case at Columbia, Wagley stood out at the University of Florida as a central figure in the field of Amazonian and Brazilian studies. Along with colleagues Marianne Schmink and Charles Wood, in 1980 Wagley founded the Amazon Research and Training Program to strengthen national and institutional cooperation between North American and Brazilian anthropology. This program in turn formed the foundation for other major projects in Brazil, including the Tropical Conservation and Development Program, begun in 1985.

Wagley's fieldwork, publications, and success in creating strong and lasting links between Brazilian and United States anthropology were sufficient to create an enduring legacy, but his professional commitment ran the full gamut of participation. He was particularly devoted to his students, chairing doctoral dissertations for both American and Brazilian students, and was recognized with the University of Florida teacher-scholar award in 1983. In 1979 he was honored with a festschrift of essays on anthropological perspectives on Brazil (Margolis and Carter 1979).

An important part of Wagley's work and legacy was formed through his years of service to anthropology and to the larger intellectual and civic community. In addition to serving as president of the American Anthropological Association and the American Ethnological Society, he was an active member of the American Academy of Arts and Sciences, the American Philosophical Society, the Council on Foreign Relations, and the Center for Inter-American Relations. He worked with the Guggenheim Foundation (1945–47) and served on the Social Science Research Council. In recognition of his work and service in Brazilian studies, he was given an award by the National Institute for

Amazon Research and received the Kalman Silvert Award from the Latin American Studies Association.

"Chuck," as he was called by his family and friends, had an openness, honesty, and lack of pretension that drew people to him (Kottak 1992). He was also described as "one of the best ethnographers our discipline has ever produced" (Barnard 1988). Many years after his fieldwork in Brazil, Wagley was remembered with such affection and respect that, even in his absence, he opened doors for other anthropologists. In the preface to his own book on his work in Brazil, anthropologist John Watanabe (1992:xi–xii) wrote that 40 years after Wagley had left the field, many townspeople still remembered him warmly, thus paving the way for Wantanabe's own eventual acceptance.

Charles Wagley died in 1991, survived by his wife, Cecilia Roxo Wagley, to whom he was married for 50 years, his daughter, Isabel Kottak (wife of anthropologist Conrad Phillip Kottak), and two grandchildren, Juliet and Nicholas. In 1992 The Charles Wagley Endowed Fellowship Fund was created at the University of Florida to honor him and his seminal work in Brazil and to continue Wagley's long tradition of supporting students and their research.

SUSAN TRENCHER

Anthony F. C. Wallace
1972

A nthony "Tony" Francis Clarke Wallace was born in Toronto, Canada, on 15 April 1923 to Dorothy Eleanor Clarke and Paul A. W. Wallace. His father taught English literature at Lebanon Valley College in Annville, Pennsylvania. While still in grade school Tony began fieldwork by collecting folklore from his Pennsylvania Dutch classmates. The elder Wallace enlisted his son's help on archival research and visits to the Iroquois community at Grand River, Ontario, for material to include in his biography of Conrad Weiser, the early 18th-century interpreter and middleman between New York, Pennsylvania, and the Six Nations Indians.

Wallace interrupted his studies of history and physics at Lebanon Valley College to volunteer for the U.S. Army in 1942, serving in Europe with the 14th Armored Division in 1944–45. After the war he returned to the University of Pennsylvania, where he received a B.A. in history in 1947. When he expressed interest in anthropology, his father sent him to Frank Speck. Wallace earned an M.A. in 1948 and Ph.D. in 1950 in anthropology. Ted Carpenter and Theodore Stern taught the courses and Speck took students on local field trips.

Already as a graduate student, Wallace had established the interests that would permeate his career: historical anthropology or ethnohistory, the relationship of psychology and culture, and the processes of cultural change. Despite Speck's Boasian-induced hostility to theories of evolution, Wallace was fascinated with the work of Sir James Frazer, combining "time perspective and change . . . across vast distances of time and space" (in Grumet 1998:107). He considered writing as a career but found himself "too data-bound to feel really comfortable with fiction" despite his continuing concern with "putting validated facts into coherent narratives," a dialectic of facts and writing that resembled the assembly of a jigsaw puzzle (in Grumet 1998:108).

Wallace argues that historical research has methodological advantages over synchronic fieldwork because archival documents provide more intimate access to a period than interviews with relative strangers. They also raise fewer ethical problems of disclosure (in Grumet 1998:108). His M.A. thesis, a psychological biography of a Delaware spokesman and contemporary of Conrad Weiser, became *King of the Delawares: Teedyuscung, 1700–1773* (1949). His 1950 dissertation on acculturation among the New York Tuscaroras, supervised by *A. Irving Hallowell* and based on two summers of fieldwork collecting Rorschach and other projective test data, revised cross-cultural personality studies to incorporate systematic intracultural variability in a "modal personality type" that remained surprisingly stable over time. During this period he underwent training analysis at the Philadelphia Psychoanalytic Institute.

The dissertation fed into *Culture and Personality* (1961, 1970) and *Religion: An Anthropological View* (1966). The former developed the concepts of mazeway, unique to each individual, and organization of diversity, around complementary rather than fully shared modeling of cultural knowledge. An adequate theory of culture and personality must deal with biology as well as culture. During the 1960s' vogue of componential analysis, Wallace studied Japanese and American kinship terms, arguing for the psychological reality or God's truth version of what the models represented.

Wallace taught sociology at the University of Pennsylvania from 1948 to 1955 and served as the research secretary for the Ford Foundation's Behavioral Research Center, participating in its interdisciplinary study of Norristown, Pennsylvania. He became senior research associate at the Eastern Pennsylvania Psychiatric Institute in 1955 and its director of clinical research in 1960. He worked on National Institute of Mental Health–funded studies of prophetic experience and paranoia, while writing *The Death and Rebirth of the Seneca* (1970). In 1961, disappointed by his colleagues' resentment over NIMH-mandated protocols for informed consent from psychiatric patients, Wallace negotiated a return to the University of Pennsylvania as professor of anthropology, with a mandate to pursue the expansion promised to Speck before his death in 1950. He served as chair for more than a decade, superintending construction of a new wing for the University Museum.

As president of the American Anthropological Association in 1971, Wallace presided over the association's reorganization as an umbrella for smaller organizations (now called sections) in an effort to stem increasing disciplinary fragmentation. The other crisis of his presidency was involvement of anthropologists with U.S. counterinsurgency movements in Latin America and Southeast Asia; Wallace argued that outside organizations should not have the power to set anthropological agendas.

Wallace's Sac and Fox report for the Indian Claims Commission on the repercussions of the Black Hawk War of 1832 became *Prelude to Disaster* (1970). He noted with wry pride: "All told, I think my ethnohistoric research supporting Indian claims wound up costing the U.S. government something like $9 billion" (in Grumet 1998:11).

The planned biography of Iroquois prophet Handsome Lake widened into a prototype for rapid cultural change, what Wallace called "revitalization movements." The theoretical treatment appeared in 1956, but the book took until 1970 to complete. Wallace then turned to the social and cultural context of technological change in his own community, Rockdale, and examined the effect of the Industrial Revolution in the local textile industry. *Rockdale* (1975) won the Bancroft Prize for American history. The companion piece, *St. Clair* (1987), described the coal mining industry in another local town where mine operators tragically ignored known safety precautions. Wallace still regrets that the appendix on assessing risk-taking behavior in a disaster-prone organization has received little anthropological attention.

The Long Bitter Trail (1993) catalogs the brutality of the Cherokee and other southern Indian removal in the 1830s and early 1840s. Wallace relates the disaster and its mismanagement to the kind of ethnic cleansing more recently illustrated in Bosnia. Failure of ethnic coexistence and greed for land provide a typological construct with ongoing implications. *Thomas Jefferson and the Indians: The Tragic Fate of the First Americans* (1999) explores the dark side of Jefferson's democracy in racism, genocide, and land speculation. For all his scientific commitment to recording linguistic vocabularies and excavating burial mounds, Jefferson was at best ambivalent about the cultural unsuitability of then-contemporary Indians for civilization. Jefferson's attitudes and resulting policies had dramatic unintended consequences. Wallace envisions a world not constrained by the limitations of Jefferson's vision, an alternative scenario in which the organization of diversity reigns.

Wallace and his wife, Elizabeth, have six children. He retired in 1988 but continues his historical research.

REGNA DARNELL

Joseph B. Casagrande
1973

J oseph Bartholomew Casagrande was born in Cincinnati, Ohio, on 14 February 1915. His father, Louis Bartholomew Casagrande, was a traveling salesman and his mother, Alma Hauskee, a beautician. He grew up in Chicago and, after his parents' divorce in his early teens, in Milwaukee. He began his undergraduate career at the University of Wisconsin intending to major in English and dedicated to sports, but he was soon converted to anthropology by taking *Ralph Linton*'s introductory course. Alexander Goldenweiser and Charlotte Gower (later Chapman) also taught courses at Wisconsin after Linton left in 1937. Casagrande was elected to Phi Beta Kappa in his junior year.

In 1940 Casagrande followed Linton to Columbia University to begin his graduate training in anthropology. Almost immediately he began the fieldwork that led to his dissertation on Oklahoma Comanche linguistic acculturation. At Columbia, in addition to his linguistic work, Casagrande explored culture and personality, joining the Kardiner-Linton seminar on the psychological analysis of primitive culture in 1940–41. He went on to study the Lac Court Oreilles Ojibwes of Wisconsin, working particularly with John Mink. His relationship with Mink is described much later in his contribution to *In the Company of Man* (Casagrande ed. 1960); Mink was both an anachronism in his traditionalism and an Ojibwe primitive philosopher as envisioned by Paul Radin.

Casagrande was drafted in 1942; after Officer Candidate School he was commissioned and served in the Italian and African campaigns. He was then posted to military intelligence in London, where he met Mary Devaney, a Scotswoman who was a captain in the British army. They married on 15 August 1945.

He returned to graduate school, but soon dropped out to support his growing family (eventually a son and three daughters) by selling encyclopedias. After a brief move back to his father's Wisconsin fishing camp, Casagrande returned to graduate school. While completing his dissertation he worked as a teaching assistant to *Charles Wagley*, a fellow student before the war. In 1948 Wagley, who was committed to fieldwork at the time, recommended that Casagrande organize the 29th International Congress of Americanists in New York the following year. Casagrande's exceptional administrative skills quickly became evident.

In 1949 and 1950 Casagrande taught at Queen's College and the University of Rochester, respectively, developing a curriculum for anthropology independent of sociology. In 1950 he began a ten-year appointment as director of fellowships for the Social Science Research Council (SSRC) in Washington, later in New York. He did not, however, entirely abandon the academy. From 1953 to 1957 he taught as adjunct associate professor at American University and attempted to revive the moribund Anthropological Society of Washington (serving as secretary from 1954 to 1957).

The SSRC sponsored John B. Carroll's Southwest Project in Comparative Psycholinguistics; Casagrande effectively coordinated 17 researchers among six ethnic groups (Navajos, Hopis, Zunis, Spanish Americans, Hopi-Tewas, and Tewas). This project was intended to test the so-called Sapir-Whorf hypothesis of linguistic relativity. Casagrande was unable to resist going beyond his administrative mandate and becoming actively engaged in the fieldwork, the human experience that he considered to lie at the core of the discipline of anthropology.

In 1960 Casagrande returned to academia as head of a newly established Department of Anthropology at the University of Illinois. His colleagues, including Julian Steward and Oscar Lewis, were well-known anthropologists but intolerant of their mutual theoretical differences; administration under these circumstances required diplomacy, "a tolerance for megalomania, and above all, an empathy for one's fellow human beings" (Thompson 1985:885). In his seven years as head, Casagrande improved the tenor of departmental relations dramatically and built a strong program at Illinois.

From 1962 until his death, Casagrande conducted fieldwork in Ecuador. He began by supervising the Columbia-Cornell-Harvard-Illinois summer field-training program in social anthropology sponsored by the Carnegie Corporation and the National Science Foundation. The program ended after five years, but Casagrande returned almost every year for his own research.

He served as president of the American Ethnological Society in 1963–64 and of the American Anthropological Association in 1972–73. His wife Mary died of cancer in 1967; he met his second wife, Mabel, in Ecuador. They were married in 1970. Casagrande was delighted when his son, Lou, decided to become an anthropologist, having accompanied his father in much fieldwork; Louis Casagrande received his Ph.D. in anthropology from the University of Minnesota in 1979.

Casagrande was a somewhat disorganized and nervous teacher in the classroom. He exemplified the discipline more comfortably in his fieldwork training of students (Thompson 1985:886). His paper on "intermediate societies" (1959) anticipated later trends in peasant studies. "Strategies for Survival: The Indians of Highland Ecuador" (1973) remains a classic comparative overview and has been widely reprinted in English and Spanish. Casagrande's specialized work was in linguistics, which he always insisted on defining in broadly anthropological terms. Linguistic colleague Kenneth Hale noted in particular his studies of "baby language, linguistic acculturation, the psychological reality of grammatical and lexical categories, problems of translation, and the principles which inhere in the structure of lexical semantic fields" (in Thompson 1985:886). His careful fieldwork records have proven useful for theoretical questions of later decades.

In the Company of Man (Casagrande ed. 1960) remains Casagrande's best-known work. It assembled 20 personal memoirs by anthropologists on the "informants" who shared cultural knowledge with them. Fieldwork was necessarily a collaborative effort in which the consultants' role as "our full partners in the study of man" was too often effaced (1960:xvi). Like Casagrande's field schools, this book helped generations of students understand how anthropologists engaged personally and intimately with individual members of cultures around the world, "a side of the discipline seldom touched upon in more technical anthropological writings" (1960:xxiii). The geographic scope of the volume underscored the expansion of American anthropology beyond the study of American Indians after World War II.

Casagrande died in Las Vegas on 2 June 1982, after suffering a stroke at a blackjack table while on a winning streak. He is remembered for a richly humanistic vision of anthropology, for his administrative skills, and for his dedication to training graduate students in the field.

REGNA DARNELL

Edward H. Spicer
1974

Edward "Ned" H. Spicer was born to Quaker parents in Cheltenham, Pennsylvania, on 29 November 1906 and grew up in Arden, Delaware. He was educated at home until the seventh grade, and then attended a Quaker school in Wilmington. His mother encouraged him to write poetry, and his father, trained as a philologist, had him copy Algonquian texts, including the whole *Walum Olum*. After graduating from high school in Louisville, Kentucky, and spending less than two months at Commonwealth College in Newallano, Louisiana, Spicer fled to New Orleans and spent a year as a seaman on freighters, going to Germany, Guatemala, and up the Great Lakes. He entered the University of Delaware in the fall of 1925, planning to be a chemist, but he switched to economics, transferred to Johns Hopkins, and then dropped out.

What was diagnosed, possibly wrongly, as pulmonary tuberculosis propelled Spicer to Arizona in 1929. He worked at the Arizona Agricultural Inspection Station in Yuma, saving money to enroll in the University of Arizona. A bank failure lost him his savings, and he was not able to enroll at the university until 1931. One advanced course in economic theory and his transferred credits allowed him to get a B.A. He also took a course in archaeology from Clara Frapps (Tanner). Under the tutelage of dean Byron Cummings he did archaeological fieldwork on most weekends. In the summer of 1932 Spicer and Cummings worked on Kinishba on the Apache reservation. Spicer also worked on King's Ruin—writing a 1933 M.A. thesis on its relationship to Prescott black-on-gray pottery—and headed a New Deal project for unemployed miners excavating and partially reconstructing Tuzigoot.

John Provinse, who arrived from the University of Chicago in 1932, urged Spicer to go there to study with Radcliffe-Brown and *Robert Redfield*, both of whom became important influences on Spicer the ethnologist. For a full scholarship, Spicer was put in charge of Redfield's office library. Spicer's seeming tuberculosis (probably coccidioidomycosis, also known as valley fever, an infection from spores of a desert fungus) recurred in 1935–36, requiring extended hospitalization and a return to a drier climate.

Spicer had met Rosamond "Roz" Brown, a fellow graduate student, in Chicago in 1934. *Fay-Cooper Cole*, the department chair, suggested she take class notes for him, so that the year of hospitalization would count as a year of residence for the Ph.D. requirement. They were married in June 1936 and began a year's fieldwork at the Yaqui (Yoeme) village of Pascua within Tucson, Arizona. Provinse instigated this fieldwork, having encountered and been intrigued by the Yaqui poet Refugio Savala. (Spicer wrote poetry and was later instrumental in the publication of Savala's *Autobiography of a Yaqui Poet* [1980].)

Spicer's dissertation, a functionalist community study focusing on the cultural persistence of uprooted Yaquis at the edges of an American city and "fictive kinship," emerged from this fieldwork, as did Rosamond's M.A. thesis on the Pascua Easter ceremony. Both were discouraged by Redfield's demands for generalization after he read what he considered their overly detailed observations of particular events. The couple interviewed young African Americans in New Orleans while Ned taught at Dillard University (1938–39) as a substitute for Allison Davis, who was working with John Dollard on his Negro Youth Project.

Spicer then filled in for Harry Getty at the University of Chicago for two years while collecting the Yaqui life histories that were published in 1988 as *People of Pascua*. In 1941–42 the Spicers did fieldwork in the Mexican Yaqui village of Potam, Sonora. During World War II Spicer was employed as a War Relocation Authority "community analyst" for the administrators of Poston, Arizona, one of the concentration camps for West Coast Japanese Americans, and thereby became one of the pioneers of applied anthropology (see Spicer 1969a, 1952; Officer 1990); he was active in the development of the Society for Applied Anthropology. However, he remained more a theorist and historian of culture change than a social engineer. In 1946 he returned to the University of Arizona, where he remained for the rest of his life.

Most of Spicer's cultural anthropological work focused on cultural systems that persisted through technological changes and intensive interethnic contact, often coercive. His magisterial *Cycles of Conquest* (1962) compares many Native peoples of the southwestern United States and northwestern Mexico. In it and in his synoptic book on the Native peoples of the whole United States (1969b), he stressed that "however influential White policies have been, the development of Indian life involves a great deal more than response to those policies" (1969b:3). Increasingly focusing on social persistence even amidst technological and cultural change, he quietly dispensed with the acculturation-to-white-majority-culture paradigm. As Adams (1990:24) suggested, Spicer, like Redfield, *Edward Sapir*, and *Ralph Linton*, was "a pragmatist at the theoretical level but an idealist at a deeper and more philosophical level."

Spicer did fieldwork with Tohono O'odhams (Papagos), Seris, and Western Apaches, but the Yaquis were the group whose history he studied most intensely (Spicer 1980, 1988), even as he and Roz continued to be observant participants in and advocates for Pascua. He also read widely on Basques, Catalans, Irish, and Welsh, and in 1969 he did some European fieldwork for an uncompleted book, *Enduring Peoples*.

Spicer was editor of the *American Anthropologist* from 1960 to 1963, president of both the American Anthropological Association and the American Philosophical Society in 1974, and was elected to the National Academy of Sciences in 1975. He retired in 1978 but continued research and musings on cultural change and cultural persistence. Both he and his life partner and later, widow, were active in civil rights and community affairs, particularly blending development and historic preservation in the Fort Lowell district of Tucson where he lived from 1946 until his death (from cancer) on 5 April 1983 (and she until her death in 1998). Both were gracious, kindly, and open to questions by their juniors. As Roz recalled, "he was an incurable optimist, always looking for the good in everything and everybody, always wanting to see what the next development would be both locally and in the world at large because 'it is so interesting' " (R. Spicer 1990:17).

STEPHEN O. MURRAY

Ernestine Friedl
1975

Ernestine Friedl served as president of the American Ethnological Society in 1967 and as president of the American Anthropological Association in 1974–75. She has been a teacher, editor, research scholar, and administrator.

Born in Hungary in 1920, Ernestine Friedl and her mother joined her father in New York in 1922. She grew up in the west Bronx with a brief period in Manhattan while her father's radio sales prospered. When the Great Depression drastically reduced her father's income, the family moved back to a one-bedroom apartment in the Bronx. To help with family finances, her mother worked hand-finishing evening gowns in New York's garment district. Like many who were adolescents during the Depression, Friedl never lost the fear of economic disaster brought on by forces outside one's own making. It was a basis for her analytical perception of circumstance as a powerful determinant in individual decision-making and destiny. The perception was reinforced by the fate of Jews in Europe. If her father had not emigrated to the United States, her small family would have been killed as were many of her relatives.

Friedl's father's respect for education and her mother's experience convinced the family that a woman needed a career, or at least enough education to permit her to earn a good living. In 1937 Friedl enrolled at Hunter College, then a municipally supported women's college for New York City residents that charged no tuition and distributed free textbooks. Acceptance of students depended only on high school grades, and the scholastic averages required for admission were very high. At Hunter, where an implicit Boasian eclecticism and the four-field approach prevailed, Friedl discovered anthropology. Her professors were all women who loved their subject and respected their students.

In 1941 Friedl enrolled in the Ph.D. program at Columbia University. There *Ralph Linton*'s concepts of culture and social structure accompanied by broad ethnographic knowledge and *Ruth Benedict*'s love of Durkheim and Mauss influenced her approach to anthropology. Linton sent Friedl to study culture and personality among the Chippewas during the summers of 1942 and 1943. She wrote an ethnohistorical dissertation on styles of leadership among the Chippewas, emphasizing social and ecological explanations rather than assumptions about immutable personality characteristics. Friedl received her Ph.D. in 1950 after having taught full-time at Brooklyn and Queens Colleges during most of her graduate-school years.

In 1942 Friedl married Harry L. Levy, a classicist 13 years her senior, and they began a personal and professional partnership that lasted until his death in 1981. Her career has been divided among teaching, research, and a strong commitment to administration. She taught for 25 years in the graduate program in anthropology at the City University of New York's Graduate Center where she was executive officer for two years. In 1973 she left New York for Duke University. She found the major change in culture, both regional and institutional, revitalizing. Her students were no longer the children of immigrants who were the first in their families to attend college but the children of educated parents they hoped to emulate. After her retirement from Duke in 1985, Friedl was an associate at the National Humanities Center, and then taught a number of semesters over a four-year period at Princeton University until 1990. The year after, she married Dr. Merel H. Harmel, a retired Duke academic anesthesiologist.

Friedl enjoys administration. She was a department chair for many years at Queens and at Duke, serving from 1980 to 1985 as dean of arts and sciences and as dean of Trinity College at Duke. Ideally, she believes administrators can create the conditions that enable academics to do their best work. They can also influence the stature of departments and universities by the standards for scholarship they promulgate and by their conceptions of the nature of universities and how they must respond to changing conditions. Friedl also served for five years on the National Science Board during President Carter's administration.

Friedl's major research has been on the anthropology of rural communities in modern Greece. In the 1950s she and John Campbell were the first American- or British-trained cultural anthropologists to study modern Greece, and indeed, among the first few to do cultural and social anthropology in Europe. Friedl was interested in studying post–World War II changes on the economics, culture, and social structure of a cash-crop farming village of Boeotia. In the 1960s she studied the history of migrants from the village to Athens; she visited the community again briefly in 1976 and for a day in 1998. These more recent data will be summarized in a new chapter to be added to a republished version of *Vasilika* (1962), her book on the village.

Early in the 1970s Friedl, who felt she had never suffered discrimination as a woman, nevertheless learned from the nascent women's movement how rare her experience had been. She wanted to learn what anthropologists knew about women's lives. Using previous studies, she wrote a small volume on power relations between men and women. She hypothesized that in hunting and gathering and horticultural societies it was the division of labor and the distribution of their products that correlated with power relationships between men and women. In her subsequent administrative life, she worked hard to encourage departments to appoint women and minority faculty.

Friedl nevertheless sustained her interest in things Greek by editing the *Journal of Modern Greek Studies* for five years. The challenge was to encourage and publish articles representing new approaches to literary studies that had been slow to influence modern Greek scholarship. In a different vein, she is currently the obituary editor for the *American Anthropologist*.

Friedl laments excessive turns to meaning at the expense of political economy in some, but by no means all, recent anthropology. She believes it has facilitated the appropriation of concepts like culture, race, and ethnicity by humanities and other scholars. These terms, she thinks, are in danger of being interpreted as biological traits and can easily slip into racism. Friedl supports an active promulgation of holistic anthropological perspectives that include biological as well as cultural, social, and historical approaches. Friedl remains a firm believer that anthropology presents the ultimate liberal education, combining the elements necessary to illuminate the human condition.

REGNA DARNELL AND ERNESTINE FRIEDL

Walter R. Goldschmidt
1976

W alter "Wally" Rochs Goldschmidt was born to Hermann
and Gretchen (Rochs) Goldschmidt in San Antonio, Texas,
on 24 February 1913. He graduated from the University
of Texas, Austin, with a B.A. cum laude in 1933 and an M.A. in 1935,
and received his Ph.D. from the University of California, Berkeley, in
1942. In 1937, a busy year for the young Texan, he married Beatrice
Lucia Gale (with whom he later had two children, Karle Gale and
Mark Stefan), and went off to do fieldwork among the Hupas and
Nomlakis of northern Oregon. At Berkeley, Goldschmidt studied under *Alfred L. Kroeber*, *Robert H. Lowie*, and Edward Gifford. He carried
out his doctoral research in farming towns in the San Joaquin Valley of
California. He has also done fieldwork among American Indians, and
in Africa among the Sebeis.

Goldschmidt's extraordinary and on-going career in anthropology has been marked by his interest in the problems of contemporary society and how anthropological knowledge can be applied toward their solution. This element of Goldschmidt's work was nurtured while he was at Berkeley by cultural geographer Carl Sauer and economists Paul Taylor and Lloyd Fisher. As Goldschmidt notes in his résumé, almost all of his work either addresses policy directly or has implications for setting policy. His early research in rural California exemplifies how, for Goldschmidt, academic and applied anthropology are always interlinked. While on the staff of the Bureau of Agricultural Economics, Goldschmidt undertook a study of two towns to determine the effects of agriculture on community structures, especially the urbanization of farming communities associated with industrialized agribusiness. This research was in part concerned with the application of existing acreage limitation law to industrial agriculture. The results of this research were published in *As You Sow* (1947, 1978) and included a report written for the U.S. Senate Committee on Small Business. This oft-cited study, reissued in an expanded edition in 1978, continues to influence work in rural studies, applied anthropology, and rural sociology. The second edition, like the first, included a report presented to a U.S. Senate subcommittee (*Small Business and the Community: The Effect of Scale of Farm Operations on Community Life*) demonstrating Goldschmidt's continued commitment to issues relevant to farmers and agribusiness as well as to the application of anthropological research. In 1996 Paul Durrenberger and Kendall Thu demonstrated the continuing viability of Goldschmidt's research findings in their research among small hog farmers in Iowa. But as Labao (1990:5) has noted, the issues raised by Goldschmidt's work "are not confined to the academic setting. The research problem is grounded in everyday life for millions of Americans."

Goldschmidt's initial interest in rural communities in the United States expanded to focus on class, values, and status. He has developed a new research instrument, the Picture Set of Values, which is designed to elicit cultural values through the use of culture-specific drawings. Several theoretical works have emerged from his research and comparative studies, including *Man's Way* (1959), *Comparative Functionalism* (1966) (described by Turner and Maryanski [1979] as rescuing the value of functionalism by "turning Malinowski on his head"), and most recently, *The Human Career* (1990).

Currently professor emeritus at the University of California, Los Angeles (UCLA), Goldschmidt held joint appointments in anthropology and sociology from 1946 to 1973, and in anthropology and psychiatry from 1970 to 1983. He served as chair of the Department of Anthropology from 1964 to 1969. His ability and willingness to serve in administrative as well as research roles has been exemplified not only at UCLA, where he was active in the creation of the African Studies Center, but also in the American Anthropological Association (AAA), where he served on the founding Board of Directors of the African Studies Association and participated in the formation of the Society for Senior Anthropologists and the Society for Psychological Anthropology. For over a decade, Goldschmidt worked with other anthropologists and filmmakers, a group that included John Adair, *Margaret Mead*, and Sol Worth, to start the National Anthropological Film Center in 1975 (now the Human Studies Film Archives).

A member of Phi Beta Kappa and Sigma Xi, Goldschmidt made exemplary contributions to anthropology as a discipline and a profession. His contributions earned him both the Medal of Honor from the International Union of Anthropological and Ethnological Sciences in 1990 and the AAA Distinguished Service Award in 1994. He has served as both the president of the AAA and the editor of the *American Anthropologist* (1956–59). In the latter role he instituted the practice of writing a friendly introduction to the articles and their authors in each issue. His numerous administrative and editorial positions include presidencies of the Southwestern Anthropological Association in 1950–51 and the American Ethnological Society in 1969–70, and editor of the *Worlds of Man*, a series of monographs on cultural ecology. He is the founding editor of *Ethos*, the official journal of the Society for Psychological Anthropology, a position he held from 1971 to 1978.

Goldschmidt has enthusiastically sought to promote interest in anthropology outside the discipline. From 1951 to 1953 he directed the Ways of Mankind Radio Project, which involved 26 radio dramatizations dealing with anthropological ideas to be used in public discussion and classrooms. Produced in association with the National Association of Educational Broadcasters, the program was published as *Exploring the Ways of Mankind*, a textbook for classroom use (1960, 3rd edition 1976). Goldschmidt used his work as a Fullbright scholar working among the Sebeis of Africa in 1953 to prepare a traveling educational photographic exhibit. He returned as director of the Culture and Ecology in East Africa Project from 1961 to 1963. This work also resulted in the publication of *Sebei Law* (1967) and *Culture and Behavior of the Sebei* (with Gale Goldschmidt, 1976).

Goldschmidt's contributions have included not only his works in the discipline but also those prepared for and about the profession, including *On Becoming an Anthropologist: A Career Pamphlet for Students* (1970); *The Uses of Anthropology* (1979), and *Anthropology and Public Policy: A Dialogue* (1983). His own graduate students have twice honored him with festschriften (Louky and Jones 1976; Kennedy and Edgerton 1982). Over the course of six decades as an anthropologist, Goldschmidt has published more than 200 works. His contributions span more than half the history of the AAA, continuing into the new century and the new millennium.

SUSAN TRENCHER

Richard N. Adams
1977

G rowing up in an academic family in Ann Arbor, Michigan, pointed Richard Newbold Adams toward scholarship, but growing up in the depression left visions of newly minted Ph.D.s selling used cars and encyclopedias, and a dismal opinion of academic salaries. After naval service in World War II, Adams shifted his major from philosophy to anthropology to deal with the more immediate world. He received a B.A. in 1947 from the University of Michigan and then an M.A. in 1949 and Ph.D. in 1951 from Yale University.

Adams conducted doctoral research in the Indian and Mestizo community of Muquiyauyo in the Mantaro Valley of Peru, an area of intermittent revolutionary activity. Muquiyauyo intrigued him by having pioneered a hydroelectric plant to supply the valley in 1920s. Back at Yale, where his mentors were *Wendell C. Bennett* and *Ralph Linton*, Adams's expression of interest in applied anthropology brought scorn from committee member *George P. Murdock*.

Eager to continue fieldwork, Adams took a position in Guatemala. Having recently toppled a dictator, Guatemala had established a National Indian Institute (IIN) as a step toward correcting centuries of suppression of that population. Its director, Antonio Goubaud Carrera, had been appointed as Guatemala's ambassador to Washington. There he requested an ethnologist from the Smithsonian Institution to assist the development of the Institute. Adams arrived in December 1950 and within weeks met Betty Hannstein. They were married the next year and have had more than 50 years of good life together; today their three children are scattered in Guatemala and the United States. Betty's Guatemalan knowledge contributed importantly to Adams's professional work.

At the IIN Adams worked with Joaquin Noval, the interim director, and staff anthropologist Juan de Dios Rosales. Noval focused on the compatibility of economic development and cultural retention at a time when most *indigenistas* were assimilationists. He believed that promoting indigenous rights was an obligation of the state, and he was driven by frustration to join the Communist Party. Adams soon began working with Nevin Scrimshaw at the Institute of Nutrition of Central America and Panama. When the Smithsonian program collapsed, he continued until late 1952 with a State Department fellowship, followed by three years with the Pan American Sanitary Bureau, working throughout Central America.

The 1954 counterrevolution backed by the CIA led to Noval's imprisonment. Although much taken with its sociology, Adams found Marxist politics uncongenial; but the Cold War made it difficult not to be perceived as a political actor. He briefly took leave to interview political prisoners and wrote (under a pseudonym at his employer's request) a report that did not support allegations against them. Adams was caught between his Guatemalan family and his friendship with Noval. Moreover, he was becoming increasing unhappy with the "developmental paradox" of public health, in which promoting population growth worsened the broader human condition, but public health officialdom refused to acknowledge this.

Adams increasingly found that his scholarship had no place in an emerging revolution. He could not embrace advocacy for either side because of the violence accompanying revolution. As he later wrote, "The only alternative I saw was to retreat to American academics" (Adams 1976). He resigned without a job in 1956 but quickly obtained a position as professor of sociology and anthropology at Michigan State University. Retreat he could, but escape he could not. Over the next two decades he was accused of being both a Communist and an agent of the CIA.

Before leaving Guatemala, Adams worked with Kalman Silvert, *John P. Gillin*, and Jorge Skinner Klee to organize a conference on Guatemalan social integration, designed to translate social science research on Guatemala into Spanish and facilitate local access to the results. Although contemporary Mayan leaders criticize the term *integration* as assimilationist, over 40 volumes were published as a result of this collaboration.

In 1962 Adams moved to the University of Texas at Austin, where he was Professor of Anthropology from 1962 to 1984 and Rapaport Centennial Professor of Liberal Arts from 1984 until his retirement in 1991 as Rapaport Professor Emeritus. From 1962 to 1967 he was assistant director and from 1986 to 1990 director of the Institute of Latin American Studies at Texas. He taught in Guatemala, Mexico, Brazil, and Argentina and was a resident scholar at the Advanced Studies Institute at Canberra, Australia. When the American and British anthropological traditions of his training proved inadequate, Adams turned to theoretical questions. He approached his research by confronting facts with their opposites, a method of "contrariness" that was comfortable for him but demonstrated his "unsuitability for the revolutionary life" (Adams 1976). He sought unstudied problems, especially around the nation-state, drawing on *Leslie A. White*'s ideas about materialism, energy dynamics, historical processes, and social evolution. The dissipative structures of Ilya Prigogine inspired him to model order from disorder in complex systems.

Adams continued empirical research in Guatemala until the late 1960s, but he had already begun exploring theoretical alternatives to Marxism. *The Second Sowing* (1967) predicted an indefinite period of lesser development for countries that had started development late. *Crucifixion by Power* (1970) explored how the structure of national power controlled and was confronted by other interests in Guatemalan society. He abandoned empirical research from about 1970 to 1985 and explored an energy model of society in four books. He spent 1969–70 in Argentina and Brazil for the Ford Foundation. Adams dropped planned Argentine urban research because of local distaste for "irrelevant" social science, but he confessed to feeling oddly like "a real anthropologist" while visiting the forest peoples with Roberta Da Matta (1976). He was finding himself increasingly comfortable as part of a community of Latin American scholars and was gradually alienated by the growing postmodernism in American anthropology.

Adams served as president of the Society for Applied Anthropology (SFAA) in 1962–63, of the Latin American Studies Association in 1968 (he was also a founder), of the American Anthropological Association in 1976–77, and vice president and chair of Section H of the American Association for the Advancement of Science for two terms (1972–73). In the early 1960s he spearheaded revision of the SFAA ethics code to reflect contemporary conflicts and priorities, later lobbying the AAA to follow suit, at the same time that applied anthropology reinvented itself as "practicing anthropology" in response to constricting academic job markets and real-world pressures on the discipline.

In the mid-1980s, anticipating retirement, Adams returned to Central American research. Since retiring he has been working and writing in Guatemala for the United Nations Development Program, the Centro de Investigaciones Regionales de Mesoamerica, and the Agency for International Development. He lives in Guatemala.

REGNA DARNELL

Francis L. K. Hsu
1978

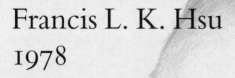

Francis L. K. Hsu, the first nonwhite president of the American Anthropological Association, was born in Juangho in southern Manchuria on 28 October 1909. After completing high school in Harbin (northern Manchuria), he earned a B.A. in sociology from the University of Shanghai in 1933. After seeing his parents for the last time in Manchuria, Hsu escaped to Beijing disguised as a laborer. He was a social worker at the Rockefeller Foundation-sponsored Medical College Hospital there from 1934–37. In 1937 he took up a four-year Boxer Indemnity fellowship at the London School of Economics, where he studied with Bronislaw Malinowski. Upon completing his Ph.D. in 1940, he took the Burma Road to the southwestern part of China controlled by the Kuomintang. He undertook the community study of Hsijou, Yunnan, a market town of about eight thousand, with un-usually high literacy and numerous wealthy families. Hsu's Hsijou field-work provided the primary empirical basis for his 1948 and 1952 books on Chinese culture. In Yunnan he met Vera Tung; they married in 1943.

In 1944 Hsu traveled to the United States on a troopship, a trip that he considered to be the beginning of his first ethnographic study of Americans. He spent a year at Columbia University, attending the famous Kardiner-Linton seminars but rejecting the Freudian emphasis on maternal child rearing and sexuality channeling as determinants of personality formation. "Instead of employing psychoanalytic terminology, I resorted to common-sense denominators" (Hsu 1948:13). Hsu took this approach not just to his first book (dedicated to *Ralph Linton* and politely critical of Kardiner's focus on early childhood treatment). He repeatedly criticized the Western analysis of the self in terms of individual psychology for failing to consider its determination by social (particularly extended family) relations.

After two years at Cornell, Hsu joined the Northwestern University faculty in 1947, where he remained until his retirement. He also had a longstanding association with the East-West Center in Honolulu.

Hsu's work combined a functionalism that was as much a reaction to as a continuation of Malinowski's with a positing of particular national characters; he conceived function as a homeostasis in which cultural heritage determines social organization (with the dominant kinship dyad being of special importance), which in turn determines individual behavior. His positing the father-son dyad as being the dominant kinship dyad in Chinese society suffices to show that his focus was social rather than psychological. It is the expectations of the generally remote father figure and the patriline that Hsu, like all orthodox Confucianists, considered most important.

From his first book, *Under the Ancestors' Shadow* (1948), onward Hsu defended the claim of a single Chinese culture with a this-worldly, hedonistic orientation. In an era in which kinship reference was the primary, if not the sole, meaning of "social structure," Hsu's (1947) demonstration that the same principles of kinship classification operating in different (Han) Chinese languages legitimated the essentialization of a singular Chinese culture. A pragmatism in linking gods and human healers was another aspect that Hsu noted in his Beijing hospital work and in observing a cholera epidemic in Yunnan, the ethnographic focus of his second book (Hsu 1952). His main thesis was that recourse to magical, scientific, and religious explanations all exist in all societies; he primarily focused on the reception of and resistance to Western scientific medicine in China during the 1930s and 1940s. The book continued to reject any characterization of Chinese as "fatalistic" or "superstitious" (Hsu 1948:260–261).

Hsu's predominant contrast between a singular (Han) "Chinese culture" and a singular (WASP) "American culture" focused on the patrilineal family-embeddedness of the former and the individualism of the latter. Looking at novels, he wrote, "Chinese novels usually concentrate on what the characters do in their social roles as generals or common men, while their Western counterparts focus on what the characters do, think and feel as individuals. There are no premodern first person Chinese novels. Second, in contrast to their Chinese counterparts, Western novels are mostly preoccupied with sex" (1978:158).

Based on 1956–57 fieldwork in India (working through interpreters) and his reading, Hsu tried to explain the world as Hindus see and feel it. In *Clan, Caste, and Club* (1963) he extended the contrast of the predominant form of identification and association beyond the nuclear family in Chinese, Indian, and American societies. In the absence of generational and occupational caste roles in America as firmly ascribed as those in the two Asian civilizations, he emphasized for Americans voluntary association. Based on fieldwork in Japan in 1964–65, Hsu (1975) wrote a book about *iemoto* as the most basic Japanese secondary grouping. It was his "deliberate procedure to ignore the time differences between the literary, artistic, folkloristic and other written materials and the sociological facts observed by my colleagues and myself" (1963:14). He was aware of the difference between prescriptive and descriptive norms, choosing to rest his inferences on the former, or in the "cogency of thesis rather than truth through formal methods" (1963:22n).

Hsu largely ignored war and the transfer of the Kuomintang government to western China during the early 1940s in order to study perennial Chinese culture and personality formation. He returned to China for nine weeks in 1972 during the Great Proletarian Cultural

Revolution and published an account with a daughter and her husband (Hsu-Balzer, Balzer, and Hsu 1974) that minimized the social upheavals and cultural changes.

Hsu frequently criticized the ethnocentrism of Anglophone anthropologists who assumed the universal relevance of their categories—in particular what he considered the undue importance assigned to "substitutes for human relations such as gods and objects and mobility or the idea of change" (1978:168)—and the universal validity of their representations. In a 1973 article in the *American Anthropologist* he assailed the tendency of western anthropologists to take data but never theories from nonwestern anthropologists: a neocolonial division of (Anglo) processing of (non-Anglo) raw materials. The force of his critique was mitigated, however, by his mostly ignoring what China-born anthropologists wrote—particularly those who had also been through London School of Economics.

Hsu died in a nursing home in Tiburon, California, on 15 December 1999.

STEPHEN O. MURRAY

Paul Bohannan
1979

P aul James Bohannan was born in Lincoln, Nebraska, in 1920.
He served in the U.S. Army from 1941 to 1946 as a captain in
the Army Security Agency, receiving the Legion of Merit. He
earned a B.A., Phi Beta Kappa with high distinction, from the University of Arizona in 1947. Upon graduation he received a Rhodes scholarship to Queen's College, Oxford, where he earned a B.Sc. in 1949
and a D.Phil. in 1951. From 1951 to 1956 he served as a university
lecturer in social anthropology at Oxford.

Bohannan returned to the United States in 1956 as assistant professor and Jonathan Edwards Preceptor, and later associate professor, at
Princeton University. In 1959 he moved to Northwestern University,
where he served as G. Stanley Harris Professor of Social Sciences from
1967 to 1975 and as chair of the Department of Anthropology from

1969 to 1972. African ethnography and economic anthropology were his preoccupations during these years. From 1974 to 1978 he was principal investigator and researcher for the Western Behavioral Sciences Institute. In 1976 Bohannan was appointed professor of anthropology at the University of California, Santa Barbara, and in 1982 he became professor of anthropology and law as well as dean of social sciences and communication at the University of Southern California, where he has been professor emeritus since his retirement in 1987.

Bohannan carried out fieldwork among the Tiv of Central Nigeria for 28 months between 1949 and 1953 and among the Wangas of Kenya for nine months in 1955. From 1958 to 1960 he directed a project on human environments in middle Africa for the National Academy of Sciences. Bohannan's publications on the Tiv, many of them coauthored with Laura Bohannan, include such diverse topics as concepts of time, farm and settlement, migration and expansion, descent, residence, the family, circumcision, justice and judgment, extraprocessual political events, politics, exchange and investment, markets, money, beauty and scarification, homicide and suicide, the artist in tribal society, and land tenure. This body of work encompasses what Bohannan views as the four central preoccupations of anthropology: ecology and economics, power and political organization, family and kinship, and religion, ideology, and worldview (1980:512).

Bohannan undertook four years of training at the Chicago Institute for Psychoanalysis from 1967 to 1971, although without obtaining clinical experience. He served on the institute's education committee from 1970 to 1974.

Bringing anthropology home to the study of North American society has preoccupied Bohannan for more than four decades. He studied American middle-class divorcees in San Francisco in 1963–64 and 1980–81 (1970), generalizing the results to divorce in a cross-cultural perspective from 1963 to 1965 (1985), as well as the mental health of children in San Diego County stepfather-headed households in 1974–75 and the invisible community of non-welfare elderly poor in San Diego center city hotels between 1974 and 1977 (leading to a more general concern with interrelationships of aging, culture, and health).

In 1978–79 he ran a seminar in dual cultural heritages for the National Endowment for the Humanities.

Bohannan's commitment to science education has been persistent. He wrote a series of popular columns in *Science* from 1980 to 1984, and served on the Board of Directors of the Biological Sciences Curriculum Study from 1972 to 1975, on the Editorial Advisory Board of the *Social Science Citation Index* from its founding until 1993, and as one of only 30 social scientists on the National Commission for the Social Studies from 1987 to 1989. He has written and collaborated on textbooks ranging from specialized topics in "marriage, family and residence" or "kinship and social organization" with John Middleton in 1968 to the personal effects of ethnographic fieldwork method with Dirk Van Der Elst (1998) to a major reworking of his overview of Africa with Philip Curtin in the fourth edition of *Africa and Africans* (1995). The latter remains as significant as its first edition in 1964, written in the throes of *uhuru* and independence movements across Africa. More general texts have presented anthropology to students and a larger public (e.g., 1963, 1991, 1995). Aggression, law, behavior, and culture are key concepts in Bohannan's works. In them he generalized from his preoccupations with African ethnography to the meaning and nature of human cultural and biological behavior. His edited volume with Margaret Gruter in 1982 is a particularly good example.

The history of anthropology has been another pervasive commitment in Bohannan's work. He has contributed to a reassessment of the seminal works of Edward Burnet Tylor, Lewis Henry Morgan, and Karl Polanyi, reviewing the work published in the early *American Anthropologist* and reformulating the concept of culture. He produced a reader in the history of anthropology with Mark Glazer (1973).

Bohannan served as director of the Social Science Research Council from 1960 to 1963, as president of the African Studies Association in 1963–64, and as president of the American Anthropological Association in 1978–79. His *African Homicide and Suicide* (1960) received the August Vollmer Award in Criminology in 1962 and the Herskovits Award in African Studies in 1972.

Bohannan's presidential address to the AAA in 1980 reviewed where

the discipline had been, acknowledged rapid change in the social context surrounding anthropology and anthropologists, asserted that in
such a state of flux "You Can't Do Nothing," and presciently predicted
the anthropology of 2000. In his view, anthropologists have been sin-
gularly unreflective. He argues that since World War II "both colonialism and the traditional forms of liberalism disappeared" (1980:510),
leaving the discipline, especially sociocultural anthropology, without a
single integrating idea. A split of private and public (political) lives,
economic globalism, postfamilial kinship, an ethic of autonomy with a
price of loneliness, and a return to religion and a "growing distrust of
science" (1980:514) seem very familiar two decades later. He predicted
game preserves overwhelming human populations, California bilin-
gualism, studying up (albeit due to the low prestige of anthropology),
and the appropriation of the culture concept by other disciplines. He
then reminded colleagues how important anthropology has been to
American public culture over the 20th century. Disciplinary reinvention will tack between sociobiology and the policy sciences, as anthropologists acknowledge the value of applying their discipline in the real
world.

In 2000 Bohannan compiled his Tiv ethnographic writings and photographs from 1949 to 1953 on CD-ROM. He continues to work on
aboriginal sin, family theory, enduring ideas in the history of anthropology, and his professional autobiography.

Paul Bohannan lives in Visalia, California.

REGNA DARNELL

Conrad M. Arensberg
1980

Conrad Maynadier Arensberg was born on 12 September 1910, in Pittsburgh, Pennsylvania, where his father was a prominent lawyer. He received his B.A. summa cum laude from Harvard University in 1931, remaining at the same institution for the Ph.D., which was granted in 1934. Arensberg was a key participant in W. Lloyd Warner's Yankee City project, which applied the methods of anthropological participant-observation fieldwork to the study of a contemporary American community.

Arensberg taught anthropology at the Massachusetts Institute of Technology from 1938 to 1941, when he was appointed associate professor and chair of the Department of Sociology and Anthropology at Brooklyn College. After one year in his new position, he entered active service in the U.S. Army's military intelligence division. After the war, in 1946,

Arensberg returned to academic life, as chair of the Department of Sociology at Barnard College. In 1952 his appointment was transferred to the graduate department of anthropology at Columbia University, a position he held until his retirement in 1979 as Buttenwieser Professor of Human Relations. Subsequent to his retirement, Arensberg remained at Columbia as a faculty member in the Columbia Teachers College Joint Program in Applied Anthropology. During his Columbia years Arensberg appreciated participating in the Kardiner seminars and the national character studies of *Margaret Mead, Ruth Benedict,* and *Francis L. K. Hsu* in the heyday of psychological anthropology as well as "the birth and diffusion of world-area studies in peasant, nomad, and plantation cultural ecology" (1981:565).

Arensberg's fieldwork in Ireland in the 1930s was among the first studies by a cultural anthropologist of a contemporary European culture or the civilization of the Old World more generally. He and his research team "had the cooperation of Government officials and the local populace, immersed themselves in the life of County Clare, working side by side with their subjects" (Thomas 1997). *The Irish Countryman* (1937), his dissertation research, summarized in lectures to the Lowell Institute in Boston in 1936, and *Culture and Community in Ireland* (1965, coauthored with Solon T. Kimball) became exemplars for such extensions of traditional anthropological subject matter. He later studied the continuity of European community characteristics in American culture.

Arensberg formulated "interaction theory" while he was a member of the Harvard Society of Fellows from 1934 to 1938. More than three decades later (1972:7–8), he still considered this a "new and growing stream of inquiry and discovery" with "no agreed-upon name, other than perhaps 'interaction theory,'" which he understood as a behavioral social science. Eliot Chapple, Douglas MacGregor, Erich Lindemann, William Foote Whyte, and Frederick Richardson were among the other students of Lloyd Warner and Everett Hughes who "imported into sociology the anthropological canons of field work, participant observation, and open-ended interviewing, by explicitly sequencing, counting and timing interaction flows" (Arensberg 1972:9).

His fascination with contemporary societies led him to ethnography in industrial settings, where he focused on the interrelationships of "social behavior, morale and productivity" (Comitas 1997:18).

Arensberg's contribution to development studies focused on the ethnography of bureaucracies. *Introducing Social Change: A Manual for Community Development, Culture and Community*, coauthored with Arthur H. Niehoff in 1964), contributed to breaking down American isolationism through direct engagement with the needs of developing communities around the globe; technical cooperation had to be phrased in terms of cultural realities. He collaborated with Kimball again in 1965 to produce a user-friendly manual for community study, *Culture and Community*, generalizing their studies in Ireland. Arensberg also undertook the study of "cultural stabilities in a modernizing India" (Comitas 1997). As research director of UNESCO's Institute for Social Sciences in Germany (1950), his specialties were the Middle East and India. He served as consultant for the U.S. Department of the Interior's Bureau of Indian Affairs (1940–42) and the U.S. Department of Agriculture (1938–40).

Arensberg was unselfconsciously multidisciplinary, collaborating productively with Eliot Chapple on measuring human relations (1942), with economist Karl Polanyi on comparing the economies of ancient empires to contemporary market systems (*Trade and Markets in the Early Empires*, 1957), and with ethnomusicologist Alan Lomax (1977) on the study of cantometrics and choreometrics. He incorporated the insights of "philosophers of science, physicists and ecologists interested in general systems theory and the integration of science" (Comitas 1997:18), blurring distinctions between anthropology and sociology, psychology, ethnography, demography, and "any other discipline he found useful in illuminating human behavior" (Thomas 1997:51).

For Arensberg, these diverse topics were interconnected, indeed inseparable. Anthropology was a natural science with human interaction as its unique subject matter. The core concept of culture was a by-product of interactional regularities associated with frequent life events, what he called "minimal sequence process modeling" (Arensberg 1972). His American Anthropological Association presidential address in 1980

(Arensberg 1981) emphasized "Cultural Holism through Interactional Systems." His holism combined social action, personal values and "adaptive and evolutionary consequence" (1981:576). The disciplinary convergence toward systems theory provided a welcome expansion for practicing anthropology, a revitalized version of applied anthropology.

Although Arensberg was a founder of the Society for Applied Anthropology, served as its president in 1945–46, and is often remembered as an applied anthropologist, he declined to distinguish between theoretical and applied anthropology. They were complementary sides of the same enterprise, in which application to real world problems provided "an essential laboratory for testing theories and models generated by the academy" (Comitas 1997). Anthropology had made "visible progress in many empirical discoveries" (1972:1); Arensberg was more concerned with the substantive than the theoretical side of anthropology. He served as editor of *Human Organization* from 1946 to 1951 and was president of the AAA in 1980–81.

Arensberg died of respiratory failure on 10 February 1997, in Hazlet, New Jersey, at the age of 86. He was survived by his wife, anthropologist Vivian Garrison, three children from a previous marriage, and two grandchildren.

REGNA DARNELL

William C. Sturtevant
1981

William Curtis Sturtevant was born on 26 July 1926 in Morristown, New Jersey. He was the first of three children of Alfred Henry Sturtevant and Phoebe Curtis Reed. His father was a pioneer in genetics, and in 1928 he moved his family to Pasadena, California, where he accepted a professorship in biology at the California Institute of Technology. His father's older brother, Edgar Howard Sturtevant, was a leading professor of linguistics at Yale University, where he specialized in Hittite and Indo-European languages.

Sturtevant earned his bachelor's degree from the University of California, Berkeley, where he studied between 1944 and 1949. His progress was interrupted by a year in the U.S. Naval Reserve (1945–46), during which he was stationed on Guam. This represented only a delay in studies that were focused and progressing well. His degree in anthropology was awarded with highest honors. Reflecting on his training at Berkeley, he has cited courses by John Rowe, Mary Haas, R. F. Heizer, David Mandelbaum, and *Robert H. Lowie* as particularly important (1955:3). Sturtevant's commitment to Native American studies within anthropology has been steadfast, having been initiated during third-grade lessons on Indian life and history. While an undergraduate, he participated in an archaeological field school at Chaco Canyon and a University of Northern Arizona Museum summer school in Mexico City. These experiences contributed to his later interest in Spanish ethnohistorical sources.

After graduating Sturtevant immediately took up graduate studies in anthropology at Yale University, earning his doctorate in 1955. At Yale he was especially influenced by anthropological linguist Floyd Lounsbury. Lounsbury's example, together with Sturtevant's training under Haas at Berkeley and Bernard Bloch at Yale, solidified his commitment to linguistic approaches within anthropology. Such methods and theories were already at the core of Americanist scholarship as consolidated by *Franz Boas*, but Sturtevant became an exemplar of this tradition during a period when it was transforming some fronts and being de-emphasized in others. Sharing Sturtevant's commitment to linguistically sophisticated ethnography was his friend and fellow-student Harold Conklin. Sturtevant's first published article was a thorough study of Seneca musical instruments written jointly with Conklin (1953). Beyond its ethnographic significance, this paper was an early example of rigorous ethnosemantic method, an approach to which both scholars later contributed theoretical works (Sturtevant 1964). Sturtevant's interest in the West Indies derived from work at Yale with *Irving Rouse* (Sturtevant 1960b).

In 1950 Sturtevant began a life-long research relationship with the Seminole people of Florida. During his doctoral research he worked most closely with Josie Billie, an important Seminole "medicine maker" (Sturtevant 1960). This early research generated a steady stream of essays in ethnography, oral history, and ethnohistory that established him as a leading figure in the anthropology of the eastern United States. Most important among these contributions is his dissertation, an ethnoscientific ethnography of Seminole medicine, ritual, and botany (1955). It stands among the most comprehensive and sophisticated studies of ethnobotany produced in the 20th century, and it remains crucial to the study of Woodland Indian cultures. Sturtevant's Seminole work was complemented by a continuation of research among the Iroquois that was also begun while he was a student at Yale. These experiences, supplemented by briefer periods of fieldwork throughout the Eastern Woodlands and a broad study of the ethnohistorical sources about it, have provided the background to his comparative studies of the region. They also informed his advocacy, in congressional testimony and other forums, for federally unrecognized Indian groups in the region (Sturtevant 1983).

Soon after graduation Sturtevant left an instructorship at Yale and a curatorship at its Peabody Museum for a position as ethnologist, and later general anthropologist, in the Smithsonian Institution's Bureau of American Ethnology. He held this position from 1956 until 1965. When the bureau merged with the Department of Anthropology in the U.S. National Museum (later the National Museum of Natural History), Sturtevant became curator of North American ethnology there. In this department he remains an active participant in the work of Smithsonian anthropology.

Most prominent among his ongoing Smithsonian projects is the *Handbook of North American Indians*, for which he serves as general editor. Published by the Smithsonian, the handbook is planned to be a 20-volume reference work summarizing anthropological, linguistic, and historical knowledge about native peoples north of Mexico. Bearing the imprint of its editor, the handbook's thoroughness has made it the essential resource for those interested in Native American societies.

Working throughout his career in museum contexts, Sturtevant has been active in the fields of museum anthropology and the study of material culture. He has advocated for the importance of museums to general anthropology (1973), developed methods for anthropological museology (1977), and conducted research on museum collections

(1967). From 1979 to 1981 he served as president of the Council for Museum Anthropology.

Sturtevant has also been an important participant in the development of ethnohistory as a subdiscipline. He served as president of the American Society for Ethnohistory in 1965–66, and his essays helped to solidify and frame this developing field (1966, 1971). The confluence of such interests and his training has also produced a commitment to the history of anthropology; he has made significant contributions to the study of early encounters between Europeans and the peoples of the New World.

In addition to the presidency of the American Anthropological Association and the organizations already noted, Sturtevant served as president of the Anthropological Society of Washington (1992–93) and the American Ethnological Society (1977). He has received numerous research grants and fellowships. Brown University awarded him the degree of L.H.D. in 1996.

In 1952 Sturtevant married Theda Maw, with whom he raised three children, Kinthi D. M., Reed P. M., and Alfred B. M. (deceased). They divorced in 1986. In 1990 he married Sally McLendon, also an anthropological linguist and Americanist.

JASON BAIRD JACKSON

M. Margaret Clark
1982

Mary Margaret Clark was born on 9 January 1925 in Amarillo, Texas. The youngest child of older parents, she grew up with siblings ten to fifteen years older. Many of her friends and schoolmates were Latino, Navajo, and Apache children. After attending local schools she entered Southern Methodist University, where she took premedical courses and received a B.S. in chemistry in 1945. She then entered Southwestern Medical School, a teaching hospital serving a largely African American and Latino population where the medical staff and students were largely white males from the middle and upper classes—a disjuncture she readily recognized as a woman already sensitized to difference, and one she found problematic. After meeting *Margaret Mead*, and having read some of her works, Clark decided to study anthropology. She entered the graduate program at the University of California, Berkeley, in 1948. There she worked most closely with *George M. Foster*, doing her dissertation research on health in a Mexican American community in San Jose, California. She received her Ph.D. in 1957.

Clark's dissertation, published in 1959 and reissued in 1970, was notable for embedding health practices in broader sociocultural contexts rather than focusing on the isolated specifics of healthcare. Also in contrast with much of the extant work at that time, it focused in part on lay practitioners, *curanderas*, who were generally women. This focus was driven by the context, in which curanderas were key participants in healthcare; it was not simply that as a woman scholar Clark turned to the role of women—rather, she questioned the dominance in the literature (at least until recently) of works emphasizing male curers, by male scholars. Clark considered many dimensions of healthcare in this Mexican American community that now seem routine but then were novel, including the social functions of illness, and the effects of cultural and linguistic differences between doctors and patients in the techniques, understandings, and effectiveness of treatment.

After receiving her Ph.D. Clark continued to study the sociocultural contexts for healthcare, working as a researcher with the U.S. Public Health Service in rural Colorado, and then in Arizona with the Navajo Health Education Project of Berkeley's School of Public Health. In 1960 she joined the Langley Porter Neuropsychiatric Institute at the University of California, San Francisco (UCSF), as a research anthropologist. Her work on aging in the urban context was among the first field research projects into cultural gerontology. *Culture and Aging*, co-authored with Barbara Gallatin Anderson (1967), drew on that research. While working at Langley Porter, Clark also lectured in the School of Medicine at the University of California, San Francisco, and in 1975 she joined with Frederick Dunn, Lucille Newman, and Christie Kiefer, at UCSF, and George Foster and James Anderson at Berkeley, to establish the Medical Anthropology Training Program at San Francisco as part of a joint doctoral program between the two institutions. Clark was appointed professor in 1975, and the following year she founded the Multidisciplinary Training Program in Applied Gerontology at UCSF. She also served as department chair in medical anthropology, and in 1980 she was named Faculty Research Lecturer, the first woman and the first social scientist to receive this highest faculty honor of the university. During her tenure at UCSF Clark also served as a consultant with the National Institute for Health and the Veterans Administration and received research funding from the National Institute for Mental Health and the National Institute on Aging.

One of the pioneering researchers in medical anthropology and cultural gerontology, and founder of two key educational programs, Clark was also active in professional organizations. She served as president of the Society for Medical Anthropology in 1972–73 and president of the American Anthropological Association in 1981–82 as well as member of the AAA Executive Board from 1974 to 1977. She was vice president (1974–75) and executive councillor (1973–76) for the Gerontological Society of America, and she served on the Executive Board of the Society for Applied Anthropology (1974–77). She was elected to the American Association for the Advancement of Science, and served on the Section H Executive Committee from 1977 to 1981. Clark received the Distinguished Mentorship award of the Gerontological Society of America in 1989 and the Malinowski Award of the Society for Applied Anthropology in 1992; the Association for Anthropology and Gerontology named their student paper award for her in recognition of her support for students.

In her candidate's statement for the presidency of the AAA (*Anthropology Newsletter*, May 1980), Clark described anthropology in terms that still resonate for many—perhaps even more so today than 20 years ago:

> In this new decade, the field of anthropology is in increasing danger of sinking into irrelevance and obscurity. The multiple crises of the modern world are challenging us to demonstrate the utility of our knowledge and skills. No longer can anthropologists remain isolated from the human problems engendered by economic crisis, massive migration and the clash of cultures, population pressure, environmental destruction and political upheaval.
>
> The massive social changes that have accompanied these crises have had immediate consequences for anthropology as a profession—jobs are scarce, research support is dwindling, training funds are vanishing. Equally

serious is the crisis we face in terms of public visibility and credibility: We seem bent upon hiding the utility of our discipline from the general public and from our political representatives—sometimes even from ourselves.

The integration of research and education and the importance of socially meaningful and useful research are themes that recur throughout Clark's career. Many of her students have gone on not just to academic careers but to work in public policy and applied research centers. Reflecting back on her shift from medicine to anthropology, Clark noted, "I became convinced that anthropology provided exactly the worldview that I had found missing in my earlier studies and that I could find no other work as satisfying to my soul" (quoted in Ames and Ablon 1994:356).

Margaret Clark retired from teaching in 1991 and lives in San Rafael, California. Since retirement she has taken a variety of courses at the Fromm Institute, a center for enrichment learning.

FREDERIC W. GLEACH

Dell Hymes
1983

D ell Hymes was born on 7 June 1927 in Portland, Oregon. He
attended public schools there and graduated from Reed
College in 1950, with a two-year interval in the U.S. Army
stationed in Korea. At Reed he studied anthropology with David French
and took a joint degree in anthropology and literature with a thesis on
the English critic, Christopher Caudwell. In 1950 he began graduate
work at Indiana University in anthropology, with minors in linguistics
and folklore. At Indiana Hymes was introduced to a broad range of
scholarship in linguistics and anthropology, studying with Carl Voegelin,
George Herzog, Fred Householder, Harold Whitehall, Harry Velten,
Thomas Sebeok, Ray Birdwhistell, Archibald Hill, Henry "Haxie"
Smith, and a visiting Kenneth Burke. "Appointed" a linguist by Voegelin
during his 1951 seminar on American Indian languages, Hymes traveled back to Oregon that summer to work on Wasco at the Warm
Springs reservation; from that initial fieldwork he developed his "life-

long devotion to Wasco" and to Native American studies (Hymes 1980a:204–05). He received his M.A. in linguistics in 1953, with a thesis analyzing Chinookan paradigms, and his Ph.D. in 1955, with a dissertation on "The Language of the Kathlamet Chinook."

In 1954 Hymes married Virginia Dosch Wolff, who, having earned a B.A. in mathematics from Queens College of the City of New York (1943), received her M.A. in anthropology from Indiana University in 1954 with a thesis on Athapaskan numeral systems. Like Dell, Virginia went on to work for more than half a century on Native American cultures and languages (particularly Sahaptin), associated as a researcher and teacher with the Universities of California (Berkeley), Pennsylvania, and Virginia, the Smithsonian Institution, the National Science Foundation, the National Endowment for the Humanities, and the Confederated Tribes of Warm Springs, Oregon. Virginia had two children by a first marriage, Katherine Wolff Unruh and Robert Wolff Hymes, adopted by Dell, and Dell and Virginia had two children together, Alison and Kenneth.

The Hymeses spent 1954–55 at the University of California, Los Angeles, where they studied with *Harry Hoijer* while Dell served as a teaching assistant in anthropology and completed his dissertation. Hoijer and *Clyde Kluckhohn* were instrumental in securing a position for Dell as a linguistic anthropologist in the Department of Social Relations at Harvard University, where the Hymeses remained until Dell was appointed associate professor of Anthropology and Linguistics at the University of California, Berkeley, in 1960; he was promoted to professor in 1964 and also served as a curator in the Robert H. Lowie Museum of Anthropology throughout his five-year stint at Berkeley. In collaboration with John Gumperz, Hymes developed the ethnography of speaking model, focusing on cross-cultural variability in the use of language as well as in its structure, which he characterized as a second type of linguistic relativity.

Dell went to the University of Pennsylvania in 1965 as a professor of anthropology. There a group of students began to test the ethnography of speaking model through fieldwork (Bauman and Sherzer 1974). Students from this period included Regna Darnell, Sheila Dauer, Judith

Irvine, Eleanor Ochs, Susan Phillips, Anne Salmond, Joel Sherzer, and T. K. Tiwari. In 1970 Hymes joined the Department of Folklore and Folklife. As dean of the Graduate School of Education from 1975 to 1987, he became deeply involved in Philadelphia's inner-city education initiatives, also theorizing the relationships of language and social inequality (1973, 1980b). Hymes was also consistently associated with the Center for Urban Ethnography. In 1987 he accepted an appointment as professor of anthropology and English at the University of Virginia, where he was honored with a chaired professorship in 1990. He retired in 1998. Virginia Hymes retired from her position as lecturer in the Department of Anthropology at the University of Virginia in 2000.

Hymes served as president of the American Folklore Society (1973–74), the Council on Anthropology and Education (1977–78), the Linguistic Society of America (1982), the Consortium of Social Science Associations (1982–84), the American Anthropological Association (1983), and the American Association of Applied Linguistics (1986). In addition to his work as an associate editor or editorial board member of many journals (such as *Journal of American Folklore, International Journal of American Linguistics, American Anthropologist, Journal of the History of the Behavioral Sciences, Dialectical Anthropology*, and *History of Anthropology*), he was the founding editor of *Language in Society*, which he edited from 1972 to 1992.

Hymes came to linguistics at a time and place in which its multiple strands (historical, formal, ethnographic, psychological, literary) were alive and well, before the Chomskian revolution narrowed the field and obscured its diverse history. He has described his career as ongoing "guerilla warfare" against the Chomskian denial of the "social, cultural context and basis of language" (1980a:206). This warfare in part accounts for important strands of his work—his devotion to the history of linguistics and anthropology (Hymes 1963, 1974a, 1983, Hymes and Fought 1975) and his pioneering work toward a fully anthropological linguistics (Hymes ed. 1964, 1966, 1971, 1973, 1974b, 1980b, Gumperz and Hymes 1972), as represented by his "ethnography of speaking" approach, his work on language and education, and his wide influence among linguistic anthropologists and sociolinguists. Equally important has been his work on Native American languages, literatures, and ethnopoetics and on the preservation and teaching of Native American languages (Hymes 1981). His recent work has focused on poetic structures of line and verse in Native American text collections, discovering patterns that seem to hold widely across languages.

Most generally, Dell Hymes has worked to link the knowledge, techniques, and histories made available by anthropology and linguistics to social justice in the broadest sense of the term, justice underpinned by "liberal, social, moral" ideals (Hymes 1980a:212). His important edited volume, *Reinventing Anthropology* (1972), compiled during protests against U.S. involvement in Vietnam as a means to reassess the future of anthropology, continues in the 21st century to focus the attention of anthropologists on the relationship of their discipline to such ideals.

RICHARD HANDLER

Nancy O. Lurie
1984–1985

N ancy Oestreich Lurie was born in Milwaukee, Wisconsin, on 29 January 1924. She grew up as the only child in a household of elders including her parents, grandparents, and a great-grandfather from whom she learned about local Potawatomi Indian settlements he visited in his boyhood. Her father served on the engineering faculty at the University of Wisconsin, Milwaukee Extension Division, and also worked at the Milwaukee Public Museum (MPM). Nancy's childhood interests suggested to her father that she might be interested in a career as an anthropologist. When she was eight years old he took her to meet Samuel A. Barrett and Will C. McKern at the museum. She resolved then and there that someday she would be the curator of anthropology at the MPM.

Lurie received her B.A. in anthropology and sociology from the University of Wisconsin in 1945, her M.A. from the University of Chicago in 1947, and her Ph.D. from Northwestern University in 1952.

At the end of her junior year, Lurie was encouraged by her major professor J. Sydney Slotkin to conduct fieldwork with the Wisconsin Winnebagos, who had hardly been studied since Paul Radin's pioneering work. Already she focused on culture change and on teaching white society respect and fairness toward Indians (Ganteaume 1989:239). During her senior year Lurie regularly visited a new friend from the previous summer, Mitchell Redcloud Sr., who was hospitalized in Madison. In addition to his ethnographic teachings, Mr. Redcloud adopted Lurie as his daughter, providing her with a Winnebago name, clan, and relatives enjoined by his decision to continue working with her after his death in 1946.

Lurie arrived at the University of Chicago just after *Sol Tax* began reorganizing the postwar anthropology program. Tax, *Fred Eggan*, and visiting professor *E. Adamson Hoebel* supervised her thesis on changing patterns of childcare and training, funded by John Whiting's comparative study of socialization across cultures. She completed her M.A. before Tax's Fox Project began, but was soon drawn to his action anthropology.

Upon graduation Lurie was hired at the Milwaukee Extension Division of the University of Wisconsin, where she taught introductory anthropology and sociology. The course, which included considerable anthropology, had been instituted a few years earlier as an evening class by Robert Ritzenthaler, McKern's successor as anthropology curator at the MPM; McKern had succeeded Barrett as director. Lurie taught there intermittently until 1953, adding a cultural anthropology course. Her doctoral work at Northwestern University comparing culture change in the Wisconsin and Nebraska Winnebagos combined ethnohistorical research with fieldwork. At Northwestern she met and married Edward Lurie, a graduate student in history; they divorced amicably in 1963.

Lurie's work as an expert witness for the U.S. Indian Claims Commission began in 1954. She served on seven cases (Lower Kutenai, Lower Kalispel, Quinaielt-Quileute, Sac and Fox et al., Winnebago, Turtle Mountain Chippewa, and Eastern Potawatomi) before the termination of the commission in 1978. In 1957 she began teaching applied anthropology at the University of Michigan, first in the extension branch and later in the School of Public Health. She could obtain a tenure-track position only after her husband left the faculty in 1961.

Mountain Wolf Woman (1961) presented the autobiography of a Winnebago woman, Mitchell Redcloud Sr.'s sister, who shared her life story as a gift to her "niece." Mountain Wolf Woman was also the sister of Crashing Thunder, Radin's famous American Indian autobiographical subject. Lurie's book provided invaluable comparative material on Winnebago life over time and from a woman's point of view.

In 1959 Lurie accepted the invitation of her fellow Chicago graduate student *June Helm* to work with the Dogribs, a northern Athabascan group in the Northwest Territories. They returned to the Dogribs in 1962 and 1967. In 1961–62 Lurie served as Sol Tax's assistant in the American Indian Chicago Conference, conceived as a "test of action anthropology on a large scale in response to Indian dissatisfaction with the federal policies of the 1950s" (Ganteaume 1989:241). Ninety tribes gathered to draft the Declaration of Indian Purpose, later presented to President John F. Kennedy. Thereafter, Lurie's action anthropology commitments were implemented in community planning surveys and project development among the Wisconsin Winnebago and the intertribal community in Milwaukee. Between 1969 and 1974 she was active in the successful Menomini struggle to repeal termination of their federal Indian status.

In 1963 Lurie joined the faculty of the newly established University of Wisconsin–Milwaukee as associate professor; her first major task was to help establish a master's program with a certificate option in museology in collaboration with the MPM. She was promoted to professor three years later. As department chair from 1967 to 1970 she helped establish a doctoral program in anthropology. In 1965–66 she was a Fullbright-Hays lecturer at the University of Aarhus, Denmark. In 1972, when Ritzenthaler retired, she fulfilled her childhood vow and became curator and head of the anthropology section of the MPM. Lurie believes public education has a potential to increase popular appreciation of anthropological contributions to the understanding of humankind. She continues to hold an adjunct appointment at the university.

In 1982 Lurie became the first American Anthropological Association president to serve a two-year term under the new reorganization. With her old field partner, president-elect June Helm, Lurie saw the AAA through major reorganization.

Throughout her career Lurie has returned repeatedly to the field. From 1982 to 1984, at a stage in her own life cycle when she was able to work appropriately with Winnebago traditionalists on such esoteric materials, she translated largely sacred songs from Frances Densmore's wax cylinders recorded half a century earlier. She also undertook ethnohistorical work on the Winnebago contribution to the Black Hawk War of 1832.

Lurie's abiding commitment has been to the four-field tradition of anthropology in teaching and museum work. The emphases in her own specialty of cultural anthropology have been on community consultation and local control of development plans, respect for her consultants, training Native American scholars, and educating mainstream society to respect Native American persons and traditions. Culture change, gender, and individual agency are the central prongs of her applied anthropology.

REGNA DARNELL

June Helm
1986–1987

B orn in Twin Falls, Idaho, on 13 September 1924, June Helm
was the only child of Julia Frances (née Dixon) and William
Jennings Helm, both from Kansas farms; they moved to Kansas City when June was six. Helm describes herself as a "typical
midwesterner" (Armstrong 1989:148).

In grade school Helm kept a scrapbook of newspaper clippings about
evolution. Before finishing high school she knew she wanted to be an
anthropologist, specifically an ethnologist. Helm's enduring commitment to anthropology led to her fostering the historical record of
American anthropology (Helm ed. 1966, 1985). Rather than "great
minds" or "grand theories," her interest lay in the social and intellectual frames constraining and channeling anthropological understandings over time.

Unlike most female (and perhaps male) anthropologists of her generation, Helm did not have a father who was a "professional man." His

274 • PRESIDENTIAL PORTRAITS

education stopped at the eighth grade; he became an able mechanic-machinist. Helm graduated from high school half a year before Pearl Harbor. With no money for college, she accepted a scholarship to a girl's finishing school in Illinois, lured by its stable of horses. Her "finishing" was brief, less than a week, once she discovered that daily chapel was required. She returned home and enrolled at the University of Kansas City, the only affordable alternative. By the fall of 1942 her father had converted used machines to war production, and the World War II boom provided ample money for Helm to transfer to the University of Chicago. She matriculated in Chicago's two-year Ph.B. program, designed to produce well-rounded and informed citizens who could then pursue specialized advanced degrees.

In 1945 Helm married Richard S. "Scotty" MacNeish, a Ph.D. candidate in archaeology, and they immediately set off to Mexico for MacNeish's dissertation fieldwork. A subsequent season in Mexico enabled Helm to carry out master's research in a rural mestizo community in Tamaupipas.

In 1949 Helm and MacNeish moved to Ottawa, where he held an appointment at the National Museum of Canada. During his summer archaeological survey of the Mackenzie River in 1950, MacNeish learned from a small community of Slaveys—a branch of the Dene Indian peoples of Canada's Northwest Territories—that they would welcome someone to teach English to their children. No all-Indian settlement in the NWT had a school. In the summer of 1951 Helm and fellow graduate student Teresa Carteretts went to the community of subarctic hunter-trappers at Jean Marie River as volunteer teachers. Like the research in Mexico, Helm's first season in northern Canada was slipped into MacNeish's field funding. The second summer at Jean Marie River saw her first research grant, $400 from the Canadian Social Science Research Council. Helm's ethnographic field data from 1951 and 1952 became the basis of her Ph.D. dissertation and her entry into the ranks of hunter-gatherer researchers.

At the start of her career Helm was buoyed by approbation of her field research by *Robert Redfield* and later by *George P. Murdock*. Nine weeks before his death, Redfield assumed the chairmanship of Helm's orals. In a note to *Sol Tax* (23 June 1928, in Helm's possession), Redfield said of her dissertation, "I much prefer this kind of perceptive and responsible reporting, with the sense of conviction of the reality which it conveys, to many a thesis that adopts the fashionable concepts and pastes them on to some facts." Helm received her Ph.D. from the University of Chicago in 1958.

Helm made brief kinship queries among other Dene—Slaveys, Chipewyans, and Hares—from 1954 to 1957. In 1959 *Nancy O. Lurie* joined her for five months among the Dogrib Dene. The Dogribs thereafter became the focus of Helm's fieldwork, which entailed ten trips between 1959 and 1979. In 1962 (Helm and Lurie 1966) and 1967 Lurie and Helm again collaborated with the Dogribs.

Helm has spent fifty years studying the culture and ethnohistory of the Mackenzie-drainage Dene (Helm 1978, 2000). She is not enamored with "theory" per se. Her research strategy has been to blend historical documentation and ethnographic field data to gain better comprehension of both. For example, she addressed issues bearing on an 18th-century Chipewyan map including evidence for 19th-century female infanticide, the Dene in the fur trade, historical changes in Dene leadership patterns, prophecy and power among the Dogribs (1994), Dene kinship and socioterritorial organization, and sociocultural change in the 19th and 20th centuries. In the 1970s she served as expert witness and land claims research advisor for the Indian Brotherhood (later the Dene First Nation), and as consultant to Canada's Mackenzie Valley Pipeline Inquiry (Helm 2000).

Helm's field research activities in the NWT ended in 1979. But in 1996 Anglo-Canadian archaeologist Tom Andrews and Dogrib John B. Zoe asked her to vet a paper they had written. It rejuvenated her commitment to the Dene, expressed in *The People of Denendeh* (Helm 2000). This volume assembled selections from Helm's published studies, unpublished field notes, essays and notes by Carterett and Lurie, and Dene oral history narratives that would otherwise be lost to the public record.

During the years Helm lived in Canada, she was a sessional lecturer at Carleton College (now University) in Ottawa and at the University of Manitoba. After she and MacNeish amicably divorced in 1958, she joined the Department of Sociology and Anthropology of the University of Iowa in 1960. In 1968 she married architect Pierce King. In 1969 the University of Iowa established the Department of Anthropology; Helm has at intervals served as department chair. Between 1993 and 1996 she chaired the newly formed American Indian and Native Studies Program.

Helm was president of the American Anthropological Association in 1986–87. She and her longtime colleague Nancy Lurie held consecutive terms, which, according to Helm, ensured them four years of the best suites at the annual meetings. Helm also served as editor of American Ethnological Society publications (1964–68), president of the Central States Anthropological Society (1970–71), chair of Section H of the American Association for the Advancement of Science (1978), associate editor of the *American Ethnologist* (1979–81), and president of the American Ethnological Society (1982–83). She was elected a fellow of the American Academy of Arts and Sciences in 1994.

Helm is professor emerita at the University of Iowa, having retired in December 1999 after 40 years of teaching. The June Helm Award for Service and Excellence, an annual peer-nominated graduate student award, was established in 1998.

SARAH ONO AND JUNE HELM

Roy A. Rappaport
1988–1989

Roy Abraham "Skip" Rappaport was born on 25 March 1926 in New York City. He enlisted in the army at the age of 17 and was awarded the Purple Heart after being wounded in action. Following the war, he obtained a B.Sc. in hotel administration from Cornell University in 1949 and opened Avaloch, a country inn in Lenox, Masschusetts. He switched to anthropology and obtained his Ph.D. in 1966 from Columbia University, the birthplace of ecological anthropology, with Andrew P. Vayda as his supervisor. Julian Steward's cultural change and Marvin Harris's cultural materialism were closely related prongs of the Columbia position (Kottak 1999:23).

Rappaport's 1962–63 fieldwork with the Tsembaga Marings in the Simbai Valley in the central highlands of Madang Territory, Papua New Guinea, focused on ritual mediation between shifting swidden horticulturalists and the world external to their valley. His study, which ultimately encompassed demography, ritual, animal husbandry, horticulture, linguistics (largely carried out by his wife, Ann), and nutrition, was part of a larger Columbia University expedition that also included Andrew and Cherry Vayda and Allison and Marek Jablonko.

Rappaport's 1966 dissertation was published two years later as *Pigs for the Ancestors: Ritual in the Ecology of a New Guinea People.* A substantially revised edition appeared in 1984. This work "became the classic case study of human ecology in a tribal society, the role of culture (especially ritual) in local and regional resource management, negative feedback, and the application of systems theory to an anthropological population" (Hart and Kottak 1999:159). Rappaport postulated that ecosystem variables remained in homeostasis (at tolerable levels for participants in the system) because ritual corrected deviations. He distinguished between cognized models, shared among members of a society, and operational models devised by the outsider-analyst.

The Maring *Kaiko* ritual sacrificed pigs to ancestral guardians during wartime. Debts to allies and ancestors alike had to be paid through this regulatory ritual before hostilities could recommence. Pigs accumulated until the women rebelled at the labor, initiating a feast that distributed surplus pigs over the region and allowed a new cycle to commence.

Rappaport revisited the Simbai Valley in 1981–82 to study the change among the Tsembaga Marings as a result of increasingly intense pressures from Western culture. *Ecology, Meaning, and Religion* (1979) was a collection of essays that had revised his early ecological work and extended its functionalism to a more formalist definition of religion and culture.

In 1965 Rappaport took a position in the Department of Anthropology at the University of Michigan, where he was Leslie A. White Professor of Anthropology, Walgreen Professor for the Study of Human Understanding, and director of the Program on Studies in Religion; he served as department chair from 1975 to 1980. His signature course in later years, The Anthropology of Religion: Ritual, Sanctity, and Adaptation, was reworked into his posthumous book *Ritual and Religion in the Making of Humanity* (1999). In addition to his "comprehensive analytical treatment of ritual" as the basis of religion, Rappaport produced a "work of prophecy," identifying a crisis both for humanity and for the global ecosystem (Hart and Kottak 1999:160). He looked to anthropology to provide an antidote to the pseudo-religion of economics that was destroying human civilization. Indeed, ritual functioned in evolution to intensify "the complex, reciprocal relationships of mutual trust that symbolic communication and social action presuppose" (Watanabe and Smuts 1999:98). Ritual, defined in terms of formality, resolved the dichotomy between sacred and profane that has plagued Western thought. Complexity could reconcile the schism between idealism and materialism, since the indeterminacy of human life precluded environmental determinism (given that humans were part of the environment).

Rappaport's later work dealt with applied anthropology, which he relabeled "engaged anthropology." During his presidency of the American Anthropological Association, Rappaport moved the profession toward active engagement with policy issues and social problems, sponsoring a number of relevant seminars. He was firmly convinced that anthropology had diagnostic potential for the disorder of American society, and he held America accountable for the inhumane face of Third World development. His AAA presidential address, "The Anthropology of Trouble" (1993) laid out his concerns for the malaises of capitalism. His intention to relocate the center of American anthropology in the study of American society was intended not so much to politicize anthropology as to "anthropologize . . . public discourse" (1993:295), taking responsibility for issues that resonate globally from our own domestic "troubles." Ethnography, the fundamental methodology of the anthropologist, was the crux of both the problem and the solution because the "domination of privileged discourse . . . threatens to make other discourses inaudible or unintelligible" (1993:301). Anthropology to date has failed to theorize social disorder and maladaptation. Rappaport asserted that political economy and interpretation must go hand in hand.

In a special issue of the *American Anthropologist* dedicated to "Ecologies for Tomorrow: Reading Rappaport Today," Kottak (1999) argues for revisions of the systems theory, functionalism, and negative feedback of 1960s ecology. Ecological and environmental issues can no longer be separated from politics and policy, while transnational and global trends preclude closed system analyses. Rappaport made the transition from culture to ecological population and acknowledged regional as well as local ecosystems, but his model was not designed for more complex societies (Kottak 1999:24). In introducing an *American Anthropologist* contemporary issues forum in his honor, Aletta Biersack emphasizes the development within Rappaport's thought over his career, from what she sees as a reductive materialism to political ecology to "the complexity of the human condition" (1999:5).

Rappaport was an environmental consultant on outer continental shelf oil leasing for the National Academy of Sciences Task Force, and on storage of nuclear waste at Yucca Mountain for the state of Nevada. He was also elected to the American Academy of Arts and Sciences.

Rappaport died after a long struggle with cancer on 9 October 1997 in Ann Arbor, Michigan. He and his wife, Ann Hart Rappaport, had two daughters. His final book, *Ritual and Religion in the Making of Humanity*, appeared posthumously in 1999.

REGNA DARNELL

Jane Buikstra
1990–1991

Jane Ellen Buikstra was born on 2 November 1945 in Evansville, Indiana. From her doctor father, who died when she was ten, Buikstra acquired her fascination with disease and her commitment to helping people. As a biological anthropologist she acknowledges a responsibility to people no longer living. From her mother she learned to distrust condescending European attitudes toward Indians and to consider the standpoint of the underdog. She collected projectile points on her family property and resonated to the mysteries of Mesa Verde, where history was unwritten and only archaeology could reveal past stories.

Buikstra received her B.A. in anthropology from DePauw University in 1967, after changing her major several times and combining area studies with courses in biological and sociocultural anthropology; she wrote her Honors thesis on salamanders. She moved to the Department of Anthropology at the University of Chicago, receiving an M.A. in 1969 and a Ph.D. in 1972. With Charles J. Merbs as her primary mentor, she aspired to study ordinary people rather than great historic figures. After one season of Arctic biology and archaeology, she switched to the Midwest where population data were likely to be more completely preserved. Her dissertation on lower Illinois River valley Hopewell consolidated a regional approach to biological variability as reflected in mortuary practices (Buikstra 1976). She has continued to work in the region (e.g., Buikstra and Charles 1999).

Buikstra's teaching career began at Northwestern University, where she served as an instructor (1970–72), assistant professor (1972–76), associate professor (1976–82), and professor (1982–86); from 1981 to 1984 she held the position of associate dean. In 1984–85 she was a resident scholar at the School of American Research in Santa Fe. She has been a research associate at the Field Museum of Natural History in Chicago (1981–), the Museum of the American Indian (1983–86), and the University of Florida (1997–), as well as an adjunct professor at Washington University in St. Louis (1986–). From 1986 to 1995 Buikstra was professor of anthropology at the University of Chicago, holding the title of Harold H. Swift Distinguished Service Professor from 1989 to 1995; she remains a research associate at the University of Chicago. Buikstra moved to the University of New Mexico in 1995 as distinguished professor in the biological anthropology program. In 2001 she was awarded the title of Leslie Spier Distinguished Professor of Anthropology, which she values particularly because *Leslie Spier* always remained a generalist in his view of anthropology.

Buikstra has conducted fieldwork in the American Midwest (with 18 projects since 1966), the Canadian Arctic (1969), Santa Fe la Vieja in Argentina (1980–82, 1984, 1987), the Marajo Expedition to Brazil (1983–86), the Programa Contisuyu in Peru (1984–), the Gatas Expedition to Spain (1986–), Cayonu Tepesi in Turkey (1988), and 12 seasons of excavations at Copán, Honduras, where she concentrated on two Early Classic royal burials, the Hunal and Margarita tombs.

The research topics arising from her intensive study of prehistoric skeletal populations across the Americas include microevolutionary change and biological response to environmental stress, bone microstructure, individuation, experimental creation, social dimensions of mortuary behavior, demography, forensics, paleopathology, paleonutrition, biological distance, and the biological impact of European colonization. Her approach has been multidisciplinary, involving collaboration with colleagues in archaeology, medicine, law enforcement, molecular biology, and chemical analysis.

The topics of her research papers, often coauthored, are predictably wide-ranging. Many of her early studies deal with the human cost of disease, including prehistoric tuberculosis in the Americas, Caribou Eskimo disease patterns, prenatal dentition, decapitation, Australopithecine vertebral pathology, and coca-chewing residues in Ancient Peruvian hair. Hers was the first American research team to isolate tuberculosis in ancient DNA. Buikstra's dissertation research with Middle Woodland mounds led her to a more general concern with monumentality and ostentation, which she pursued in New World Mayan and Peruvian contexts as well as in Bronze Age Spain; desert preservation provided a more diverse tissue base accessible to analysis. She studied cemeteries and mounds in their symbolic dimensions, as sacred landscapes, and approached biocultural adaptation through topics as diverse as the diet and changing fertility of early humans in America, at the transition to agriculture, and the intragroup effects of Macaque social group fission. The biological implications of changing subsistence strategies can be reconstructed from human remains. Chemical analysis of excavated bone, including the effects of burning on bone and metal-ion exchange, alternate in her work with more traditional techniques of osteology and forensics. Throughout her career Buikstra has maintained a commitment to rigorous standards of data collection in approaching the population biology of the past. She has synthesized the state of the field as well as reported on her own research projects (e.g. Buikstra and Cook 1992, Buikstra and Konigsberg 1985).

Buikstra has defended the value of scientific study of human remains in relation to the difficult issues of repatriation and reburial (Buikstra and Gordon 1981). In both technical and popular publications, she has defended the rights of local communities over human remains that have a known cultural continuity. She argues, however, that ancient remains can be understood only through science.

Buikstra served as president of the American Association of Physical Anthropologists from 1985 to 1987 as well as president of the American Anthropological Association. During her AAA presidency she emphasized the need for long-term financial stability and facilitated representation of anthropological expertise to the general public. She remains committed to the breadth of anthropology as a discipline whose core value is tolerance—both of multiple approaches within the field and of the diversity of humankind, which is our long-established subject matter. Buikstra was elected to the National Academy of Sciences in 1987 and has served on the executive board and the ethics committee of the American Board of Forensic Anthropology since 1994.

REGNA DARNELL

Annette Weiner
1992–1993

T he anthropologist whom the Trobrianders named "Anna" was
born Annette Barbara Cohen on 14 February 1933 in Phila
delphia. She was the oldest of four children and the only daughter of Archibald and Phyllis Cohen, both in business. She attended the
Philadelphia High School for Girls and became an x-ray technician.
Annette married her first husband, Martin Weiner, in 1951; her children, Linda Weiner Hoffman and Jonathan Weiner, were born to this
marriage, which ended in divorce in 1973. Her second marriage, in
1979, to philosophy professor Robert Paltier, also ended in divorce
three years later. In 1987 Weiner married anthropologist William E.
Mitchell, a specialist in Pacific cultures and now emeritus at the University of Vermont; they were together at the time of her death on 7
December 1997.

Weiner anticipated a recent trend by beginning her academic career
as a nontraditional student, attending college after establishing a family. By 1964, when she entered the University of Pennsylvania, she was

also a trained artist and had established herself in publishing. Weiner was vice president of Murette Publishing Company in Chester, Pennsylvania, from 1960 to 1964; she had also worked at M&N Publishing Company in New York City, cofounding and copublishing *Lady's Circle* (1963–64), a relatively popular but conventional women's magazine of the period. At Murette, Weiner wrote and published a series of children's foreign-language learning books that drew on her art training: *Let's Color in French*, *Let's Color in Spanish*, *Let's Color in German*, and *Let's Color in Hebrew*.

Weiner intended to continue studying art in college until she encountered anthropology in her sophomore year, as she herself would later explain:

> I felt very diminished by the fact that I had not [gone to college]. . . . I got married when I was very young and I had two children and I found myself searching for something else to fill out my life, something to do intellectually. Although I was by no means an intellectual, I hadn't even read any literature of note. I read pop best sellers at the time.
>
> And for a while when I started at Penn, I decided I would be an art major and then I decided where would that really take me? Would I end up teaching art in some place? And that idea didn't seem very interesting to me. . . .
>
> So I found anthropology along the way as an undergraduate because someone I knew gave me a copy of Hortense Powdermaker's *Stranger and Friend*. I found there this romantic notion of living in New Guinea. And she studied with Malinowski. Then she worked in the South of the United States and then she worked in Hollywood. What could be more spectacular? It was all so wonderful. I had never really heard of anthropology before and there I was and I was totally convinced that that was it. Love at first sight. And I thought that this person Malinowski must be really important because she's always referring to him. So I went and I ordered a hardback of *Argonauts of the Western Pacific*. I had only read this book and there I had *Argonauts*. I mean, about six years later I'd be there! It was quite unbelievable that this was going to be my life. (Kirshenblatt-Gimblett and Myers 1997)

Upon finishing her bachelor's degree in 1968 she went on to graduate work in anthropology at Bryn Mawr, where she worked with *Frederica de Laguna* and *A. Irving Hallowell*, finishing her Ph.D. in 1974.

In her doctoral fieldwork Weiner did not at first intend to revise Bronislaw Malinowski's classic rendition of Trobriand culture, but, consonant with her training, to focus on the art and economics of wood carving, especially for tourism: "Since carving for the tourists was the villagers' major source of Western cash, I planned to examine both how cash affected the traditional exchanges of men's valuables and how much change had occurred in the traditional carving designs and techniques" (Weiner 1988:20). But her observation of women's practices and activities, especially their involvement in mortuary rituals and exchange, led her to theorize the central role of gender in sociocultural processes of production and reproduction.

Weiner's published dissertation (1976) quickly placed her at the forefront of an emerging anthropology of gender, yet it also transcended it. Her work is still acknowledged as a major contribution to social theory, particularly as regards kinship, gender, social organization, cultural reproduction, and exchange. She elaborated on the importance of exchange by problematizing reciprocity in her other two major publications (Weiner and Schneider 1989, Weiner 1992): "she challenged the simplistic 'gift'/'commodity' dichotomy for exchange and argued that exchange should be understood as having the capacity to express identity and to produce hierarchy—ranked or valued difference" (Beidelman and Myers 1998:27).

Weiner taught at Franklin and Marshall College (1973–74) and then at the University of Texas, Austin (1974–80). In 1980 she was recruited by New York University, where the loss of its chair because of criminal activity had plunged the department of anthropology into a crisis. She served as chair from 1981 to 1991, restoring the department to high standing through curricular reorganization and inspired faculty recruitment, proving her talent for recognizing scholarly potential. Her administrative success at NYU was acknowledged through a sequence of promotions: appointments to the David B. Kriser distinguished professorship in anthropology, which she held from 1984 until her death, dean of social science (1993–96), and dean of the Graduate School of Arts and Sciences (1991–96), a position she relinquished when her illness progressed.

At the American Anthropological Association, Weiner occupied a series of positions that culminated in her election as president (1992–93). Unfortunately, she was absent from the 1993 meeting over which she was meant to preside, as she was undergoing surgery for the cancer that eventually ended her life. In recognition of her contributions to anthropology, academia, and the organization, Weiner received the AAA Distinguished Service medal in 1997.

For those of us who were her students, Weiner was as influential as a person as she was for her scholarship. She has been accurately portrayed as stylish, romantic, brilliant, strong, creative, impressive, and generous, but also as formidable, fearless, and forthright (New York University 1998). Following her wishes, Weiner's daughter, Linda, took "Anna's" ashes to the Trobriand Islands in the spring of 1998 and scattered them in the sea.

VILMA SANTIAGO–IRIZARRY

James Peacock
1994–1995

J ames Lowe "Jim" Peacock III was born on Halloween, 31 October
1937, in Montgomery, Alabama. The family moved often, especially during the war when his father was in the army, and Peacock
attended first grade in four different schools. Much of his youth was
spent in southern Georgia. At the age of 13 he began taking summer
jobs, working as an agricultural laborer, door-to-door salesman, elec-
trician apprentice, and sports coordinator for the state mental hospital
in Delaware, a work camp position. He planned to go to the College of
William and Mary in Virginia, but at the last minute decided instead to
go to Florida State University. The following year he transferred to
Duke University, majoring in psychology, which he had become interested in through reading during high school. In his senior year at Duke,
Peacock took an anthropology course with Weston LaBarre, who also
took him and a friend, Christopher Crocker, to the 1958 American
Anthropological Association meetings in Washington. There he heard

Alfred L. Kroeber and Alan Lomax. The experience reinforced his feeling that anthropology was more interesting and exciting than the experimental psychology he had been studying.

Peacock completed his B.A. in Psychology in 1959 and applied to graduate programs in anthropology; he chose Harvard University because of its department of social relations, which offered the possibility of combining his experience in psychology with his developing anthropological interests. *Clyde Kluckhohn* died after Peacock's first year at Harvard, and he studied with Talcott Parsons, Robert Bellah, *Cora Du Bois*, and David Maybury-Lewis. There he also met Thomas Kirsch, another graduate student, and the two became good friends; it was Kirsch who steered Peacock toward Parsons, and toward working in Southeast Asia. Student gatherings at Hayes Bickford, a cheap Harvard Square café, contributed to Peacock's (and others') development of theoretical perspectives and lasting social connections. In 1961 Peacock went to Yale University for language studies, and there he met fellow Georgian and music student Florence Turner Fowler; they married on 4 August 1962 and left for Indonesia together the next day.

The Peacocks spent a year in Surabaya, living in the slums and doing fieldwork on theater at the height of the Sukarno period, shortly before the massacres depicted in the movie *The Year of Living Dangerously*. They returned to Cambridge in 1963, where their first daughter was born, and Jim received his Ph.D. in 1965. He then began teaching at Princeton, where he helped create a Ph.D. program in anthropology, but he left in 1967 to teach at the University of North Carolina, Chapel Hill—taking advantage of the opportunity to return to the South. There he was promoted to associate professor in 1970 and professor in 1973. He chaired the anthropology department from 1975 to 1980 and in 1990–91 and the faculty from 1991 to 1994, cochaired a Research Institute on the South in Comparative Perspective, and has taught as a visitor at Princeton, Yale, and the University of California at San Diego. He is currently Kenan Professor of Anthropology, professor of comparative literature, and director of the University Center for International Studies. Peacock was elected to the American Academy of

Arts and Sciences and the Order of the Golden Fleece in 1995, and also that year received the Thomas Jefferson Award of the University of North Carolina, which recognized leadership in the faculty.

Peacock's dissertation research was published in 1968 (*Rites of Modernization: Symbolic and Social Aspects of Indonesian Proletarian Drama*), and in June 1969 the family—including two daughters by that time—returned to Southeast Asia for further research. Florence and the girls had to come back in December, but Jim remained for eight months, working in Muslim training camps in Indonesia. This work contributed to two volumes published in 1978. He returned to Indonesia in 1979, 1988, and 1996. Also in the late 1960s, Peacock worked with Tom Kirsch to prepare a textbook, *The Human Direction: An Evolutionary Approach to Social and Cultural Anthropology*, published in 1970 and reissued in 1973 and 1980, with a Japanese translation published in 1975. During this period he also wrote *Consciousness and Change* (1975), drawing on the works of Emile Durkheim and Max Weber along with psychological and symbolic anthropology, particularly the work of Victor Turner, to implicate symbol-systems in processes of change; the emphases on historical process and modernity hearken to more recent trends in anthropology, although the approaches differ.

Returning to the southeastern United States afforded Peacock the opportunity to turn his anthropological lens in that direction, and in the 1970s he did research on psychology and culture in religious and psychiatric institutions, faith healing, southern Protestantism and family life, and alcoholism. In some of these projects he collaborated with Ruel Tyson, a colleague in religious studies at the University of North Carolina. Later they wrote together on Appalachian Primitive Baptists (1989). Peacock's work continues a University of North Carolina tradition, begun by Howard Odum, of professional involvement in local issues, which Peacock extended to the legislature and local communities.

In many ways Peacock's work can be characterized, as he did himself in the preface to *Consciousness and Change*, as broadly synthetic across space, time, theoretical perspectives, and disciplinary boundaries: "Such symbolic forms as those of religion, art, ideology, fantasy, dream, and neurosis are customarily treated as separate phenomena, the specialties of separate fields such as the sociology and anthropology of religion, literary criticism, political science, psychology, psychiatry, and psychological anthropology. I strive to show commonalities and linkages, to set forth a unifying framework capable of synthesizing these several phenomena and fields of study" (1975:ix–x). Jim Peacock lives in Chapel Hill with his wife Florence, who has sung professionally in the United States and abroad; all three daughters have grown up and moved out.

FREDERIC W. GLEACH

Yolanda T. Moses
1996–1997

Born on 27 September 1946 and raised in California, Yolanda T. Moses graduated from Perris Union High School in 1964. As a youth, she considered teaching, pharmacy, and social work as potential professions prior to pursuing a career in anthropology and in higher education. Financial hardship had prevented her parents from finishing college, but Moses earned an associate's degree with honors from San Bernardino Valley College in 1966, going on to receive a B.A. in sociology, summa cum laude, from California State University–San Bernardino in 1968.

Moses was disillusioned by sociology's characterization of African American families as deviant: "there was nothing in my life that I had experienced that was abnormal" (Moses interview). As she considered programs for graduate study, she recalled *Margaret Mead's* positive response during a presentation at San Bernadino to a question she had asked about the rise of the Black Power movement in America. She learned that Mead was an anthropologist, and that was a factor in her decision to pursue graduate work in anthropology. In 1970 Moses was among 78 students nationwide to earn one of the Ford Foundation's first round of graduate fellowships aimed at increasing the number of minority Ph.D. students, which at the time was less than 1 percent in all fields of study. She completed her master's and doctoral degrees in anthropology at the University of California–Riverside (UCR) in 1976 with highest honors.

Since none of UCR's anthropology faculty focused on women's issues at the time, Moses first worked with a Caribbeanist (Paul Hooks) and later a Latin Americanist (Michael Kearney) on issues of political identity in Montserrat as the island moved from colonial to independent status. She saw these questions as related to the discourse on racial colonization within the United States at the time. However, her field research hit a snag almost immediately when she learned that Montserrat had decided it was too poor to become independent. Thinking quickly about other phenomena she was observing in the field, she decided to look at the status of women in Montserrat's remittance society. Her study, which involved family and communication networks with Trinidad and Jamaica, was a precursor to current globalization studies of diaspora. Moses's was among the first studies to consider Caribbean women across classes. She later analyzed the role of education in shaping bifurcated family and professional spheres among middle-class women in Kenya.

Having conducted fieldwork on issues of ethnicity/race, class, gender, and education, Moses made a name for herself in multicultural education and cultural diversity. She describes her commitment: "I am a person who takes America literally when it calls itself a democracy. The cornerstone, to me, of a thriving democracy is to have the voices of all of its citizens involved in creating, strengthening, and leading the social institutions in this country. That will not happen unless we have the diversity of all our population involved with higher education. We have talked a good game about it, and it's now time for us to really think strategically about how to make it happen. Democratic engagement in diversity is an investment in the future of democracy. It's no less than that." (Moses interview)

After early visiting professorships at the State University of New York–Plattsburgh and the University of Tennessee–Knoxville, Moses was a professor of social science (anthropology) at California State Polytechnic University (Pomona) from 1977 to 1988. While at Pomona, she also headed the Ethnic and Women's Studies Department and served as dean of the School of Liberal Arts from 1985 to 1988. Between 1988 and 1993 Moses was the vice president for academic affairs at California State University–Dominguez Hills. Then, in 1993, she was appointed president of the City College of New York (CCNY), the largest of the City University of New York's nine campuses. She says her biggest challenge in that position was trying to create an inclusive teaching, learning, and research community within a university environment that valued and rewarded hierarchical structures. Also during her tenure at CCNY, from 1995 to 1997, Moses served as president of the American Anthropological Association, challenging the organization to "look at our history as we think about our future on the eve of the millennium, and . . . reclaim our legacy of defining what race means in the U.S." (Moses interview). She was particularly pleased that the AAA's statement on race was placed on the organization's website, and that the Census Bureau took the AAA's recommendations on race under advisement for the next census. In 2000 Moses was named president of the American Association for Higher Education. She aspires to promote national access to quality higher education and to study the impact of technology on the academy.

In characterizing her administrative work, Moses notes that

Everything that I've learned as an anthropologist I can use in some way as an administrator. . . . What anthropology teaches is how to see the big picture. But you also understand the dynamics of human interaction in large complex hierarchies and organizational structures. Anthropology has trained us, also, to be observers of human behavior in microsettings as well. This has helped me over the years in bringing different groups of people together, problem solving, trying to come to consensus, and deciding when there is no consensus when authority has to be used. In all of these situations, anthropology gives me the ability to fine-tune my decisions. (Moses interview)

Moses's personal life includes collecting antiques, reading, playing racquetball, and spending time with her husband of 28 years, James F. Bawek. Her daughters, Shana and Antonia, are both pursuing careers in anthropology. "I hope to raise another generation of feminist anthropologists of color who can ... bring that anthropological perspective with them to whatever work they do." (Moses interview). She advises, "Pursue your dream, whatever it is. Because in this society— 21st-century United States—you're still going to find discrimination. You're still going to find racism; you're still going to find sexism. But you're just going to have to roll over it" (Moses interview).

L. KAIFA ROLAND

Jane H. Hill
1998–1999

Jane Hassler Hill was born in Berkeley, California, on 27 October 1939. Her father was a physicist and her mother a botanist. Both parents were on the faculty at the University of California, Los Angeles, though her father spent most of his career in industry; the UCLA Botanical Garden is named after Hill's mother: the Mildred E. Mathias Garden. Except for a brief two-year period at UCLA's University Elementary School, Hill attended public schools in Los Angeles.

Hill's roots in academia led her to a scholarly career from the outset. She first attended Reed College but transferred to University of California, Berkeley, after two years, graduating in 1960 with a B.A. and the departmental award in anthropology. She took classes with Clifford Geertz, Robert Murphy, John Rowe, *Sherwood Washburn*, and Seth Leacock, among others. Herbert Landar at Reed and William Jacobsen at Berkeley were also significant influences at this stage of Hill's career, even though both were junior faculty at the time. Hill originally wanted to be an archaeologist, but the Berkeley Field School did not admit women at the time—ostensibly to avoid digging extra latrines. David French, who had mentored her at Reed, and William Shipley at Berkeley were the first instructors to inculcate in her an interest in the anthropology of language.

A sentimental breakup led Hill to study anthropology at UCLA instead of the University of Pennsylvania, where she had originally planned to initiate her graduate career. The new program in linguistics at UCLA had space for a last-minute applicant, which also contributed to her eventual entry into what was shaping up to be her life's work in linguistic anthropology. By then Hill had already spent two summers in Peru, participating in an ethnopharmacological expedition led by her mother and by Dermot Taylor of the UCLA Medical School. This first taste of Latin American fieldwork further shaped her career trajectory.

At the time, UCLA required students to spend several days being tested in order to determine what coursework they required. On the strength of her excellent training at Reed and Berkeley, Hill tested so well that she was not required to do any coursework. But, to her credit, she decided to take courses with Pedro Carrasco, Aidan Southall, M. G. Smith, Phil Newman, and Joseph Birdsell. She continued her work in linguistics under the guidance of William Bright, *Harry Hoijer*, and Robert Stockwell. While doing her master's degree in linguistics at UCLA, she met her future husband and professional collaborator, Kenneth C. Hill, whom she married in August 1961; they had three children, Eric, Harold, and Amy. After obtaining her M.A. in 1962, Hill decided to go on to a Ph.D in anthropology.

Hill wrote her dissertation on Cupeño grammar, a Uto-Aztecan language of southern California, and defended it in 1966. By an interesting coincidence, her work with a small community of the language's last indigenous speakers became her first incursion into issues of language "death." Shortly after Hill wrote her dissertation, the then-archivist of the Lowie Museum at Berkeley, Dale Valory, found a batch of field notes on Cupeño collected by one of *Alfred L. Kroeber*'s students, Paul-Louis Faye. With funding from the American Philosophical Society, Hill worked on the notes, remarking upon the differences between Faye's documentation and hers. This led her to study the structural effects of language attrition among members of speech communities and to her work among Nahuatl speakers, where larger speech communities would facilitate statistical analysis.

Hill and her husband spent years researching the Mexicano Nahuatl–speaking communities in the Malinche region of Puebla and Tlaxcala, originally focusing on the structural impact of language obsolescence. While doing this fieldwork she began to move away from her roots in American structural linguistics, becoming more interested in how speakers use speech strategically and manipulate their knowledge of local speech repertoires. She was also influenced by then-emerging theoretical paradigms on the relationship between language, culture, and society: Hymes's initial elaboration of an ethnography of speaking, ethnomethodology, and Bakhtin/Volosinov, once translations of his work began to appear in the United States in the early 1980s, (Hill 1985).

This intellectual shift led to one of Hill's first major publications, *Speaking Mexicano* (1986), coauthored with her husband. It also placed her at the forefront of new lines of inquiry in linguistic anthropology that have significantly advanced the field in the last 20 years (Blount 1995, Grillo 1988). Eventually, Hill's interest in speakers' strategic deployment of linguistic resources led to her work on language and racism, which establishes how Anglo-American speakers exploit language's indexicality by using deficient, ungrammatical, and spurious forms of Spanish (thus, "mock" Spanish) to racialize Latinos (e.g., Hill 1993).

Hill began her teaching career at Wayne State University, where she became departmental head and active in the American Association of University Professors' union efforts. Since 1983 she has taught at the University of Arizona, where she holds the title Regents Professor. This location has facilitated a return to her first interest, Native American languages. In addition to her work on "mock" Spanish, racism, and ideology, she is currently studying Tohono O'odham dialectology with Ofelia Zepeda. The speech community's interest in having better access to the material has led her to revisit her dissertation work on

Cupeño grammar. Hill has also been working recently on historical linguistics, especially within the context of the history of the Uto-Aztecan peoples.

Hill's apparently placid scholarly life has been disrupted by family illness. One of Hill's three children—her daughter, Amy—was diagnosed with schizophrenia and died at a relatively early age. The Southern Arizona chapter of the Alliance for the Mentally Ill was a crucial resource for Hill and her family in coping with this illness.

Hill sees herself as a linguist working within the "Boasian synthesis." She is interested in how the study of language can contribute to a synthetic understanding of the human condition and its history. She has challenged a deterministic perspective in relating language distribution and human history and sees herself as a generalist who has not been able to resist tangents, precisely as the Boasian synthesis so productively presupposes. Hill's service as president of the American Anthropological Association demonstrated the breadth of her anthropological vision across subdisciplines and specializations. In addition to anthropological societies, Hill is a member of the American Academy of Arts and Sciences.

VILMA SANTIAGO–IRIZARRY

Louise Lamphere
1999–2001

Louise Lamphere was born in St. Louis, Missouri, in October 1940; her younger sister was born in February 1943. She grew up in Denver, imbibing from childhood the identity of a Westerner. Her mother, Miriam Bretschneider Lamphere, came from a German-American family in Golden, Colorado. Louise's maternal grandfather worked for the railroad, and then taught himself geology and explored oil fields, first for Sinclair Oil and later independently. His oil investments survived the Great Depression, allowing him to build a large house in East Denver. He was a workaholic patriarch who controlled the women of his family. Louise's father, Harold Lamphere, was the son of a Northern Irish mother, who ran a boarding house to put her son through college, and a jack-of-all-trades father from Montana. Harold became a patent lawyer, making a modest living. In 1945 the family returned to Denver, living near Miriam's parents in a white middle-class Protestant neighborhood where Louise attended public school. In 1954 her father died of a heart attack at age 49; her mother became even more dependent on her parents, who supported the small family. Louise attended a large urban high school where her academic abilities kept her an outsider. She graduated first in her class, edited the school newspaper in her senior year, had her own telephone, and drove a red convertible.

Lamphere entered Stanford University in 1958, receiving her B.A. in 1962. In her first year she converted to atheism and social science, majoring in sociology; she wrote an honors thesis in the interdisciplinary program Social Thought and Institutions. Her role models were Harvard-trained; she enjoyed seminar evenings in faculty homes but failed to notice that the wives had neither independent careers nor secure jobs at Stanford. Lamphere spent a year in Germany with Stanford Abroad, acquired a network of friends, and began to study anthropology in her final two years.

With a National Science Foundation grant, Lamphere entered the interdisciplinary Social Relations Department at Harvard, receiving an M.A. in 1966 and a Ph.D. in 1968. Her graduate cohort was middle-class and about half women, although the undergraduate program was dominated by elite private school alumni. *Cora Du Bois* was the only tenured woman in Anthropology, Sociology, and Psychology.

Fieldwork on the Navajo Reservation took Lamphere back to the West, although overseas fieldwork was considered more prestigious. She lived with Navajo families, initially as part of the Harvard/Cornell/Columbia field school that placed students in Ramah, the Navajo community studied by *Clyde Kluckhohn*. Although she has never mastered the language, this initial fieldwork established relationships with Navajo women that persist today. She was attracted to values of autonomy and cooperation, in a place where women's roles were not subordinated to those of men (Lamphere 1977). Despite cultural change and widespread social problems, this distinctive culture persists. Her forthcoming book, *Weaving Together Women's Lives: Three Generations in a Navajo Family* builds a personal narrative around a shared political economy, demonstrating how fieldwork has become more dialogic, and how "home" and "field" may be indistinguishable when one works in the United States.

After a year at the University of Rochester, in 1968 Lamphere accepted a tenure-track assistant professorship in the all-male Department of Sociology and Anthropology at Brown University. Consciousness-raising through the antiwar and women's movements increasingly merged politics and professional life. Personal rebellion against permanent-waved hair, make-up, skirts, and conventional marriage led her to wonder "how women in other classes and ethnic groups dealt with issues of marriage, ordinary wage jobs, and child rearing" (Lamphere MS:10). In 1971–72, at the London School of Economics on an NSF postdoctoral fellowship, she tried to find out. On her return she moved into a "collective house" with a group that included her partner Peter Evans (father of her son Peter Bret); this location and support network anchored her life in Providence, Rhode Island.

Despite an excellent publication record and supportive graduate students, Lamphere was denied tenure in 1974, without prior warning. An internal grievance committee acknowledged that procedures were not followed but denied any discrimination or breach of academic freedom. Lamphere filed a Title VII class-action suit in federal court. Brown University consistently refused to provide documentation (which ultimately demonstrated sexist allusions and collusion to deny her tenure). Brown's new president urged an out-of-court settlement. In September 1977 Lamphere and three of her colleagues received tenure or damages; the settlement mandated a procedure at Brown for women alleging discrimination, establishing a claims fund and an affirmative action monitoring process. Lamphere returned to Brown in 1979.

The Lamphere case transformed Brown University's hiring practices and was almost unique in effectively mobilizing class action against discrimination in faculty hiring and retention (Sizer 1991, Abel 1981). The case documented Brown's appalling gender record. Brown discharged the consent decree only in 1992, with conditions. Lamphere believes that "suing Brown was the most important thing I have done" (MS:20).

Lamphere taught at the University of New Mexico as an associate professor in 1976–77 and 1978–79, remaining as an adjunct professor during the years in which she returned to Brown (1979–85). In 1985 she was promoted to professor at Brown and then returned to New Mexico, where she became professor of anthropology (1986), University Regents Professor (1999), and Distinguished Professor (2001).

Feminism easily spilled over into the classroom. Lamphere collaborated with Michelle Rosaldo at Stanford in editing *Woman, Culture, and Society* (1974), which has sold over 60,000 copies. The central problematic was sexual asymmetry and the universality of female subordination. In 1997 Lamphere edited *Situated Lives: Gender and Culture in Everyday Life* with Helena Ragoné and Patricia Zavella.

Much of Lamphere's recent work analyzes ethnicity, power, and gender in contemporary American society. She studied the cultural shift from working daughters to working mothers among immigrant women in the industrialized Northeast (Lamphere 1987), and then turned to how working mothers manage family and factory in the Sunbelt (Lamphere et al. 1993). Her edited *Structuring Diversity: Ethnographic Perspectives on the New Immigration* (1992) reports on a team project studying newcomers and established residents in six American cities. Both at Brown and at New Mexico, she has done fieldwork in the communities where she lives.

Lamphere was president of the American Ethnological Society from 1987 to 1989 and of the American Anthropological Association from 1999 to 2001. She received the Conrad Arensberg Award from the Society for the Anthropology of Work in 1994, the Society for the Anthropology of North America Prize for Critical Study of North America from the Society for the Anthropology of North America in 1995, and the Squeaky Wheel Award of the AAA Status of Women Committee in 1998.

REGNA DARNELL

Donald Brenneis
2001–2003

D onald Lawrence "Don" Brenneis was born on 2 February
1946 in San Francisco, California. He earned his B.A. in 1967
from the Anthropology and Humanities Honors Program at
Stanford University, where Robert Textor guided his emergent focus
on political anthropology. On 5 July 1969 Brenneis married Wynne
Furth, who also had a B.A. from Stanford and went on to earn a J.D.
from the Harvard Law School and to practice law in California. The
couple has one daughter, Valance Elisabeth Furth Brenneis, who is currently teaching in a New York City public school.

In 1969 Brenneis entered the graduate program in Social Anthropology at Harvard University, where he received his Ph.D. in 1974. At
Harvard he worked with Klaus-Friedrich Koch, Keith Kernan, and
Claudia Mitchell-Kernan, all of whom helped shape his interests in the
intersection of language and social and political life. Brenneis made a
preliminary field trip to Fiji during the summer of 1970, returning for

extended work between 1971 and 1973, and for summer research in 1975 and 1980. Funded by a U.S. National Institute of Mental Health grant for which Koch was the principal investigator, Brenneis conducted research in a Fiji Indian community, Bhatgaon, on village-level dispute management. Brenneis's position as a research associate on the NIMH grant also involved supervising research projects on dispute settlement by students of the University of the South Pacific in Suva, Fiji. Wynne participated actively in fieldwork on Fiji, doing research in a Fijian magistrate's court, where her specialization in municipal and administrative law, coupled with a keen ethnographic eye and ear, served her well. Wynne's legal training and experience has also contributed to Don's analyses of dispute resolution processes and legal systems.

In a steady stream of essays over more than 20 years, Brenneis has explored the social consequentiality of talk and other kinds of performance, concentrating on local genres and psychological-aesthetic principles, the constructive role of audiences in aesthetic performances, and the creative "invention" of Hindu traditions from India in the radically different context of Fiji Indian communities. The Bhatgaon material in particular led Brenneis to the question of how people who think they should be treated as equals interact, a state of affairs growing out of the leveling of Indian caste distinctions that the historical experience of emigration entailed in Fiji. In Bhatgaon, Brenneis found a corresponding democratization of both sacred and secular knowledge, and his studies of Fiji Indian *talanoa* (idle chatter or gossip), *pancayat* (a public event for the mediation of disputes), *bhajan* (devotional songs), and other genres consistently explored the link between social relationships (including the norms that inform them) and the performances that bring them to life and transform them.

In collaboration with Fred Myers, Brenneis coedited *Dangerous Words: Language and Politics in the Pacific* (1984). In their seminal introduction to this volume, Brenneis and Myers addressed the ways in which social actors draw upon language in order to reproduce the local political order; as regards egalitarian societies, they challenged conventional assumptions about egalitarianism as a "natural" condition of unranked small-scale societies. Brenneis documents how, through the use of particular speech genres, participants in dispute resolution processes purposely reconstitute "equality" and deflect conflict among social actors who have differential access to material and symbolic resources. The focus on the interconnections among language, law, social structure, and political processes was an important contribution to contemporary scholarship, as it stressed the constitutive role of language in social practice.

In the mid-1990s Brenneis pursued his research on the relationship between performance and egalitarian social relations in a new venue when (putting to good use his, by then, extensive editorial experience) he began work on peer review and related practices at the National Science Foundation (Brenneis 1994). He argued that on review panels the work of negotiating an ongoing amiable sociability among peers could make it difficult to find truly innovative research proposals (Brenneis 1999). During this period he also coedited, with Ronald Macaulay, *The Matrix of Language* (1996), a reader in contemporary linguistic anthropology.

Brenneis taught at Pitzer College (Claremont, California) from 1973 to 1996, beginning as an assistant professor, winning promotion to associate professor in 1979 and to professor in 1984, and serving as acting dean of the Faculty in 1985. In 1996 he moved to the University of California, Santa Cruz, as professor and chair of the Anthropology Board of Studies. Throughout his career he has been extraordinarily active both in editorial work and in the governance of professional associations. In 1982–83 he served as the editor of the *Newsletter of the Association for Political and Legal Anthropology* (precursor to POLAR) and in 1989 he began a five-year term as editor of *American Ethnologist*. Brenneis (personal communication) described his work with *American Ethnologist* as "intellectually exhilarating" and "a wonderful way to get a sense of the diversity and vitality of what we're all up to." He has also served on the editorial board of *Papers in Pragmatics* (1986–89), *Cultural Anthropology* (1995–2000), and *Ethos* (1997–) as well as on the Publications Committee of the American Anthropological Association (1994–97).

In addition to editorial responsibilities, Brenneis has served as program chair or cochair for annual meetings of the Association for Social

Anthropology in Oceania (1981, 1982), the California Folklore Society (1985), and the Society for Cultural Anthropology (1990, 1992). He was a member of the Board of Directors of the Society for Cultural Anthropology from 1988 to 1993 and served as the representative of the American Ethnological Society to the American Association for the Advancement of Science from 1995 to 1998.

RICHARD HANDLER

References

Listed for each biographee are works cited in the biographical sketch, along with the principal sources of information on the biographees and selected works by them. Not specifically cited are general sources of personal data such as listings in *Who's Who*, *Contemporary Authors*, *Modern Men and Women of Science*, *Biographical Index*, and so forth; these sources are readily available through the Biography and Genealogy Master Index, an online reference tool maintained by The Gale Group and available through most major research libraries.

Complete lists of publications are available for many of these biographees, typically in an obituary in a professional journal or a festschrift or other memorial collection. For some, however, these wonderful research tools seem never to have been prepared, and they have become exceptional in more recent years as many publishers feel they are a waste of valuable publication space. Future researchers will lament this decision.

Where Are Their Papers?

The professional archives of anthropologists can end up in a variety of locations, from home institutions to research libraries; often papers are in multiple locations, and some of these locations can be difficult to find. Some people begin archiving their papers long before death; for others it is a postmortem decision made by the family or colleagues. Certain letters and memos have circulated in copies passed from hand to hand for decades. Many documents are destroyed, lost, or uncataloged; some even *should* be destroyed, to protect confidentiality agreements, for example. Others may be archived with a date restriction, not to be seen until a certain time has passed. The researcher must be sensitive to such issues when doing archival research.

When in doubt as to the location of someone's papers, a good starting point is always the National Anthropological Archives at the Smithsonian Institution. They maintain on their website a catalog of locations for anthropologists' papers; at this time the url is *http://www.nmnh.si.edu/naa/other_archives.htm*, but it can always be found by searching from the Smithsonian homepage. Also, many libraries now have their archival holdings cataloged and available through Research Libraries Information Network (RLIN); a reference librarian can help with this resource.

For convenience, we have included here the known major locations for the papers of the American Anthropological Association presidents, as we have record of them. This list may not be exhaustive, so the researcher should inquire creatively for other possible sources.

Archive Abbreviations

AMNH:	American Museum of Natural History, Department of Anthropology, New York
APS:	American Philosophical Society Library, Philadelphia
ASHL:	Alaska State Historical Library, Juneau
ASM:	Arizona State Museum Archives, University of Arizona, Tucson
BU–H:	Haffenreffer Museum of Anthropology, Brown University, Providence RI
BMC:	Bryn Mawr College, Department of Anthropology, Bryn Mawr PA
BSU:	Ball State University, Department of Anthropology Archives, Muncie IN
CathU:	Catholic University, Department of Archives, Manuscripts, and Museum Collections, Washington DC
CMC:	Canadian Museum of Civilization Archives (formerly National Museum of Man), Ottawa
CU–B:	Columbia University, Butler Library, New York
FMA:	Field Museum of Natural History Archives, Chicago
HU–P:	Pusey Library, Archives, Harvard University, Cambridge
Iowa:	University of Iowa Libraries, Iowa City
LC:	Library of Congress, Manuscript Division, Washington DC
MAI:	Museum of the American Indian, Heye Foundation, Archives, now located in the National Museum of the American Indian Archives, Silver Spring MD
MNA:	Museum of Northern Arizona, Harold S. Colton Research Center, Flagstaff
MNM:	Museum of New Mexico Library, Santa Fe
MPM:	Milwaukee Public Museum
NAA:	National Anthropological Archives, Smithsonian Institution, Washington DC
NAES:	NAES College Archives, Chicago
NL:	Newberry Library, Chicago

NMAA:	Library of the National Museum of American Art and the National Portrait Gallery, Smithsonian Institution, Washington DC
NWT:	Northwest Territories Archives, Prince of Wales Northern Heritage Center, Yellowknife
Penn:	University of Pennsylvania, University Museum Archives, Philadelphia
PM:	Peabody Museum of Archaeology and Ethnology, Harvard University, Cambridge
RC–S:	Schlesinger Library, Radcliffe College, Cambridge
Swarth:	Friends Historical Library, Swarthmore College, Swarthmore PA
SWM:	Southwest Museum, Braun Research Library, Los Angeles
UC:	University of Chicago Library
UCB:	University of California, Berkeley
UCB–B:	Bancroft Library, University of California, Berkeley
UCR:	University of California, Riverside
UCLA:	University of California, Los Angeles
UCSD:	Melanesian Archive, University of California, San Diego
UF:	University of Florida, Gainesville
UIUC:	University of Illinois at Urbana-Champaign, University Archives
UM–B:	Bentley Historical Library, University of Michigan, Ann Arbor
UWM:	Golda Meir Library, Archives, University of Wisconsin-Milwaukee
Vassar:	Vassar College Libraries, Poughkeepsie NY
WHC:	Western History Collections, University of Oklahoma, Norman

Introduction and Suggested Readings

Included here in addition to the works cited in the introduction is a selection of works dealing with facets of the past century of American anthropology. These are intended only to suggest starting points for further reading. Not specifically listed but also recommended are the four volumes *American Anthropology: Selected Papers from the "American Anthropologist,"* edited by Frederica de Laguna (1888–20), George W. Stocking Jr. (1921–45), Robert F. Murphy (1946–70), and Regna Darnell (1971–95), and the volumes (nine at present) in the *History of Anthropology* series published by the University of Wisconsin Press, edited by George Stocking (vols. 1–8) and Richard Handler (vols. 9–). We also suggest the *History of Anthropology Newsletter, Historiographia Linguistica,* and the *Journal of the History of the Behavioral Sciences* for articles in disciplinary history. Soon it will be possible to download the full text of articles on the history of anthropology published in the *American Anthropologist* from the Web site of the General Anthropology Division of the AAA, a project undertaken by Jonathan Marks.

AAA. 1966. American Anthropological Association. 1966. American Anthropological Association Council Meeting, Saturday, 20 November 1965, Denver co. *American Anthropologist* 68: 759–773.

Ames, Michael M. 1992. *Cannibal Tours and Glass Boxes: The Anthropology of Museums.* Vancouver: University of British Columbia Press.

Baker, Lee D. 1998. *From Savage to Negro: Anthropology and the Construction of Race, 1896–1954.* Berkeley: University of California Press.

Barkan, Elazar. 1992. *The Retreat of Scientific Racism: Changing Concepts of Race in Britain and the United States between the World Wars.* Cambridge: Cambridge University Press.

Bieder, Robert E. 1986. *Science Encounters the Indian, 1880–1920: The Early Years of American Ethnology.* Norman: University of Oklahoma Press.

———. 1992. The Collecting of Bones for Anthropological Narratives. *American Indian Culture and Research Journal* 16(2): 21–35.

Boas, Franz. 1902. The Foundation of a National Anthropological Society. *Science* n.s., 15(386): 804–809.

———. 1940. The Aims of Ethnology [1888]. In *Race, Language and Culture.* New York: Macmillan.

Bowler, Peter J. 1986. *Theories of Human Evolution: A Century of Debate, 1844–1944.* Baltimore: Johns Hopkins University Press.

Brew, J. O., ed. 1968. *One Hundred Years of Anthropology.* Cambridge: Harvard University Press.

Clifford, James. 1988. *The Predicament of Culture: Twentieth-Century Ethnography, Literature, and Art.* Cambridge: Harvard University Press.

Cohn, Bernard S. 1981. Anthropology and History in the 1980s: Towards a Rapprochement. *The Journal of Interdisciplinary History* 12:227–252.

Cole, Douglas. 1985. *Captured Heritage: The Scramble for Northwest Coast Artifacts.* Seattle: University of Washington Press.

———. 1999. *Franz Boas: The Early Years, 1858–1906.* Seattle: University of Washington Press.

Darnell, Regna, ed. 1974. *Readings in the History of Anthropology.* New York: Harper and Row.

———. 1998. *And Along Came Boas: Continuity and Revolution in Americanist Anthropology.* Amsterdam: John Benjamins.

———. 2001. *Invisible Genealogies: A History of Americanist Anthropology.* Lincoln: University of Nebraska Press.

Deloria, Vine Jr. 1969. Anthropologists and Other Friends. In *Custer Died for Your Sins.* New York: Macmillan.

———. 1973. Some Criticisms and a Number of Suggestions. In *Anthropology and the American Indian: A Symposium.* San Francisco: The Indian Historian Press.

———. 1995. *Red Earth, White Lies: Native Americans and the Myth of Scientific Fact.* New York: Scribner.

Eggan, Fred. 1943. The American Anthropological Association. *American Association for the Advancement of Science Bulletin* 2(5): 38.

Erickson, Paul A., and Liam D. Murphy, eds. 2001. *Readings for a History of Anthropological Theory*. Peterborough and New York: Broadview Press.

Frantz, Charles. 1974. Structuring and Restructuring of the American Anthropological Association. Paper presented at the American Anthropological Association annual meeting; on file at AAA offices.

Gacs, Ute, Aisha Khan, Jerrie McIntyre, and Ruth Weinberg, eds. 1989. *Women Anthropologists: Selected Biographies*. Urbana: University of Illinois Press.

Givens, Douglas R. 1992. *Alfred Vincent Kidder and the Development of Americanist Archaeology*. Albuquerque: University of New Mexico Press.

Gould, Stephen Jay. 1983. *Mare's Eggs and Hen's Teeth*. New York: Norton.

Greenwood, Davydd. 1999. "Inhumanities" and "Inaction" Research: An Uncertain Future for Anthropology. *Anthropology Newsletter* 40(4): 56.

Hallowell, A. Irving. 1960. The Beginnings of Anthropology in America. In *Selected Papers from the American Anthropologist*, Frederica de Laguna, ed. Evanston: Row, Peterson and Co.

———. 1965. The History of Anthropology as an Anthropological Problem. *Journal of the History of the Behavioral Sciences* 1: 24–38.

Harris, Marvin. 1968. *The Rise of Anthropological Theory*. New York: Thomas Crowell.

Harrison, Ira E., and Faye V. Harrison, eds. 1999. *African-American Pioneers in Anthropology*. Urbana: University of Illinois Press.

Helm, June, ed. 1966. *Pioneers of American Anthropology: The Uses of Biography*. American Ethnological Society Monograph 43. Seattle: University of Washington Press.

Helms, Mary W. 1988. *Ulysses Sail: An Ethnographic Odyssey of Power, Knowledge, and Geographical Distance*. Princeton: Princeton University Press.

Hinsley, Curtis M. 1994. *The Smithsonian and the American Indian: Making a Moral Anthropology in Victorian America*. Washington: Smithsonian Institution Press. [originally published as *Savages and Scientists*, 1981]

Hockett, Charles. 1979. Forgotten Goals and Unfinished Business in Anthropology. *American Anthropologist* 81:640–643.

Hodgen, Margaret T. 1964. *Early Anthropology in the Sixteenth and Seventeenth Centuries*. Philadelphia: University of Pennsylvania Press.

Honigmann, John J. *The Development of Anthropological Ideas*. Homewood IL: The Dorsey Press.

Hymes, Dell. 1983. *Essays in the History of Linguistic Anthropology*. Amsterdam: John Benjamins.

Hymes, Dell, ed. 1972. *Reinventing Anthropology*. New York: Pantheon Books.

———, ed. 1974. *Studies in the History of Linguistics: Traditions and Paradigms*. Bloomington: Indiana University Press.

Judd, Neil M. 1967. *The Bureau of American Ethnology: A Partial History*. Norman: University of Oklahoma Press.

Kehoe, Alice B. 1998. *The Land of Prehistory: A Critical History of American Archaeology.* New York: Routledge.

Kehoe, Alice B., and Mary Beth Emmerichs, eds. 1999. *Assembling the Past: Studies in the Professionalization of Archaeology.* Albuquerque: University of New Mexico Press.

Kroeber, A. L. 1959. The History of the Personality of Anthropology. *American Anthropologist* 61: 398–403.

Kuper, Adam. 1999. *Culture: The Anthropologists' Account.* Cambridge: Harvard University Press.

Lowie, Robert H. 1937. *The History of Ethnological Theory.* New York: Rinehart and Co.

Mark, Joan. 1980. *Four Anthropologists: An American Science in its Early Years.* New York: Science History Publications.

McGee, W J. 1902. A Proposed American Anthropologic Association. *Science* n.s., 15(391): 1035–1036.

———. 1903. The American Anthropological Association. *American Anthropologist* n.s., 5: 178–192.

Michrina, Barry. 2001. Brightness in San Francisco. *Anthropology News* 42(1): 58–59.

Murra, John V., ed. 1976. *American Anthropology: The Early Years.* 1974 Proceedings of the American Ethnological Society. St. Paul: West.

Murray, Stephen O. 1994. *Theory Groups and the Study of Language in North America.* Amsterdam: John Benjamins.

Ortiz, Alfonso. 1973. An Indian Anthropologist's Perspective on Anthropology. In *Anthropology and the American Indian: A Symposium.* San Francisco: The Indian Historian Press.

Parezo, Nancy J., ed. 1993. *Hidden Scholars: Women Anthropologists and the Native American Southwest.* Albuquerque: University of New Mexico Press.

Patterson, Thomas C. 2001. *A Social History of Anthropology in the United States.* Oxford: Berg.

Radin, Paul. 1966. *The Method and Theory of Ethnology: An Essay in Criticism* [1933]. New York: Basic Books.

Reader, John. 1981. *Missing Links: The Hunt for Earliest Man.* Boston: Little, Brown.

Reyman, Jonathan E., ed. 1992. *Rediscovering Our Past: Essays on the History of American Archaeology.* Aldershot, Hampshire UK: Avebury.

Silverman, Sydel, ed. 1981. *Totems and Teachers: Perspectives on the History of Anthropology.* New York: Columbia University Press.

Spencer, Frank. 1997. *History of Physical Anthropology: An Encyclopedia.* New York: Garland.

Spencer, Frank, ed. 1982. *A History of Physical Anthropology, 1930–1980.* New York: Academic Press.

Stocking, George W. 1960. Franz Boas and the Founding of the American Anthropological Association. *American Anthropologist* 62: 1–17.

———. 1968. *Race, Culture, and Evolution: Essays in the Historiography of Anthropology.* New York: Free Press.

———. 1987. *Victorian Anthropology*. New York: Free Press.

———. 1992. *The Ethnographers Magic and Other Essays in the History of Anthropology*. Madison: University of Wisconsin Press.

Sturtevant, William C. 1966. Anthropology, History, and Ethnohistory. *Ethnohistory* 13 (1–2): 1–51.

Thoresen, Timothy H. H. 1975. *Toward a Science of Man: Essays in the History of Anthropology*. The Hague: Mouton.

Trencher, Susan. 2000. *Mirrored Images: American Anthropology and American Culture*. 1960–1980. Westport CT: Bergin and Garvey.

Valentine, Lisa Philips, and Regna Darnell, eds. 1999. *Theorizing the Americanist Tradition*. Toronto: University of Toronto Press.

Voget, Fred W. 1975. *A History of Ethnology*. New York: Holt, Rinehart and Winston.

Willey, Gordon R. 1988. *Portraits in American Archaeology: Remembrances of some Distinguished Americanists*. Albuquerque: University of New Mexico Press.

Willey, Gordon R. and Jeremy A. Sabloff. 1980. *A History of American Archaeology*, second edition. San Francisco: W. H. Freeman and Co.

Winters, Christopher, ed. 1991. *International Dictionary of Anthropologists*. New York: Garland.

Zimmerman, Larry J. 1992. Archaeology, Reburial, and the Tactics of a Discipline's Self-Delusion. *American Indian Culture and Research Journal* 16(2): 37–56.

References for Individual Sketches

W J MCGEE, 1902–1904
Papers: LC, NAA

Darnell, Regna. 1998. *And Along Came Boas: Continuity and Revolution in Americanist Anthropology*. Amsterdam and Philadelphia: John Benjamins.

Hinsley, Curtis M., Jr. 1981. *Savages and Scientists: The Smithsonian Institution and the Development of American Anthropology 1846–1910*. Washington DC: Smithsonian Institution.

Hodge, Frederick Webb. 1912. W J McGee. *American Anthropologist* 14: 683–687.

McGee, Emma. 1915. *The Life of W J McGee*. Farley IA: privately printed.

McGee, W J. 1897. The Bureau of American Ethnology. In *The Smithsonian Institution 1846–96*, G. Brown Goode, ed. Washington DC: Devine Press.

———. 1898. The Seri Indians. *17th Annual Report of the Bureau of American Ethnology*, 1–334. Washington DC: GPO.

———. 1899. The Trend of Human Progress. *American Anthropologist* 1: 401–447.

———. 1901. Man's Place in Nature. *American Anthropologist* 3: 1–13.

West, Terry. 1992. *W J McGee and Conservation as Applied Anthropology*. Washington DC: USDA Forest Service.

FREDERIC WARD PUTNAM, 1905–1906
Papers: AMNH, PM

Dexter, Ralph. 1970. The Role of F. W. Putnam in Founding the Field Museum. *Curator* 13: 21–36.

Dexter, Ralph W. 1979. The Impact of Evolutionary Theories on the Salem Group of Agassiz Zoologists (Morse, Hyatt, Packard, Putnam). *Essex Institute Historical Collections* 115(3): 129–171.

Dixon, Roland B. 1915. Frederic W. Putnam. *Harvard Graduate's Magazine* 24: 305–308.

Kroeber, A. L. 1915. Frederic Ward Putnam. *American Anthropologist* n.s., 17: 712–718.

Patterson, Thomas C. 2001. *A Social History of Anthropology in the United States.* Oxford: Berg.

Tozzer, Alfred M. 1935. Frederic Ward Putnam, 1839–1915. *National Academy of Science, Biographical Memoirs* 16: 125–153.

FRANZ BOAS, 1907–1908
Papers: AMNH, APS, CU–B, FMA

Boas, Franz. 1888. *The Central Eskimo.* Bureau of American Ethnology Annual Report 6. Washington DC: GPO.

———. 1911a. Introduction to the *Handbook of American Indian Languages.* Washington DC: Smithsonian Institution.

———. 1911b. *The Mind of Primitive Man.* New York: Macmillan.

———. 1940. *Race, Langage and Culture.* New York: Free Press.

Cole, Douglas. 2000. *Franz Boas: The Early Years, 1858–1906.* Vancouver: Douglas and McIntyre.

Darnell, Regna. 1998. *And Along Came Boas: Continuity and Revolution in Americanist Anthropology.* Amsterdam: John Benjamins.

———. 2001. *Invisible Genealogies: A History of Americanist Anthropology.* Lincoln: University of Nebraska Press.

Franz Boas, 1858–1942. Memoir 61 of the American Anthropological Association. *American Anthropologist* 45(3, pt. 2). 1943.

Goldschmidt, Walter, ed. 1959. *The Anthropology of Franz Boas: Essays on the Centennial of His Birth.* American Anthropological Association Memoir 89. *American Anthropologist* 61 (5, pt. 2).

Jonaitis, Aldona, ed. 1995. *A Wealth of Thought: Franz Boas on Native American Art.* Seattle: University of Washington Press.

Lévi-Strauss, Claude, and Didier Eribon. 1991. *Conversations with Claude Lévi-Strauss.* Paula Wissing, trans. Chicago: University of Chicago Press.

Lowie, Robert H. 1947. Franz Boas, 1858–1942. *National Academy of Science, Biographical Memoirs* 24: 303–322.

Stocking, George W., Jr. 1968. *Race, Culture and Evolution: Essays in the Historiography of Anthropology.* New York: Free Press.

Stocking, George W., Jr., ed. 1974. *The Shaping of American Anthropology, 1883–1911.* New York: Basic Books.

WILLIAM HENRY HOLMES, 1909–1910
Papers: NAA, NMAA

Hinsley, Curtis M. 1994. *The Smithsonian and the American Indian: Making a Moral An-thropology in Victorian America*. Washington DC: Smithsonian Institution. [origi-nally published as *Savages and Scientists*, 1981]

Holmes, William Henry. 1884. Prehistoric Textile Fabrics of the United States, Derived from Impressions on Pottery. In *Third Annual Report of the Bureau of American Ethnology*. Washington DC: GPO.

———. 1885. Evidences of the Antiquity of Man on the Site of the City of Mexico. *Transactions of the Anthropological Society of Washington* 3: 68–81.

———. 1892. Modern Quarry Refuse and the Paleolithic Theory. *Science* 20: 295–297.

———. 1897. Stone Implements of the Potomac-Chesapeake Tidewater Province. In *Fifteenth Annual Report of the Bureau of American Ethnology*. Washington DC: GPO.

———. 1903. Aboriginal Pottery of the Eastern United States. *Twentieth Annual Report of the Bureau of American Ethnology*. Washington DC: GPO.

———. 1906. Decorative Art of the Aborigines of Northern America. In *Anthropologi-cal Papers Written in Honor of Franz Boas*. New York: Stechert.

———. 1909. Biographical Memoir of Lewis Henry Morgan, 1818–1881. *Biographical Memoirs of the National Academy of Sciences* 6: 219–239.

Hough, Walter. 1933. William Henry Holmes. *American Anthropologist* n.s., 35: 752–765.

Judd, Neil M. 1967. *The Bureau of American Ethnology: A Partial History*. Norman: Uni-versity of Oklahoma Press.

Mark, Joan. 1980. William Henry Holmes. In *Four Anthropologists: An American Science in its Early Years*. New York: Science History Publications.

Stocking, George W. 1968. The Scientific Reaction Against Cultural Anthropology, 1917–1920. In *Race, Culture, and Evolution: Essays in the Historiography of Anthro-pology*. New York: Free Press.

Willey, Gordon R., and Jeremy A. Sabloff. 1980. *A History of American Archaeology*, sec-ond edition. San Francisco: W. H. Freeman and Co.

JESSE WALTER FEWKES, 1911–1912
Papers: NAA

Anon. 1916. Fewkes, Jesse Walter. *The National Cyclopædia of American Biography* 15: 32–33.

Fewkes, Jesse Walter. 1890. On the Use of the Edison Phonograph in the Preservation of the Languages of the American Indians. *Nature* 41: 560.

———. 1898. The Winter Solstice Ceremony at Walpi. *American Anthropologist* o.s., 11: 65–87, 101–115.

———. 1903. Hopi Katchinas, Drawn by Native Artists. In *Twenty-First Annual Report of the Bureau of American Ethnology*. Washington DC: GPO.

———. 1907. The Aborigines of Porto Rico and Neighboring Islands. In *Twenty-Fifth Annual Report of the Bureau of American Ethnology*. Washington DC: GPO.

———. 1912. Casa Grande, Arizona. In *Twenty-Eighth Annual Report of the Bureau of American Ethnology*. Washington DC: GPO.

———. 1919. Designs on Prehistoric Hopi Pottery. In *Thirty-Third Annual Report of the Bureau of American Ethnology*. Washington DC: GPO.

———. 1922. Prehistoric Island Culture Areas of America. In *Thirty-Fourth Annual Report of the Bureau of American Ethnology*. Washington DC: GPO.

Hinsley, Curtis M. 1994. *The Smithsonian and the American Indian: Making a Moral Anthropology in Victorian America*. Washington DC: Smithsonian Institution. [originally published as *Savages and Scientists*, 1981]

Hough, Walter. 1931. Jesse Walter Fewkes. *American Anthropologist* n.s., 33: 92–97.

———. 1934. Biographical Memoir of Jesse Walter Fewkes, 1850–1930. *National Academy of Sciences Biographical Memoirs* 15: 259–283.

ROLAND B. DIXON, 1913–1914
Papers: PM

Bernstein, Bruce. 1993. Roland Dixon and the Maidu. *Museum Anthropology* 17 (2): 20–26.

Brigham, Clarence Saunders. 1935. Roland Burrage Dixon. *Proceedings of the American Antiquarian Society* 45: 13–14.

de Laguna, Frederica, ed. 2002. *American Anthropology, 1888–1920: Selected Papers from the "American Anthropologist."* Lincoln: University of Nebraska Press. [originally published as *Selected Papers from the American Anthropologist, 1888–1920*, 1960]

Dixon, Roland B. 1928. *The Building of Cultures*. New York: Charles Scribner's Sons.

Hooton, Earnest. 1935. Roland Burrage Dixon. *Proceedings of the American Antiquarian Society* 45: 770–774.

Kroeber, A. L. 1936. Roland Burrage Dixon. *American Anthropologist* 38: 294–297.

Moos, Katherine. 1975. *Race Theory in American Ethnology: Roland B. Dixon and Alfred Kroeber, 1900–1930*. Unpublished bachelor's thesis, Radcliffe College.

Morison, Samuel Eliot. 1930. *The Development of Harvard University Since the Inauguration of President Eliot, 1869–1929*. Cambridge: Harvard University Press.

Tozzer, A. M. 1936. Roland Burrage Dixon. *American Anthropologist* 38: 291–294.

Tozzer, Alfred, Gregory Baxter, and Henry Hubbard. 1935. *Minute on the Life and Services of Roland Burrage Dixon*. Harvard University Gazette *30(23): 93–94.*

FREDERICK WEBB HODGE, 1915–1916
Papers: MAI, SWM, UCB-B, UCLA

Anderson, Arthur J. O. 1958. Frederick Webb Hodge, 1864–1956. *Hispanic American Historical Review* 38(2): 263–267.

Anon. 1956. Dr. Frederick Webb Hodge, 1864–1956. *The Masterkey* 30(6): 176–178.

Cole, Fay-Cooper. 1957. Frederick Webb Hodge, 1864–1956. *American Anthropologist* 59: 517–520.

Curtis, Edward S. 1907–1930. *The North American Indian, Being a Series of Volumes Pictur-*

ing and Describing the Indians of the United States and Alaska. Cambridge UK: The University Press and the Plimpton Press.

Exposition of Indian Tribal Arts, Inc. 1931. *Introduction to American Indian Art*. New York: Exposition of Indian Tribal Arts.

Hinsley, Curtis M. 1994. *The Smithsonian and the American Indian: Making a Moral Anthropology in Victorian America*. Washington DC: Smithsonian Institution. [originally published as *Savages and Scientists*, 1981]

Hodge, Frederick Webb. 1921. *Turquoise work of Hawikuh, New Mexico*. Leaflets of the Museum of the American Indian, Heye Foundation, 2. New York: Museum of the American Indian, Heye Foundation.

———. 1923. *Circular kivas near Hawikuh, New Mexico*. Contributions from the Museum of the American Indian, Heye Foundation, 7(1). New York: Museum of the American Indian, Heye Foundation.

———. 1937. *History of Hawikuh, New Mexico, One of the So-Called Cities of Cíbola*. Los Angeles: The Southwest Museum.

Hodge, Frederick Webb, ed. 1907–1910. *The Handbook of American Indians North of Mexico*. Bureau of American Ethnology Bulletin 30. Washington DC: GPO.

Hodge, Frederick Webb, and Theodore H. Lewis, eds. 1907. *Spanish Explorers in the Wouthern United States, 1528–1543*. New York: C. Scribner's Sons.

Judd, Neil M., M. R. Harrington and S. K. Lothrop. 1957. Frederick Webb Hodge— 1864–1956. *American Antiquity* 22(4): 401–404.

Powell, Lawrence Clark. 1954. Sky, Sun, and Water: The Southwest of Frederick Webb Hodge. *Southwest Review* 39(3): 157–165.

Smith, Watson, Richard B. Woodbury and Nathalie F. S. Woodbury. 1966. *The Excavation of Hawikuh by Frederick Webb Hodge: Report of the Hendricks-Hodge Expedition, 1917–1923*. Contributions from the Museum of the American Indian, Heye Foundation, 20. New York: Museum of the American Indian, Heye Foundation.

ALFRED L. KROEBER, 1917–1918
Papers: UCB-B, APS, LC

Golla, Victor, ed. 1984. *The Sapir-Kroeber Correspondence, 1905–1925*. Berkeley: Survey of California and Other Indian Languages.

Hymes, Dell. 1961. Alred Louis Kroeber. *Language* 37: 1–28.

Kroeber, Alfred L. 1909. Classificatory Systems of Relationship. *Journal of the Royal Anthropological Institute* 39: 77–84.

———. 1917. The Superorganic. *American Anthropologist* 19: 163–213.

———. 1923. *Anthropology*. New York: Harcourt Brace.

———. 1925. *Handbook of the Indians of California*. Bureau of American Ethnology Bulletin 78. Washington DC: GPO.

———. 1939. *Cultural and Natural Areas of Native North America. University of California Publications in American Archaeology and Ethnology* 38.

———. 1944. *Configurations of Culture Growth.* Berkeley: University of California Press.

———. 1948. *Anthropology,* second edition. New York: Harcourt Brace.

———. 1952. *The Nature of Culture.* Chicago: University of Chicago Press.

———. 1957. *Style and Civilization.* Berkeley: University of California Press.

———. 1963. *An Anthropologist Looks at History.* Berkeley: University of California Press.

Kroeber, Theodora. 1970. *Alfred Kroeber: A Personal Configuration.* Berkeley: University of California Press.

Rowe, John Howland. 1962. Alfred Louis Kroeber, 1876–1960. *American Antiquity* 27: 395–415.

Steward, Julian H. 1973. *Alfred Kroeber.* New York: Columbia University Press.

CLARK WISSLER, 1919–1920
Papers: BSU, AMNH

Darnell, Regna. 1998. *And Along Came Boas: Continuity and Revolution in Americanist Anthropology.* Amsterdam: John Benjamins.

Freed, Stanley A., and Ruth S. Freed. 1983. Clark Wissler and the Development of Anthropology in the United States. *American Anthropologist* 85: 800–825.

Kroeber, A. L. 1948. In Memory of Clark Wissler. In Memorial Service for Dr. Clark Wissler. Manuscript, American Museum of Natural History, Department of Anthropology Archives: 1–4.

Reed, James S. 1980. Clark Wissler: A Forgotten Influence in American Anthropology. Unpublished Ph.D. dissertation in anthropology, Ball State University.

Spier, Leslie. 1921. The Sun Dance of the Plains Indians: Its Development and Diffusion. *American Museum of Natural History, Anthropological Papers* 16: 451–527.

Wissler, Clark. 1912. Ceremonial Bundles of the Blackfoot Indians. *American Museum of Natural History, Anthropological Papers* 7: 65–289.

———. 1917. *The American Indian.* New York: Douglas C. McMurtrie.

———. 1923. *Man and Culture.* New York: Thomas Y. Crowell.

Wissler, Clark, ed. 1916. Societies of the Plains Indians. *American Museum of Natural History, Anthropological Papers* 11.

———, ed. 1921. Sun Dance of the Plains Indians. *American Museum of Natural History, Anthropological Papers* 16.

WILLIAM CURTIS FARABEE, 1921–1922
Papers: PM, Penn

Anon. 1925a. William Curtis Farabee. *Art and Archaeology* 20(2): 92, 96.

———. 1925b. William Curtis Farabee. *American Journal of Physical Anthropology* 8: 452.

———. 1935. Farabee, William Curtis. *The National Cyclopædia of American Biography* 24: 207–208.

Brew, J. O. 1968. Introduction. In *One Hundred Years of Anthropology*, J. O. Brew, ed. Cambridge: Harvard University Press.

Colton, Harold S. 1961. Reminiscences in Southwest Archaeology: IV. *Kiva* 26(3): 1–7.

de Milhau, Louis J. 1940. Spregisandur Holiday. In *Explorers Club Tales*. New York: Tudor.

Farabee, William Curtis. 1917. A Pioneer in Amazonia: The Narrative of a Journey from Manaos to Georgetown. *The Bulletin of the Geographical Society of Philadelphia* 15: 57–103.

———. 1918. *The Central Arawaks*. Anthropological Publications 9. Philadelphia: The University Museum.

———. 1922. *The Indian Tribes of Eastern Peru*. Papers of the Peabody Museum of American Archaeology and Ethnology, Harvard University, 10. Cambridge: Peabody Museum.

———. 1924. *The Central Caribs*. Anthropological Publications 10. Philadelphia: The University Museum.

WALTER HOUGH, 1923–1924
Papers: NAA

Glenn, James R. 1991. Hough, Walter. In *International Dictionary of Anthropologists*, Christopher Winters, ed. New York: Garland.

Hough, Walter. 1988. Distribution of the Fire-Syringe. *American Anthropologist* 1: 294–295.

———. 1890. Aboriginal Fire-Making. *American Anthropologist* 3: 359–71.

———. 1897. The Hopi in Relation to their Plant Environment. *American Anthropologist* 10: 33–44.

———. 1898. Environmental Interrelations in Arizona. *American Anthropologist* 11: 133–155.

———. 1900. Oriental Influences in Mexico. *American Anthropologist* 2: 66–74.

———. 1907. *Antiquities of the Upper Gila and Salt River Valleys in Arizona and New Mexico*. Bureau of American Ethnology Bulletin 35. Washington DC: GPO.

Judd, Neil M. 1936. Walter Hough: An Appreciation. *American Anthropologist* 38: 471–481.

———. 1967. *The Bureau of American Ethnology: A Partial History*. Norman: University of Oklahoma Press.

ALEŠ HRDLIČKA, 1925–1926
Papers: NAA

Bower, B. 2000. Ishi's Long Road Home. *Science News* 157: 24–25.

Harper, Kenn. 2000. *Give Me My Father's Body: The Life of Minik, the New York Eskimo*. South Royalton VT: Steerforth.

Hecht, J. M. 1977. A Vigilant Anthropology: Léonce Manouvrier and the Disappearing Numbers. *Journal of the History of the Behavioral Sciences*. 33: 221–240.

Hrdlička, A. 1901. An Eskimo Brain. *American Anthropologist* 3: 454–500.

————. 1908. Physical Anthropology and its Aims. *Science* 28: 41–42.

————. 1916. The Brain Collection of the U.S. National Museum. *Science* 44: 739.

————. 1920. *Anthropometry*. Philadephia: The Wistar Institute of Anatomy and Biology.

————. 1927. The Neanderthal Phase of Man. *Journal of the Royal Anthropological Institute* 58: 247–274.

————. 1930. *The Skeletal Remains of Early Man*. Washington DC: Smithsonian Institution.

————. 1925. *The Old Americans*. Baltimore: Williams and Wilkins.

Kroeber, Theodora. 1961. *Ishi in Two Worlds: A Biography of the Last Wild Indian in North America*. Berkeley: University of California Press.

Montagu, M. F. A. 1944. Aleš Hrdlička, 1869–1943. *American Anthropologist* 46: 113–117.

Schultz, A. H. 1943. Aleš Hrdlička, 1869–1943. *Biographical Memoirs of the National Academy of Sciences* 23: 305–338.

Spencer, F. 1979. Aleš Hrdlička, M.D., 1869–1943: A Chronicle of the Life and Work of an American Physical Anthropologist. Ph.D. dissertation, Department of Anthropology, University of Michigan.

Stewart, T. D. 1940. [Biographical Sketch of Aleš Hrdlička]. *American Journal of Physical Anthropology* 26: 3–40.

MARSHALL H. SAVILLE, 1927–1928

Papers: AMNH, MAI

Anon. 1935. Marshall H. Saville. *Maya Research* 2(3): 297–298.

————. 1940. Saville, Marshall Howard. *The National Cyclopædia of American Biography* 28: 468–469.

————. 1956. *The History of the Museum*. Museum of the American Indian, Heye Foundation, Indian Notes and Monographs Misc. Series 55.

Brigham, Clarence Saunders. 1935. Marshall Howard Saville. *Proceedings of the American Antiquarian Society* n.s., 45(2): 151–153.

McVicker, Donald E. 1992. The Matter of Saville: Franz Boas and the Anthropological Definition of Archaeology. In *Rediscovering Our Past: Essays on the History of American Archaeology*, Jonathan E. Reyman, ed. Aldershot, Hampshire UK: Avebury.

Saville, Marshall H. 1907–10. *The Antiquities of Manabi, Ecuador: A Preliminary Report*. Contributions to South American Archeology: The George G. Heye Expedition. New York: Irving Press.

————. 1913. Precolumbian Decoration of the Teeth in Ecuador, With Some Account of the Occurrence of the Custom in Other Parts of North and South America. *American Anthropologist* 15(3): 377–394.

ALFRED M. TOZZER, 1929–1930

Papers: PM

Gailey, Christine Ward. 1989. Eleanor Burke Leacock (1922–1987). In *Women Anthro-*

pologists: Selected Biographies, Ute Gacs, Aisha Khan, Jerrie McIntyre, and Ruth Weinberg, eds. Urbana: University of Illinois Press.

Lothrop, S. K. 1955. Alfred Marston Tozzer, 1876–1954. *American Anthropologist* 57: 614–618.

Phillips, Philip. 1955. Alfred Marston Tozzer—1877–1954. *American Antiquity* 21(1): 72–80.

Spinden, Herbert Joseph. 1947. Alfred Marston Tozzer, 1877–1954. *Biographical Memoirs of the National Academy of Sciences* 30: 382–397.

Tozzer, Alfred M. 1911. Preliminary Study of the Prehistoric Ruins of Tikal, Guatemala. *Memoirs of the Peabody Museum* 5(2): 93–135.

———. 1913. Preliminary Study of the Prehistoric Ruins of Nakum, Guatemala. *Memoirs of the Peabody Museum* 5(2): 144–201.

———. 1944. *Okinawan Studies*. 3 vols. Honolulu: Office of Strategic Services.

———. 1957. *Chichén Itzá and Its Cenote of Sacrifice: A Comparative Study of Contemporaneous Maya and Toltec*. Memoirs of the Peabody Museum of Archaeology and Ethnology 11–12. Cambridge: Peabody Museum.

GEORGE G. MACCURDY, 1931
Papers: PM

Hencken, Hugh. 1948. George Grant MacCurdy, 1863–1947. *Bulletin of the American School of Prehistoric Research* 16: iv–xxii.

Hooton, Earnest A. 1950. George Grant MacCurdy, 1863–1947. *American Anthropologist* 52: 513–515.

McCown, Theodore D. 1948. George Grant MacCurdy, 1863–1947. *American Anthropologist* 50: 516–524.

MacCurdy, George Grant. 1902. The Teaching of Anthropology in the United States. *Science* 15: 211–216.

———. 1905. The Eolithic Problem—Evidences of a Rude Industry Antedating the Paleolithic. *American Anthropologist* 7: 425–479.

———. 1919. The Academic Teaching of Anthropology in Connection with other Departments. *American Anthropologist* 21: 49–60.

———. 1924. *Human Origins: A Manual of Prehistory*. 2 vols. New York: D. Appleton.

MacCurdy, George Grant, ed. and contributor. 1937. *Early Man*. New York: J.B. Lippincott.

JOHN R. SWANTON, 1932
Papers: APS, NAA, RC-S

Bringhurst, Robert. 1999. *A Story as Sharp as a Knife: The Classical Haida Mythtellers and Their World*. Vancouver BC: Douglas & McIntyre and Lincoln: University of Nebraska Press.

Fenton, William N. 1959. John Reed Swanton. *American Anthropologist* 61: 663–668.

————. 1991. Frank G. Speck's Anthropology (1881–1950). In *The Life and Times of Frank G. Speck 1881–1950*, Roy Blankenship, ed. Philadephia: University of Pennsylvania Department of Anthropology.

Judd, Neil M. 1967. *The Bureau of American Ethnology: A Partial History*. Norman: University of Oklahoma Press.

Kroeber, Alfred L. 1940. The Work of John R. Santon. In *Essays in Historical Anthropology of North America*. Smithsonian Miscellaneous Collections 100: 1–9.

Lonergay, David. 1999. John Reed Swanton. *American National Biography* 25: 192–193. New York: Oxford University Press.

Murray, Stephen O. 1983. Historical Inferences from Ethnohistorical Data: Boasian Perspectives. *Journal of the History of the Behavioral Sciences* 19: 335–340.

Steward, Julian. 1960. John Reed Swanton. *Biographical Memoirs of the National Academy of Sciences* 34: 328–349.

Swanton, John R. 1905. The Social Organization of American Tribes. *American Anthropologist* 7: 663–673.

————. 1911. *Indian Tribes of the Lower Mississippi Valley and Adjacent Coast of the Gulf of Mexico*. Bureau of American Ethnology Bulletin 43. Washington DC: GPO.

————. 1939a. *Final Report of the United States De Soto Expedition Commission* H.R. Doc. 71, 76th Congress. Washington DC.

————. 1939b. Some Thoughts on the Problem of Progress and Decline. *Science* 89: 253–258.

————. 1942. *Source Material on the History and Ethnology of the Caddo Indians*. Bureau of American Ethnology Bulletin 132. Washington DC: GPO.

————. 1952. *Indians of the Southeastern United States*. Bureau of American Ethnology Bulletin 145. Washington DC: GPO.

Swanton, John R., and Roland B. Dixon. *Primitive American History*. American Anthropologist *16: 376–412.*

FAY-COOPER COLE, 1933–1934
Papers: UC

Cole, Fay-Cooper. 1931. Race Problems as Seen by the Anthropologist. *The Scientific Monthly* 32: 80–82.

————. 1933. *The Long Road from Savagery to Civilization*. Baltimore: Williams & Williams, in cooperation with the Century of Progress Exposition.

Cole, Mabel Cook. 1916. *Philippine Folk Tales*. Chicago: A. C. McClurg & Co.

————. 1929. *Savage Gentlemen*. New York: D. Van Nostrand.

Cole, Mabel Cook, and Fay-Cooper Cole. 1940. *The Story of Primitive Man: His Earliest Appearance and Development*. Chicago: University of Knowledge.

Eggan, Fred. 1963. Fay-Cooper Cole, 1881–1961. *American Anthropologist* 65: 641–648.

————. 1974. Among the Anthropologists. *Annual Review of Anthropology* 3: 1–19.

Jennings, Jesse D. 1962. Fay-Cooper Cole, 1881–1961. *American Antiquity* 27: 573–575.

Rydell, Robert W. 1993. *World of Fairs: The Century-of-Progress Expositions*. Chicago: University of Chicago Press.

Stocking, George W. 1979. *Anthropology at Chicago: Tradition, Discipline, Department*. Chicago: University of Chicago Library.

Willey, Gordon R., and Jeremy A. Sabloff. 1980. *A History of American Archaeology*, second edition. San Francisco: W. H. Freeman and Co.

ROBERT H. LOWIE, 1935
Papers: AMNH, APS, UCB-B, UCR

Casagrande, Joseph B. 1960. *In the Company of Man: Twenty Portraits of Anthropological Informants*. New York: Harper Torchbbooks.

Darnell, Regna. 1998. *And Along Came Boas: Continuity and Revolution in Americanist Anthropology*. Amsterdam: John Benjamins.

DuBois, Cora, ed. 1960. *Lowie's Selected Papers in Anthropology*. Berkeley: University of California Press.

Lowie, Robert H. 1908. The Test Theme in North American Mythology. *Journal of American Folklore* 21: 97–148.

———. 1917. *Culture and Ethnology*. New York: Douglas C. McMurtrie.

———. 1920. *Primitive Society*. New York: Boni and Liveright.

———. 1924. *Primitive Religion*. New York: Boni and Liveright.

———. 1935. *The Crow Indians*. Lincoln: University of Nebraska Press.

———. 1937. *The History of Ethnological Theory*. New York: Farrar and Rinehart.

———. 1954. *Toward Understanding Germany*. Chicago: University of Chicago Press.

———. 1956. Reminiscences of Anthropological Currents in America Half a Century Ago. *American Anthropologist* 58: 995–1016.

———. 1959. *Robert H. Lowie Ethnologist: A Personal Record*. Berkeley: University of California Press.

Robert F. Murphy, ed. 1972. *Robert H. Lowie*. New York: Columbia University Press.

Parsons, Elsie Clews, ed. 1922 [1967]. *American Indian Life*. Lincoln: University of Nebraska Press.

Radin, Paul. 1958. Robert H. Lowie, 1883–1957. *American Anthropologist* 60: 358–375.

HERBERT J. SPINDEN, 1936
Papers: AMNH, BU-H

Anon. 1938. Spinden, Herbert Joseph. *The National Cyclopædia of American Biography*, volume E: 73–74.

———. 1942. [Bibliography of] Herbert J. Spinden. *Boletín bibliográfico de antropología americana* 6(1–3): 209–215.

———. 1967. Dr. Spinden Dead; Indian Authority. *New York Times*, 24 October 44.

Martin, Paul S. 1974. Early Development in Mogollon Research. In *Archaeological Researches in Retrospect*, Gordon R. Willey, ed. Cambridge MA: Winthrop.

Spinden, Herbert J. 1917. The Origin and Distribution of Agriculture in America. In *Proceedings of the Nineteenth International Congress of Americanists*, F. W. Hodge, ed. Washington DC.

———. 1928. *Ancient Civilizations of Mexico and Central America*. Handbook Series 3, third edition. New York: American Museum of Natural History.

———. 1933. *Songs of the Tewa; Preceded by an Essay on American Indian Poetry, With a Selection of Outstanding Compositions from North and South America; An Appendix Contains Original Tewa Texts and Explanatory Notes*. New York: Exposition of Indian Tribal Arts.

Weeren, John S. 1997. Finding Aid. Association on American Indian Affairs Archives. Public Policy Papers; Department of Rare Books and Special Collections; Princeton University Library. Available at *http://infoshare1.princeton.edu:2003/libraries/firestone/rbsc/finding_aids/aaia/aaia.html*.

Will, G. F. and H. J. Spinden. 1906. *The Mandans: A Study of Their Culture, Archaeology and Language*. Papers of the Peabody Museum of American Archaeology and Ethnology. Cambridge: Peabody Museum.

Willey, Gordon R. 1981. Spinden's Archaic Hypothesis. In *Antiquity and Man: Essays in Honor of Glyn Daniel*, John D. Evans, Barry Cunliffe, and Colin Renfrew, eds. London: Thames and Hudson.

Willey, Gordon R., and Jeremy A. Sabloff. 1980. *A History of American Archaeology*, second edition. San Francisco: W. H. Freeman and Co.

NELS C. NELSON, 1937
Papers: AMNH

Anon. 1964. Nels Nelson, 88, Ex-Curator, Dies. *New York Times*, 6 March, 31.

Barton, D. R. 1941. Mud, Stones, and History. *Natural History* 47(5): 293–96, 303.

Hast, Adele. 1981. Nelson, Nels Christian. In *Dictionary of American Biography*, Supplement 7, 1961–65. New York: Charles Scribner's Sons.

Spier, Leslie. 1931. N. C. Nelson's Stratigraphic Technique in the Reconstruction of Prehistoric Sequences in Southwestern America. In *Methods in Social Science: A Case Book*, Stuart A. Rice, ed. Chicago: University of Chicago Press.

Willey, Gordon R., and Jeremy A. Sabloff. 1980. *A History of American Archaeology*, second edition. San Francisco: W. H. Freeman and Co.

EDWARD SAPIR, 1938
Papers: CMC, APS, UC

Darnell, Regna. 1990. *Edward Sapir: Linguist, Anthropologist, Humanist*. Berkeley: University of California Press.

Hymes, Dell, and John Fought. 1975. American Structuralism. In *Current Trends in*

    Linguistics 10, Historiography of Linguistics, Thomas A. Sebeok, ed. The Hague: Mouton.

Sapir, Edward. 1916. *Time Perspective in Aboriginal American Culture: A Study in Method.* Canadian Department of Mines, Geological Survey, Memoir 90, Anthropological Series 13.

———. 1921. A Bird's Eye View of American Languages North of Mexico. *Science* 54: 408.

———. 1921. *Language: An Introduction to the Study of Speech.* New York: Harcourt, Brace and Company.

———. 1925. Sound Patterns in Language. *Language* 1: 37–51.

———. 1933. La Réalité psychologique des phonèmes. *Journal de Psychologie Normale et Pathologiqe* 30: 247–265.

———. 1949. *Selected Writings of Edward Sapir in Language, Culture, and Personality*, David Mandelbaum, ed. Berkeley: University of California Press.

DIAMOND JENNESS, 1939
Papers: CMC, NWT

Canada. 1997. *First Nations in Canada.* Ottawa: Indian and Northern Affairs Canada.

de Laguna, Frederica. 1971. Diamond Jenness, C.C. *American Anthropologist* 73(1): 248–254.

Jenness, Diamond, and A. Ballantyne. 1920. *The Northern D'Entrecasteaux.* Oxford: Clarendon.

Jenness, Diamond. 1923. *The Copper Eskimos.* Report of the Canadian Arctic Expedition, 1913–1918, vol. 12.

———. 1925. A New Eskimo Culture in Hudson Bay. *Geographical Review* 15: 428–437.

———. 1928. *The People of the Twilight.* New York: Macmillan.

———. 1932. *The Indians of Canada.* National Museum of Canada Bulletin 65, Anthropological Series 15. Ottawa: National Museum of Canada.

———. 1962–68. *Eskimo Administration.* 5 vols. Montreal: Arctic Institute of North America.

Jenness, Stuart E., ed. 1991. *Arctic Odyssey: The Diary of Diamond Jenness, 1913–1916.* Hull, Quebec: Canadian Museum of Civilization.

Kulchyski, Peter. 1993. Anthropology in the Service of the State: Diamond Jenness and Canadian Indian Policy. *Journal of Canadian Studies* 28(2): 21–29.

Taylor, William E., Jr. 1988. Jenness, Diamond. *The Canadian Encyclopedia*, second edition, 2:1108. Edmonton: Hurtig.

JOHN M. COOPER, 1940
Papers: CathU, NAA

Anon. 1950. Bibliography of John Montgomery Cooper. *Primitive Man* 23(3): 66–84.

Cooper, John M. 1917. *Analytical and Critical Bibliography of the Tribes of Tierra del Fuego and Adjacent Territory*. Bureau of American Ethnology Bulletin 63. Washington DC: GPO.

———. 1925. If Evolution Were a Fact. *Catholic World* 121: 721–728.

———. 1931a. *Children's Institutions: A Study of Programs and Policies in Catholic Children's Institutions in the United States*. Philadelphia: Dolphin.

———. 1931b. Contraception and Altruistic Ethics. *International Journal of Ethics* 41: 443–460.

———. 1934. Mental Disease Situations in Certain Cultures—A New Field for Research. *Journal of Abnormal and Social Psychology* 24: 10–17.

———. 1942. Areal and Temporal Aspects of Aboriginal South American Culture. *Primitive Man* 15: 1–38.

Flannery, Regina. 1950. John Montgomery Cooper, 1881–1949. *American Anthropologist* 52(1): 64–74.

Furfey, Paul Hanly. 1950. John Montgomery Cooper: 1881–1949. *Primitive Man* 23(3): 49–65.

Lowie, Robert H. 1949. John Montgomery Cooper (1881–1949). *Boletín bibliográfico de antropologia americana* 12(2): 289–292.

Métraux, Alfred. 1950. The Contribution of the Rev. Father Cooper to South American Ethnography. *Primitive Man* 23(3): 39–48.

Tibesar, Leopold H. 1950. Doctor Cooper Initiates the Catholic Anthropological Conference. *Primitive Man* 23(3): 35–38.

ELSIE CLEWS PARSONS, 1941

Papers: APS, CU-B

Babcock, Barbara A., and Nancy J. Parezo. 1988. *Daughters of the Desert: Women Anthropologists and the Native American Southwest, 1880–1980*. Albuquerque: University of New Mexico Press.

Deacon, Desley. 1997. *Elsie Clews Parsons: Inventing Modern Life*. Chicago: University of Chicago Press.

Falk, Julia S. 1999. *Women, Language and Linguistics*. London: Routledge.

Friedlander, Judith. 1989. Elsie Clews Parsons. In *Women Anthropologists: Selected Biographies*, Ute Gacs, Aisha Khan, Jerrie McIntyre, and Ruth Weinberg, eds. Urbana: University of Illinois Press.

Goldfrank, Esther. 1978. *Notes on an Undirected Life As One Anthropologist Tells It*. New York: Queens College Press.

Hare, Peter. 1985. *A Woman's Quest for Science: Portrait of Anthropologist Elsie Clews Parsons*. New York: Prometheus.

Kroeber, Alfred. 1943. Elsie Clews Parsons. *American Anthropologist* 45: 252–255.

Parsons, Elsie Clews. 1906. *The Family*. New York: G. P. Putnam's Sons.

———. 1936. *Mitla: Town of the Souls*. Chicago: University of Chicago Publications in Anthropology.

————. 1939. *Pueblo Indian Religion*. 2 vols. Chicago: University of Chicago Publications in Anthropology.

————. 1943. Folk-lore of the Antilles, French and English. *Memoirs of the American Folklore Society* 26.

————. 1945. *Peguche, Canton of Otavalo, Province of Imbabura, Ecuador: A Study of Andean Indians*. Chicago: University of Chicago Press.

Zumwalt, Rosemary. 1992. *Wealth and Rebellion: Elsie Clews Parsons, Anthropologist and Folklorist*. Urbana: University of Illinois Press.

A. V. KIDDER, 1942
Papers: APS, MNM, PM

Adams, Jenny L. 1994. *Pinto Beans and Prehistoric Pots: The Legacy of Al and Alice Lancaster*. Arizona State Museum Archaeological Series 183. Tucson: University of Arizona.

Givens, Douglas R. 1992. *Alfred Vincent Kidder and the Development of Americanist Archaeology*. Albuquerque: University of New Mexico Press.

Greengo, Robert E. 1968. Alfred Vincent Kidder, 1885–1963. *American Anthropologist* 70: 320–325.

Judd, Neil M. 1960. Reminiscences in Southwest Archaeology: II. *Kiva* 26(1): 1–6.

Kidder, A. V. 1915. Pottery of the Pajarito Plateau and of Some Adjacent Regions in New Mexico. *Memoirs of the American Anthropological Association* 2: 407–462.

————. 1924. *An Introduction to the Study of Southwestern Archaeology, With a Preliminary Account of the Excavations at Pecos*. Papers of the Phillips Academy Southwestern Expedition 1. New Haven: Yale University Press.

————. 1931. *The Pottery of Pecos, Volume 1: The Dull-Paint Wares*. Papers of the Phillips Academy Southwestern Expedition 5. New Haven: Yale University Press.

————. 1932. *The Artifacts of Pecos*. Papers of the Phillips Academy Southwestern Expedition 6. New Haven: Yale University Press.

————. 1937. A Program for Maya Research. *Hispanic American Historical Review* 17: 160–169.

————. 1940. Archaeological Problems of the Highland Maya. In *The Maya and Their Neighbors*, C. L. Hay, ed. New York: D. Appleton-Century.

————. 1960. Reminiscences in Southwest Archaeology: I. *Kiva* 25(4): 1–32.

Kidder, Alfred Vincent, and Samuel G. Guernsey. 1919. *Archeological Explorations in Northeastern Arizona*. Bureau of American Ethnology Bulletin 65. Washington DC: GPO.

Kluckhohn, Clyde. 1940. The Conceptual Structure in Middle American Studies. In *The Maya and Their Neighbors*, C. L. Hay, ed. New York: D. Appleton-Century.

Taylor, Walter W. 1948. *A Study of Archeology*. American Anthropological Association Memoir 69.

Wauchope, Robert. 1965. Alfred Vincent Kidder, 1885–1963. *American Antiquity* 31: 149–171.

Willey, Gordon R. 1967. Alfred Vincent Kidder: October 29, 1885–June 11, 1963. *Biographical Memoirs of the National Academy of Sciences* 39: 292–322.

Woodbury, Richard B. 1973. *Alfred V. Kidder*. New York: Columbia University Press.

Zumwalt, Rosemary Lévy. 1992. *Wealth and Rebellion: Elsie Clews Parsons, Anthropologist and Folklorist*. Urbana: University of Illinois Press.

LESLIE SPIER, 1943
Papers: MNA, UCB-B

Amoss, Pamela T. 1989. Erna Gunther (1896–1982). In *Women Anthropologists: Selected Biographies*, Ute Gacs, Aisha Khan, Jerrie McIntyre, and Ruth Weinberg, eds. Urbana: University of Illinois Press.

Basehart, Harry W. and W.W. Hill. 1965. Leslie Spier, 1893–1961. *American Anthropologist* 67: 1258–1277.

Mandelbaum, David G. 1962. Leslie Spier, 1893–1961. *The Eastern Anthropologist* 15(2): 172–175.

Spencer, Robert F. 1987. Leslie Spier, December 13, 1893–December 3, 1961. *National Academy of Sciences Biographical Memoirs* 57: 430–458.

Spier, Leslie. 1918. *The Trenton Argillite Culture*. Anthropological Papers of the American Museum of Natural History 22(4). New York: American Museum of Natural History.

———. 1921. *The Sun Dance of the Plains Indians: Its Development and Diffusion*. Anthropological Papers of the American Museum of Natural History 16(7). New York: American Museum of Natural History.

———. The Distribution of Kinship Systems in North America. *University of Washington Publications in Anthropology* 1: 69–88.

———. 1929. Problems Arising from the Cultural Position of the Havasupai. *American Anthropologist* 31: 213–222.

Taylor, Walter W. 1963. Leslie Spier, 1893–1961. *American Antiquity* 28: 379–381.

ROBERT REDFIELD, 1944
Papers: UC

Baker, Lee D. 1999. *From Savage to Negro*. Berkeley: University of California Press.

Gamio, Manuel. 1930. *Mexican Immigration to the United States: A Study of Human Migration and Adjustment*. Chicago: University of Chicago Press.

Godoy, Ricardo. 1978. The Background and Context of Redfield's *Tepoztlán*. *Journal of the Steward Anthropological Society* 10: 47–79.

Redfield, Robert. 1928. *A Plan for a Study of Tepoztlán, Morelos*. Ph.D. dissertation, University of Chicago.

———. 1929. The Antecedents of Mexican Immigration to the United States. *American Journal of Sociology* 35: 433–438.

———. 1930. *Tepoztlán, A Mexican Village: A Study of Folk Life*. Chicago: University of Chicago Press.

———. 1941. *The Folk Culture of the Yucatan*. Chicago: University of Chicago Press.

————. 1950. *A Village that Chose Progress: Chan Kom Revisited*. Chicago: University of Chicago Press.

————. 1953. *The Primitive World and Its Transformation*. Ithaca NY: Cornell University Press.

————. 1955. *The Little Community*. Chicago: University of Chicago Press.

————. 1956. *Peasant Society and Culture: An Anthropological Approach to Civilization*. Chicago: University of Chicago Press.

————. 1962. *Human Nature and the Study of Society*, Margaret Park Redfield, ed. Chicago: University of Chicago Press.

Redfield, Robert, and Alfonso Villa Rojas. 1934. *Chan Kom: A Maya Village*. Chicago: University of Chicago Press.

Rubinstein, Robert A. 1991. *Fieldwork: The Correspondence of Robert Redfield and Sol Tax*. Boulder CO: Westview.

Singer, Milton, and James Redfield. 1999. Robert Redfield. *American National Biography*, 20:251–253. New York: Oxford University Press.

Thomas, W. I., and Florian Znaniecki. 1927 [1918]. *The Polish Peasant in America and Europe*. New York: Knopf.

Villa Rojas, Alfonso. 1979. Fieldwork in the Mayan region of Mexico. In *Long-Term Field Research in Social Anthropology*, George M. Foster et al., eds. New York: Academic Press.

NEIL M. JUDD, 1945
Papers: NAA

Brew, J. O. 1978. Neil Merton Judd, 1887–1976. *American Anthropologist* 80: 352–354.

Judd, Neil M. 1924. Report on Illegal Excavations in Southwestern Ruins. *American Anthropologist* 26: 428–432.

————. 1926. *Archaeological Excavations North of the Rio Colorado*. Bureau of American Ethnology Bulletin 82. Washington DC: GPO.

————. 1929. The Present Status of Archaeology in the United States. *American Anthropologist* 31: 401–418.

————. 1954. The Material Culture of Pueblo Bonito. *Smithsonian Miscellaneous Collections* 124: xii–398.

————. 1959. Pueblo Del Arroyo, Chaco Canyon, New Mexico. *Smithsonian Miscellaneous Collections* 138: vii–222.

————. 1967. *The Bureau of American Ethnology: A Partial History*. Norman: University of Oklahoma Press.

————. 1968. *Men Met Along the Trail: Adventures in Archaeology*. Norman: University of Oklahoma Press.

Woodbury, Richard B. 1993. *Sixty Years of Southwestern Archaeology: A History of the Pecos Conference*. Albuquerque: University of New Mexico Press.

RALPH LINTON, 1946
Papers: Swarth

Linton, Adelin, and Charles Wagley. 1971. *Ralph Linton*. New York: Columbia University Press.

Linton, Ralph. 1923. The Material Culture of the Marquesas Islands. *Bishop Museum Memoirs*: 253–471.

———. 1924. Totemism and the A.E.F. *American Anthropologist* 26: 296–300.

———. 1925. Archaeology of the Marquesas Islands. *Bishop Museum Bulletin* 23.

———. 1933. The Tanala: A Hill Tribe of Madagascar. *Field Museum of Natural History, Anthropological Series* 22.

———. 1936. *The Study of Man: An Introduction*. New York: Appleton-Century.

———. 1945. *The Cultural Background of Personality*. New York: Appleton-Century.

———. 1955. *The Tree of Culture*. New York: Knopf.

———. 1956. *Culture and Mental Disorders*. George Devereux, ed. Springfield IL: Thomas.

Linton, Ralph, ed. 1940. *Acculturation in Seven American Indian Tribes*. New York: Appleton-Century.

———, ed. 1945. *The Science of Man in the World Crisis*. New York: Columbia University Press.

Linton, Ralph, Robert Redfield, and Melville Herskovits. 1936. Memorandum for the Study of Acculturation. *American Anthropologist* 38: 149–152.

RUTH BENEDICT, JANUARY–MAY 1947
Papers: APS, Vassar

Benedict, Ruth Fulton. 1922. The Vision in Plains Culture. *American Anthropologist* 24: 1–23.

———. 1934. *Patterns of Culture*. Boston: Houghton Mifflin.

———. 1935. *Zuni Mythology*. 2 vols. New York: Columbia University Contributions to Anthropology.

———. 1940. *Race: Science and Politics*. New York: Modern Age.

———. 1946. *The Chrysanthemum and the Sword: Patterns of Japanese Culture*. Boston: Houghton Mifflin.

———. 1948. Anthropology and the Humanities. *American Anthropologist* 50: 585–593.

———. 1970. Synergy: Some Notes of Ruth Benedict, selected by Abraham Maslow and John J. Honigmann. *American Anthropologist* 72: 320–333.

Caffrey, Margaret. 1989. *Ruth Benedict: Stranger in this Land*. Austin: University of Texas Press.

Geertz, Clifford. 1988. *Works and Lives: The Anthropologist as Author*: 102–128. Stanford: Stanford University Press.

Lapsley, Hilary. 1999. *Margaret Mead and Ruth Benedict: The Kinship of Women*. Amherst: University of Massachusetts Press.

Mead, Margaret, ed. 1959. *An Anthropologist at Work: Selected Writings of Ruth Benedict*. Boston: Houghton Mifflin.

————. 1974. *Ruth Benedict.* New York: Columbia University Press.

Mintz, Sidney. 1981. Ruth Benedict. In *Totems and Teachers,* Sydel Silverman, ed. New York: Columbia University Press.

Modell, Judith. 1983. *Ruth Benedict: Patterns of a Life.* Philadelphia: University of Pennsylvania Press.

Young, Virginia Heyer. Beyond Relativism. Unpublished MS.

CLYDE KLUCKHOHN, MAY–DECEMBER 1947
Papers: HU-P, Iowa

Kluckhohn, Clyde. 1927. *To the Foot of the Rainbow.* New York: Century.

————. 1944. Navajo Witchcraft. *Papers of the Peabody Museum of Archaeology and Ethnology, Harvard University,* 22, no. 2.

————. 1949. *Mirror for Man.* New York: McGraw Hill.

————. 1962. *Culture and Behavior: The Collected Essays of Clyde Kluckhohn,* Richard Kluckhohn, ed. New York: The Free Press.

————. 1958. The Scientific Study of Values and Contemporary Civilization. *Proceedings of the American Philosophical Society* 102: 469–476.

Kluckhohn, Clyde, and Dorothea Leighton. 1946. *The Navaho.* Cambridge: Harvard University Press.

————. 1947. *Children of the People.* Cambridge: Harvard University Press.

Kluckhohn, Clyde, and Henry A. Murray, ed. 1948. *Personality in Nature, Society and Culture.* New York: Knopf.

Kluckhohn, Florence, and Fred Strodbeck. 1961. *Variations in Value Orientations.* New York: Row, Peterson.

Kroeber, A. L., and Clyde Kluckhohn. 1952. Culture: A Critical Review of Concepts and Definitions. *Papers of the Peabody Museum of Archaeology and Ethnology, Harvard University,* 47, no. 1.

Lamphere, Louise. 1979. Long Term Research among the Navajo. In *Long-Term Field Research in Social Anthropology,* George M. Foster, Thayer Scudder, Elizabeth Colson, and Robert V. Kemper, eds. New York: Academic Press.

Parsons, Talcott, and Evon Z. Vogt. 1962. Clyde Kluckhohn. *American Anthropologst* 64 (1, part 1): 140–161.

Taylor, Walter W., John L. Fischer, and Evon Z. Vogt. 1973. *Culture and Life: Essays in Memory of Clyde Kluckhohn.* Carbondale: Southern Illinois Press.

HARRY SHAPIRO, 1948
Papers: AMNH

Davenport, Charles B., and Morris Steggerda. 1929. *Race Crossing in Jamaica.* Washington DC: Carnegie Institution.

Fischer, Eugen. 1913. *Die Rehobother Bastards und das Basterdierungsproblem beim Menschen.* Jena: Gustav Fischer Verlag.

Lasker, Gabriel Ward. 1999. *Happenings and Hearsay: Reflections of a Biological Anthropologist.* Detroit: Savoyard Books.

Shapiro, Harry L. 1936. *The Heritage of the Bounty.* New York: Simon and Schuster. Reissue; New York: Doubleday, 1962.

———. 1939. *Migration and Environment.* New York: Oxford University Press.

———. 1944. Anthropology's Contribution to Inter-Racial Understanding. *Science* 99: 373–376.

Spencer, Frank. 1996. Harry Lionel Shapiro 1902–1990. *Biographical Memoirs of the National Academy of Sciences* 70: 3–21.

A. IRVING HALLOWELL, 1949
Papers: APS

American Philosophical Society. 1995. Alfred Irving Hallowell Papers 1892–1981, MS coll. no. 26. Description and guide, typescript. Philadelphia.

Hallowell, A. Irving. 1942. *The Role of Conjuring in Saulteaux Society.* Philadelphia: Publications of the Philadelphia Anthropological Society, vol. 2.

———. 1955. *Culture and Experience.* Philadephia: University of Pennsylvania Press.

———. 1976. *Contributions to Anthropology: Selected Papers of A. Irving Hallowell.* Chicago: University of Chicago Press.

———. 1992. *The Ojibwa of Berens River, Manitoba: Ethnography into History,* Jennifer S. H. Brown, ed. Fort Worth: Harcourt Brace College Publishers.

Spiro, Melford, 1976. Alfred Irving Hallowell 1892–1974. *American Anthropologist* 78: 608–611.

Wallace, Anthony F. C., 1980. Alfred Irving Hallowell. National Academy of Sciences, *Biographical Memoirs,* 51: 195–213.

RALPH BEALS, 1950
Papers: NAA, UCB-B

Beals, Ralph L. 1932. The Comparative Ethnography of Northern Mexico. *Ibero-Americana* 2: 93–226.

———. 1933. Ethnology of the Nisenan. *University of California Publications in American Archaeology and Ethnology* 31: 335–414.

———. 1943. The Aboriginal Culture of the Cahita Indians. *Ibero-Americana* 19: 1–94.

———. 1945a. *The Contemporary Culture of the Cahita Indians.* Bureau of American Ethnology Bulletin 142. Washington DC: GPO.

———. 1945b. Ethnology of the Western Mixe Indians. *University of California Publications in American Archaeology and Ethnology* 42: 1–176.

———. 1946. *Cherán: A Sierra Tarascan Village.* Smithsonian Institution Institute of Social Anthropology Contribution 2. Reprint; Norman: University of Oklahoma Press, 1998.]

———. 1951. Urbanism, Urbanization, and Acculturation. *American Anthropologist* 53: 1–10.

———. 1966. *Community in Transition: Nayón, Ecuador.* Los Angeles: UCLA Latin American Center.

———. 1969. *The Politics of Social Research.* Chicago: Aldine.

———. 1975. *The Peasant Marketing System of Oaxaca, Mexico.* Berkeley: University of California Press.

———. 1976. Anthropology and Government. *Anthropology UCLA* 8: 159–174.

———. 1978. Sonoran Fantasy or Coming of Age? *American Anthropologist* 80: 355–362.

———. 1979. Julian Steward: The Berkeley Days. *Papers of the Julian Steward Anthropological Society* 6: 3–15.

———. 1982a. Fifty Years in Anthropology. *Annual Reviews in Anthropology* 11: 1–23.

———. 1982b. Unanticipated Consequences of Planned Cultural Change. In *Culture and Ecology*, J. Kennedy and R. Edgerton, eds. Washington DC: American Anthropological Association.

Beals, Ralph L., and Harry Hoijer. 1953. *An Introduction to Anthropology.* First edition. New York: Macmillan.

Beals, Ralph L., and Norman D. Humphrey. 1957. *The Frontier in Learning: The Mexican Student in the United States.* Minneapolis: University of Minnesota Press.

Dillon. Diane L. 1977. Ralph Beals, Anthropologist and Educator. Unpublished Interview Transcripts, UCLA Oral History Program.

Goldschmidt, Walter. 1986. Ralph Leon Beals. *American Anthropologist* 88: 947–953.

Spicer, Edward H. 1962. *Cycles of Conquest: The Impact of Spain, Mexico and the United States on the Indians of the Southwest, 1533–1960.* Tucson: University of Arizona Press.

WILLIAM W. HOWELLS, 1951
Papers: PM

Howells, William W. *1944.* Mankind So Far. *Garden City* : Doubleday Doran.

———. *1948.* The Heathens: Primitive Man and His Religions. *Garden City NY: Doubleday.*

———. 1954. *Back of History: The Story of Our Own Origins.* Garden City NY: Doubleday.

———. 1992. Yesterday, Today and Tomorrow. *Annual Review of Anthropology* 21: 1–17.

Spencer, Frank. 1997. Howells, William White (1908–). In *History of Physical Anthropology: An Encyclopedia*, Frank Spencer, ed. New York: Garland.

Giles, Eugene, Hallam L. Movius Jr., Harry L. Shapiro, George R. Holcomb, and Michael Crichton. 1976. The Measure of a Man: William White Howells. In *The Measures of Man*, Eugene Giles and Jonathan S. Friedlaender, eds. Cambridge: Peabody Museum Press.

Lasker, Gabriel Ward. 1999. *Happenings and Hearsay: Reflections of a Biological Anthropologist.* Detroit: Savoyard Books.

WENDELL C. BENNETT, 1952
Papers: AMNH

Bennett, Wendell C. 1934. Excavations at Tiahuanaco. *American Museum of Natural History Anthropological Papers* 34(3): 357–494.

———. 1939. Archaeology of the North Coast of Peru: An Account of Exploration and Excavation in Virú and Lambayeque Valleys. *American Museum of Natural History Anthropological Papers* 37(1): 1–154.

———. 1943. The Position of Chavin in Andean Sequences. *Proceedings of the American Philosophical Society* 86(2): 323–327.

Bennett, Wendell C., ed. 1948. *A Reappraisal of Peruvian Archaeology*. Society for American Archaeology Memoir 4.

———. and Junius Bird. 1949. *Andean Culture History*. New York: American Museum of Natural History Handbook Series 15.

———. and Robert Zingg. 1935. *The Tarahumara: An Indian Tribe of Northern Mexico*. Chicago: University of Chicago Press.

Kidder, Alfred V. II. 1954. Wendell Clark Bennett, 1905–1953. *American Anthropologist* 56: 269–273.

Rouse, Irving. 1954. Wendell C. Bennett, 1905–1953. *American Antiquity* 3: 265–270.

FRED EGGAN, 1953
Papers: UC

Eggan, Fred, ed. 1937. *Social Organization of North American Tribes*. Chicago: University of Chicago Press.

———. 1950. *Social Organization of the Western Pueblos*. Chicago: University of Chicago Press.

———. 1954. Social Anthropology and the Method of Controlled Comparison. *American Anthropologist* 56: 743–761.

———. 1966. *The American Indian: Perspectives for the Study of Social Change*. Chicago: Aldine.

———. 1974. Among the Anthropologists. *Annual Review of Anthropology* 3: 1–19.

———. 1975. *Essays in Social Anthropology and Ethnology*. Chicago: University of Chicago Press.

Fogelson, Raymond D. 1979. Eggan, Fred. *Encyclopedia of the Social Sciences: Biographical Supplement* 18: 163–166.

Vogt, Evon Z., Jr. 1992. Frederick Russell Eggan. *Biographical Memoirs of the National Academy of Sciences* 68: 84–100.

Schusky, Ernest L. 1989. Fred Eggan: Anthropologist Full Circle. *American Ethnologist* 16: 142–157.

JOHN O. BREW, 1954
Papers: ASM, PM

Adams, Jenny L. 1994. *Pinto Beans and Prehistoric Pots: The Legacy of Al and Alice Lancaster*. Arizona State Museum Archaeological Series 183. Tucson: University of Arizona.
Brew, John O. 1946. The Archaeology of Alkali Ridge, Southeastern Utah, With a Review of the Prehistory of the Mesa Verde Division of the San Juan and Some Observations on Archaeological Systematics. *Papers of the Peabody Museum, Harvard*, 21.
———. 1961. Salvage in River Basins: A World View. *Archaeology* 14(4): 233–235.
Brew, John O., ed. 1968. *One Hundred Years of Anthropology*. Cambridge: Harvard University Press.
Montgomery, Ross Gordon, Watson Smith, and John O. Brew. 1949. Franciscan Awatovi: The Excavation and Conjectural Reconstruction of a 17th-Century Spanish Mission Establishment at a Hopi Indian Town in Northeastern Arizona. *Papers of the Peabody Museum, Harvard*, 36.
Whitehill, Walter Muir. 1969. John Otis Brew. In *Analecta Biographica: A Handful of New England Portraits*. Brattleboro VT: The Stephen Greene Press.
Woodbury, Richard B. 1990. John Otis Brew, 1906–1988. *American Antiquity* 55(3): 452–459.

GEORGE P. MURDOCK, 1955

Goodenough, Ward H. 1979. George P. Murdock. *International Encyclopedia of the Social Sciences, Biographical Supplement* 18: 554–559. New York: Free Press.
———. 1988. George Peter Murdock's Contributions to Anthropology: An Overview. *Behavior Science Research* 22: 1–9.
Murdock, George P. 1934. *Our Primitive Contemporaries*. New York: Macmillan.
———. 1949. *Social Structure*. New York: Macmillan.
———. 1964. The Kindred. *American Anthropologist* 66: 129–132.
Murdock, George P., ed. and trans. 1931. *The Evolution of Culture, by Julius Lippert*. New York: Macmillan.
Spoehr, Alexander. 1985. George Peter Murdock (1897–1985). *Ethnology* 24: 307–317.
Whiting, John W. M. 1986. George Peter Murdock (1897–1985). *American Anthropologist* 88: 682–686.

EMIL W. HAURY, 1956
Papers: ASM

Crown, Patricia L. 1993. Remembrance of Emil W. Haury. *Kiva* 59(2): 261–265.
Haury, Emil W. 1932. *Roosevelt 9:6, A Hohokam Site of the Colonial Period*. Medallion Papers 11. Globe AZ: Gila Pueblo.

———. 1935.Tree-rings:The Archaeologist's Time-piece. *American Antiquity* 1(2): 98–108.

———. 1936. *The Mogollon Culture of Southwestern New Mexico*. Medallion Papers 20. Globe AZ: Gila Pueblo.

———. 1945. The Excavation of Los Muertos and Neighboring Ruins in the Salt River Valley, Southern Arizona. *Papers of the Peabody Museum, Harvard* 34, no. 1.

———. 1950. *The Stratigraphy and Archaeology of Ventana Cave, Arizona*. Tucson: University of Arizona Press and University of New Mexico Press.

———. 1986. *Emil W. Haury's Prehistory of the American Southwest*, J. Jefferson Reid and David E. Doyel, eds. Tucson: University of Arizona Press.

———. 1995. Wherefore a Harvard Ph.D.? *Journal of the Southwest* 37(4): 710–733.

Reid, J. Jefferson Reid. 1993. Emil Walter Haury, 1904–1992. *Kiva* 59(2): 242–259.

Smith, Watson. 1987. Emil Haury's Southwest: A Pisgah View. *Journal of the Southwest* 29(1): 107–120.

Steere, Peter L. 1993. The Writings of Emil W. Haury: An Annotated Bibliography. *Kiva* 59(2): 205–241.

Thompson, Raymond Harris, Caleb Vance Haynes Jr., and James Jefferson Reid. 1997. Emil Walter Haury: May 2, 1904–December 5, 1992. *Biographical Memoirs of the National Academy of Sciences* 72: 150–174.

E. ADAMSON HOEBEL, 1957
Papers: APS

Cohoe. 1964. *A Cheyenne Sketchbook*, commentary by E. Adamson Hoebel and Karen Daniels Petersen. Norman: University of Oklahoma Press.

Gibbs, James Lowell Jr. 1979. Hoebel, E. Adamson. In *International Encyclopedia of the Social Sciences, Biographical Supplement*, vol. 18, David L. Sills, ed. New York: Free Press.

Miller, Frank C. 1995. E. Adamson Hoebel (6 November 1906–23 July 1993). *Proceedings of the American Philosophical Society* 139(1): 105–108.

Pospisil, Leopold. 1973. E. Adamson Hoebel and the Anthropology of Law. *Law & Society Review* 7(4): 537–569.

Rohrl, Vivian J., M. E. R. Nicholson, and Mario D. Zamora. 1992. *The Anthropology of Peace: Essays in Honor of E. Adamson Hoebel*. Studies in Third World Societies, Publication 48 (parts 1 and 2). Williamsburg VA: College of William and Mary, Department of Anthropology.

Schwartz, Richard D. 1973. To Ad Hoebel–With Thanks. *Law & Society Review* 7(4): 531–532.

Wallace, Ernest, and E. Adamson Hoebel. 1952. *The Comanches: Lords of the South Plains*. Norman: University of Oklahoma Press.

HARRY HOIJER, 1958
Papers: APS

Beals, Ralph. 1977. Harry Hoijer. *American Anthropologist* 79: 105–110

Beals, Ralph L., and Harry Hoijer. 1953. *An Introduction to Anthropology*. First edition. New York: Macmillan.

Fromkin, Victoria. 1977. Harry Hoijer. *Language* 53: 169–173.

Gumperz, John, and Stephen Levinson. 1996. *Rethinking Linguistic Relativity*. Cambridge: Cambridge University Press.

Hoijer, Harry. 1933. Tonkawa, an Indian language of Texas. *Handbook of American Indian Languages* 3: 1–148

———. 1945. Navajo Phonology. *University of New Mexico Publications in Anthropology* 1.

———. 1951 Cultural Implications of some Navaho Linguistic Categories. *Language* 27: 111–120

———. 1956 Lexicostatistics: A Critique. *Language* 32: 49–60

———. 1972. *Tonkawa Texts*. University of California Publications in Linguistics 73.

Hoijer, Harry, ed. 1946. *Linguistic Structures of Native America*. New York: Viking Fund Publications in Anthropology, 6.

———, ed. 1954. *Language in Culture*. American Anthropological Association, Memoir 79.

Hoijer, Harry, and Edward Sapir. 1967. *The Phonology and Morphology of the Navaho Language*. Berkeley: University of California Press.

Landar, Herbert. 1977. Harry Hoijer: An Annotated Bibliography. *International Journal of American Linguistics* 43: 339–354.

Lucy, John. 1992. *Language Diversity and Thought: A Reformulation of the Linguistic Diversity Hypothesis*. Cambridge: Cambridge University Press.

SOL TAX, 1959
Papers: NAA, NAES, NL, UC

Ablon, Joan. 1979. The American Indian Chicago Conference. In *Currents in Anthropology: Essays in Honor of Sol Tax*, Robert Hinshaw, ed. The Hague: Mouton.

Blanchard, David. 1979. Beyond Empathy: The Emergence of an Action Anthropology in the Life and Career of Sol Tax. In *Currents in Anthropology: Essays in Honor of Sol Tax*, Robert Hinshaw, ed. The Hague: Mouton.

Gearing, Fred, Robert McC. Netting and Lisa R. Peattie, eds. 1960. *Documentary History of the Fox Project, 1948–1959: A Program in Action Anthropology, Directed by Sol Tax*. Chicago: University of Chicago Department of Anthropology.

Heise, Kenan. 1995. Professor Sol Tax; Was Anthropologist at U. of C. *Chicago Tribune*, 7 January, sec. 1, 19.

Hinshaw, Robert. 1979. Tax, Sol. In *International Encyclopedia of the Social Sciences, Biographical Supplement*, vol. 18. David L. Sills, ed. New York: Free Press.

Johansen, Bruce E., and Donald A. Grinde Jr. 1997. Tax, Sol. In *The Encyclopedia of Native American Biography: Six Hundred Life Stories of Important People, from Powhatan to Wilma Mankiller*. New York: Henry Holt and Co.

Kennedy, Randy. 1995. Sol Tax, 87, Anthropologist Who Founded Journal, Dies. *New York Times*, 8 January, 32.

Rubinstein, Robert A. 1991. A Conversation with Sol Tax. *Current Anthropology* 32(2): 175–183.

———, ed. 1991. *Fieldwork: The Correspondence of Robert Redfield and Sol Tax.* Boulder CO: Westview.

Stocking, George W. 2000. "Do Good, Young Man": Sol Tax and the World Mission of Liberal Democratic Anthropology. In *Excluded Ancestors, Inventible Traditions: Essays Toward a More Inclusive History of Anthropology*, Richard Handler, ed. Madison: University of Wisconsin Press.

Tax, Sol. 1931. An Algerian Passover. *American Hebrew*, 3 April, 548.

———. 1952. Action Anthropology. *América Indígena* 12: 103–106.

———. 1953. *Penny Capitalism: A Guatemalan Indian Economy.* First edition. Washington DC: GPO.

———. 1988. Pride and Puzzlement: A Retro-introspective Record of 60 Years of Anthropology. *Annual Review of Anthropology* 17: 1–21.

Tax, Sol, ed. 1967. *The Draft: A Handbook of Facts and Alternatives.* Chicago: University of Chicago Press.

Tax, Sol, ed. 1968. *The People vs. the System: A Dialogue in Urban Conflict.* Chicago: Acme.

MARGARET MEAD, 1960

Papers: LC, AMNH

Bateson, Gregory, and Margaret Mead. 1942. *Balinese Character.* New York: Special Publications of the New York Academy of Sciences, Series II.

Bateson, Mary Catherine. 1984. *With a Daughter's Eye: A Memoir of Margaret Mead and Gregory Bateson.* New York: William Morrow.

Freeman, Derek. 1983. *Margaret Mead and Samoa: The Making and Unmaking of an Anthropological Myth.* Cambridge: Harvard University Press.

Howard, Jane. 1984. *Margaret Mead: A Life.* New York: Simon and Schuster.

Mead, Margaret. 1928. *Coming of Age in Samoa: A Psychological Study of Primitive Youth for Western Civilization.* New York: William Morrow.

———. 1930. *Growing up in New Guinea.* New York: William Morrow.

———. 1935. *Sex and Temperament in Three Primitive Societies.* New York: William Morrow.

———. 1942. *And Keep Your Powder Dry.* New York: William Morrow.

———. 1972. *Blackberry Winter: My Early Years.* New York: William Morrow.

———. 1974. *Ruth Benedict.* New York: Columbia University Press.

Mead, Margaret, ed. 1959. *An Anthropologist at Work: Writings of Ruth Benedict.* Boston: Houghton Mifflin.

———, ed. 1977. *Letters from the Field, 1925–1975.* New York: Harper and Row.

Mead, Margaret, and Rhoda Métraux, eds. 1953. *The Study of Culture at a Distance.* Chicago: University of Chicago Press.

Métraux, Rhoda. 1980. Margaret Mead: A Biographical Sketch. *American Anthropologist* 82: 262–269.

Yans-McLaughlin, Virginia. 1989. Margaret Mead. In *Women Anthropologists: Selected Biographies,* Ute Gacs, Aisha Khan, Jerrie McIntyre, and Ruth Weinberg, eds. Urbana: University of Illinois Press.

GORDON R. WILLEY, 1961

Vogt, Evon Z., and Richard M. Leventhal, eds. 1983. *Prehistoric Settlement Patterns: Essays in Honor of Gorgon R. Willey.* Albuquerque: University of New Mexico Press.
Willey, Gordon R. 1974. The Virú Valley Settlement Pattern Study. In *Archaeological Researches in Retrospect,* G. R. Willey, ed. Cambridge MA: Winthrop.
———. 1988. *Portraits in American Archaeology: Remembrances of Some Distinguished Americanists.* Albuquerque: University of New Mexico Press.
———. 1990. *New World Archaeology and Culture History: Collected Essays and Articles.* Albuquerque: University of New Mexico Press.
Willey, Gordon R., ed. 1964. *Prehistoric Settlement Patterns in the New World.* New York: Viking Publications in Anthropology 23.
Willey, Gordon R., and Philip Phillips. 1958. *Method and Theory in American Archaeology.* Chicago: University of Chicago Press.
Willey, Gordon R., and Jeremy A. Sabloff. 1974. *A History of American Archaeology.* London: Thames and Hudson.

SHERWOOD WASHBURN, 1962
Papers: UCB-B

DeVore, I. 1992. An interview with Sherwood Washburn. *Current Anthropology* 33: 411–423.
Haraway, D. 1988. Remodelling the Human Way of Life: Sherwood Washburn and the New Physical Anthropology, 1950–1980. In *Bones, Bodies, Behavior: Essays on Biological Anthropology,* George W. Stocking, ed. History of Anthropology 5. Madison: University of Wisconsin Press.
Marks, J. 2000. Sherwood Washburn, 1911–2000. *Evolutionary Anthropology* 9: 225–226.
Washburn, S. L. 1951. The New Physical Anthropology. *Transactions of the New York Academy of Sciences* Series II, 13: 298–304.
———. 1963. The Study of Race. *American Anthropologist* 65: 521–531.
———. 1983. Evolution of a Teacher. *Annual Review of Anthropology* 12: 1–24.
Washburn, S. L., ed. 1961. *The Social Life of Early Man.* Chicago: Aldine.
———, ed. 1963. *Classification and Human Evolution.* Chicago: Aldine.

MORRIS E. OPLER, 1963

Gesensway, Deborah, and Mindy Roseman. 1987. *Beyond Words: Images from America's Concentration Camps.* Ithaca NY: Cornell University Press.

Harris, Marvin. 1968. *The Rise of Anthropological Theory*. New York: Thomas Crowell.

Opler, Marvin K., ed. 1959. *Culture and Mental Health*. New York: Macmillan.

Opler, Morris. 1942. *An Apache Life-Way: The Economic, Social and Religious Institutions of the Chiracahua Indians*. Chicago: University of Chicago Press.

———. 1969. *Apache Odyssey: A Journey Between Two Worlds*. New York: Holt.

Opler, Morris, and Edward F. Castetter. 1936. *The Ethnobiology of the Chiricahua and Mescalero Apache*. Albuquerque: University of New Mexico Press.

Opler, Morris, and Harry Hoijer. 1938. *Chiracahua and Mescalero Apache Texts*. Chicago: University of Chicago Press.

Opler, Morris, and Henry F. Dobyns, eds. 1966. *Recommendations for Future Research on the Process of Cultural Change*. Ithaca: Comparative Studies of Cultural Change, Department of Anthropology, Cornell University.

Stocking, George W., Jr. 1968. *Race, Culture and Evolution: Essays in the Historiography of Anthropology*. New York: Free Press.

Williams, Gerry C., and Carolyn Peel, eds. 1977. *Essays in Anthropology in Honor of Morris Edward Opler*. Norman: University of Oklahoma Press.

Zamora, Mario D., et al., eds. 1971. *Themes in Culture: Essays in Honor of Morris E. Opler*. India: Kaymangii.

LESLIE A. WHITE, 1964
Papers: NAA, UM–B

Barrett, Richard A. 1989. The Paradoxical Anthropology of Leslie White. *American Anthropologist* 91: 986–999.

Beardsley, Richard K. 1976. An Appraisal of Leslie White's Scholarly Influence. *American Anthropologist* 78: 617–620.

Carneiro, Robert L. 1981. Leslie A. White. In *Totems and Teachers: Perspectives on the History of Anthropology*, Sydel Silverman, ed. New York: Columbia University Press.

Kroeber, Alfred L. 1948. White's View of Culture. *American Anthropologist* 50: 405–415.

Service, Elman R. 1976. Leslie Alvin White, 1900–1975, with bibliography compiled by Beth Dillingham. *American Anthropologist* 78: 612–629.

White, Leslie A. 1949. *The Science of Culture: A Study of Man of Civilization*. New York: Farrar Strauss.

———. 1959. *The Evolution of Culture: The Development of Civilization to the Fall of Rome*. New York: McGraw-Hill.

———. 1963. *The Ethnography and Ethnology of Franz Boas*. Austin: Texas Memorial Museum Bulletin 6.

———. 1966. *The Social Organization of Ethnological Theory*. Houston: Rice University Studies 52(4).

———. 1975. *The Concept of Cultural Systems: A Key to Understanding Tribes and Nations*. New York: Columbia University Press.

ALEXANDER SPOEHR, 1965

American Anthropological Association. 1966. American Anthropological Association Council Meeting, Saturday, November 20, 1965, Denver, Colorado. *American Anthropologist* 68: 759–773.

———. 1967. American Anthropological Association Council Meeting, Saturday, November 19, 1966, Pittsburgh, Pennsylvania. *American Anthropologist* 69: 371–783.

Boggs, Stephen T. 1965. The Arts and Humanities Bill. *Fellow Newsletter* 6(5): 1–2.

Heise, Kenan. 1992. Anthropologist, Curator Alexander Spoehr. *Chicago Tribune* 2 July, sec. 3, 11.

Martin, Paul S., Carl Lloyd, and Alexander Spoehr. 1938. Archaeological Works in the Ackman-Lowry Area, Southwestern Colorado, 1937. *Field Museum of Natural History Anthropological Series* 23(2): 217–304.

Oliver, Douglas. 1996. Alexander Spoehr, August 23, 1913–June 11, 1992. *National Academy of Sciences Biographical Memoirs* 69: 294–313.

Spoehr, Alexander. 1942. Kinship Systems of the Seminole. *Field Museum of Natural History Anthropological Series* 33(2): 29–114.

———. 1947. Changing Kinship Systems: A Study in the Acculturation of the Creeks, Cherokees, and Choctaws. *Field Museum of Natural History Anthropological Series* 33(4): 151–235.

———. 1973. *Zamboanga and Sulu: An Archaeological Approach to Ethnic Diversity*. Ethnology Monographs 1, Department of Anthropology, University of Pittsburgh.

———. 1980. *Protein from the Sea: Technological Change in Philippine Capture Fisheries*. Ethnology Monographs 3, Department of Anthropology, University of Pittsburgh.

JOHN P. GILLIN, 1966
Papers: PM

Anon. 1973. Dr. John P. Gillin. Anthropologist. *New York Times*, 5 August, 53.

———. 1979. Gillin, John Philip. *The National Cyclopedia of American Biography* 58: 429–431.

Gillin, John Lewis, and John Philip Gillin. 1942. *An Introduction to Sociology*. New York: Macmillan.

Gillin, John P. 1938. *Archaeological Investigations in Nine Mile Canyon, Utah (During the Year 1936)*. Bulletin 28(11), University of Utah, Salt Lake City.

———. 1947. *Moche: A Peruvian Coastal Community*. Publication 3, Institute of Social Anthropology, Smithsonian Institution. Washington DC.

———. 1948a. *The Ways of Man: An Introduction to Anthropology*. New York: Appleton-Century.

———. 1948b. Magical Fright. *Psychiatry* 11: 387–400.

———. 1951. *The Culture of Security in San Carlos: A Study of a Guatemalan Community of Indians and Ladinos*. Publication 16, Middle American Research Institute, Tulane University, New Orleans.

———. 1969. *Human Ways: Selected Essays in Anthropology*. Pittsburgh: University of Pittsburgh Press.

Gillin, John P., ed. 1954. *For a Science of Social Man*. New York: Macmillan.

Reina, Ruben E. 1976. John Phillip [*sic*] Gillin, 1907–1973. *American Anthropologist* 78: 79–86.

FREDERICA DE LAGUNA, 1967
Papers: ASHL, BMC, NAA, Penn

de Laguna, Frederica. 1934. *The Archaeology of Cook Inlet, Alaska*. Philadelphia: University of Pennsylvania Press.

———. 1937. *The Arrow Points to Murder: The Crime Club*. New York: Doubleday Doran.

———. 1938. *Fog on the Mountain: The Crime Club*. New York: Doubleday Doran.

———. 1947. *The Prehistory of Northern North America as Seen from the Yukon*. Memoirs of the Society for American Archaeology 3.

———. 1956. *Chugach Prehistory: The Archaeology of Prince William Sound, Alaska*. Seattle: University of Washington Publications in Anthropology 13.

———. 1960. *The Story of a Tlingit Community: A Problem in the Relationship between Archaeological, Ethnological, and Historical Methods*. Bureau of American Ethnology Bulletin 172. Washington DC: GPO.

———. 1968. Presidential Address, 1967: On Anthropological Inquiry. *American Anthropologist* 70: 469–476.

———. 1972. *Under Mount Saint Elias: The History and Culture of the Yakutat Tlingit*. Washington DC: Smithsonian Institution Press.

———. 1977. *Voyage to Greenland: A Personal Initiation into Anthropology*. New York: W. W. Norton.

———. 2000. *Travels among the Dena*. Seattle: University of Washington Press.

de Laguna, Frederica, ed. 1991. *The Tlingit Indians*, by G. T. Emmons. Seattle: University of Washington Press.

———, ed. 2002. *American Anthropology, 1888–1920: Selected Papers from the "American Anthropologist."* Lincoln: University of Nebraska Press.

de Laguna, Frederica, and Kaj Birket-Smith. 1938. *The Eyak Indians of the Copper River Delta, Alaska*. Copenhagen: Levin and Munksgaard.

Ferzacca, Steve. 1998. Frederica de Laguna and her Reunion Under Mount Saint Elias. *Expedition* 40: 27–43.

Grinev, A. V. 2000. Frederica de Laguna and her Contribution to the Study of the Native Population of Alaska. *Anthropology and Archaeology of Eurasia* 38: 11–23.

McClelland, Catherine. 1989a. Frederica de Laguna. In *Women Anthropologists: Selected Biographies*, Ute Gacs, Aisha Khan, Jerrie McIntyre, and Ruth Weinberg, eds. Urbana: University of Illinois Press.

———. 1989b. Frederica de Laguna and the Pleasures of Anthropology. *American Ethnologist* 16: 766–785.

IRVING ROUSE, 1968

Griffin, James B. 1978. An Appreciation of Irving Benjamin Rouse. In *Archaeological Essays in Honor of Irving B. Rouse*, Robert C. Dunnell and Edwin S. Hall, eds. The Hague: Mouton.

Renfrew, Colin. 1974. [Review of] Irving Rouse: *Introduction to Prehistory: A Systematic Approach. Antiquity* 48(191): 244–246.

Rouse, Irving. 1938. Contributions to the Prehistory of the Ft. Liberté Region, Haiti. Ph.D. dissertation, Yale University.

———. 1939. *Prehistory in Haiti: A Study in Method.* Yale University Publications in Anthropology 21.

———. 1941. *Culture of the Ft. Liberté Region, Haiti.* Yale University Publications in Anthropology 24.

———. 1953. The Circum-Caribbean Theory: An Archaeological Test. *American Anthropologist* 55: 188–200.

———. 1965. The Place of "Peoples" in Prehistoric Research. *Journal of the Royal Anthropological Institute* 95(1): 1–15.

———. 1972. *Introduction to Prehistory: A Systematic Approach.* New York: McGraw-Hill.

———. 1986. *Migrations in Prehistory: Inferring Population Movement from Cultural Remains.* New Haven: Yale University Press.

———. 1992. *The Tainos: Rise and Decline of the People Who Greeted Columbus.* New Haven: Yale University Press.

Rouse, Irving, and José M. Cruxent. 1963. *Venezuelan Archaeology.* New Haven: Yale University Press.

Siegel, Peter E. 1996. An Interview with Irving Rouse. *Current Anthropology* 37(4): 671–689.

Sued Badillo, Jalil. 1992. Facing up to Caribbean History. *American Antiquity* 57(4): 599–607.

CORA DU BOIS, 1969
Papers: HU-P, PM, RC-S, UC

Du Bois, Cora. 1935. Wintu Ethnography. *University of California Publications in American Archaeology and Ethnology* 36(1): 1–148.

———. 1937. Some Anthropological Perspectives on Psycho-Analysis. *Psycho-Analytic Review* 24(3): 246–263.

———. 1944. *The People of Alor.* Minneapolis: University of Minnesota Press.

———. 1949. *Social Forces in Southeast Asia.* Minneapolis: University of Minnesota Press.

———. 1970. Studies in an Indian Town. In *Women in the Field: Anthropological Experiences*, Peggy Golde, ed. Chicago: Aldine.

———. 1980. Some Anthropological Hindsights. *Annual Review of Anthropology* 9: 1–15.

Seymour, Susan. 1989. Cora Du Bois (1903–). In *Women Anthropologists: Selected Biographies*, Ute Gacs, Aisha Khan, Jerrie McIntyre, and Ruth Weinberg, eds. Urbana: University of Illinois Press.

GEORGE M. FOSTER, 1970

Brandes, Stanley. 1988. *Power and Persuasion: Fiestas and Social Control in Rural Mexico.* Philadelphia: University of Pennsylvania Press.

Foster, George M. 1976. Graduate Study at Berkeley, 1935–1941. *Anthropology* UCLA 8: 9–18.

———. 1979a. Fieldwork in Tzintzuntzan: The First Thirty Years. In *Long-Term Field Research in Social Anthropology*, G. Foster et al., eds. New York: Academic Press.

———. 1979b. The Institute of Social Anthropology. In *The Uses of Anthropology*, Walter Goldschmidt, ed. Washington DC: American Anthropological Association.

———. 1986. The Changing Culture of the Anthropological Profession in the United States. *Southwestern Anthropological Association Newsletter* 6(1): 5–11.

Foster, Mary LeCron, and Stanley H. Brandes, eds. 1980. *Symbol as Sense: New Approaches to the Analysis of Meaning.* New York: Academic Press.

Kemper, Robert V. 1977. *Migration and Adaptation: Tzintzuntzan Peasants in Mexico City.* Beverly Hills CA: Sage.

CHARLES WAGLEY, 1971
Papers: UF

Kottak, Conrad Phillip. 1992. Charles Wagley. *Anthropology Newsletter* 33(4): 5.

Margolis, Maxine L., and William E. Carter. 1979. *Brazil, Anthropological Perspectives: Essays in Honor of Charles Wagley.* New York: Columbia University Press.

Wagley, Charles. 1949. *The Tenetehara Indians of Brazil: A Culture in Transition.* New York: Columbia University Press.

———. 1952. *Race and Class in Rural Brazil.* Paris: UNESCO.

———. 1953. *Amazon Town: A Study of Man in the Tropics.* New York: Macmillan.

———. 1963. *An Introduction to Brazil.* New York: Columbia University Press.

———. 1974. *Man in the Amazon.* Gainesville: University Press of Florida.

Wagley, Charles, and Marvin Harris. 1958. *Minorities in the New World: Six Case Studies.* New York: Columbia University Press.

Watanabe, John. 1992. *Maya Saints and Souls in a Changing World.* Austin: University of Texas Press.

ANTHONY F. C. WALLACE, 1972
Papers: APS

Grumet, Robert S. 1998. An Interview with Anthony F. C. Wallace. *Ethnohistory* 45: 103–107.

Wallace, Anthony F. C. 1949 [1995]. *King of the Delawares: Teedyuscung, 1700–1763.* Syracuse: Syracuse University Press.

———. 1956. Revitalization Movements. *American Anthropologist* 58: 264–281.

———. 1961 [1970]. *Culture and Personality.* New York: Random House.

———. 1966. *Religion: An Anthropological View*. New York: Random House.

———. 1970a. *The Death and Rebirth of the Seneca*. New York: Knopf.

———. 1970b. *Prelude to Disaster*. Springfield: Illinois State Historical Society.

———. 1975. *Rockdale: The Growth of an American Village in the Early Industrial Revolution*. New York: Knopf.

———. 1987. *St. Clair: A Nineteenth-Century Coal Town's Experience with a Disaster-Prone Industry*. New York: Knopf.

———. 1993. *The Long Bitter Trail*. New York: Hill and Wang.

———. 1999. *Thomas Jefferson and the Indians: The Tragic Fate of the First Americans*. Cambridge: Harvard University Press.

JOSEPH B. CASAGRANDE, 1973

Papers: UIUC

Casagrande, Joseph. 1948. Comanche Baby Language. *International Journal of American Linguistics* 14: 11–14.

———. 1954–55. Comanche Linguistic Acculturation. *International Journal of American Linguistics* 20: 140–151, 217–237; 21: 8–25.

———. 1959. Some Observations on the Study of Intermediate Societies. In *Intermediate Societies, Social Mobility, and Communication*, Verne R. Ray, ed. Seattle: University of Washington Press.

———. 1973. Strategies for Survival: The Indians of Highland Ecuador. In *Contemporary Cultures of Latin America*, Dwight B. Heath, ed. New York: Random House and Knopf.

Casagrande, Joseph, ed. 1960. *In the Company of Man: Twenty Portraits by Anthropologists*. New York: Harper.

Thompson, Stephen I. 1985. Joseph Bartholomew Casagrande (1915–1982). *American Anthropologist* 87: 883–888.

EDWARD H. SPICER, 1974

Papers: ASM

Adams, William Y. 1990. Edward Spicer, Historian. *Journal of the Southwest* 32: 18–26.

Gallaher, Art Jr. 1984. Edward Holland Spicer. *American Anthropologist* 86: 380–385.

Officer, James E. 1990. Edward Spicer and the Application of Anthropology. *Journal of the Southwest* 32: 18–35.

Savala, Refugio. 1980. *Autobiography of a Yaqui Poet*. Tucson: University of Arizona Press.

Spicer, Edward H. 1940 *Pascua*. Chicago: University of Chicago Press.

———. 1952. *Human Problems in Technological Change*. New York: Sage.

———. 1954. *Potam*. American Anthropological Association, Memoir 77.

———. 1962. *Cycles of Conquest: The Impact of Spain, Mexico and the United States on the Indians of the Southwest*. Tucson: University of Arizona Press.

———. 1969a. *Impounded People*. Tucson: University of Arizona Press.

———. 1969b. *A Short History of the Indians of the United States.* New York: Van Nostrand.

———. 1971. Persistent Cultural Systems. *Science* 175: 795–800.

———. 1980. *The Yaquis: A Cultural History.* Tucson: University of Arizona Press.

———. 1988. *People of Pascua.* Tucson: University of Arizona Press.

Spicer, Rosamond B. 1990. A Full Life, Well-Lived. *Journal of the Southwest* 32: 3–17.

ERNESTINE FRIEDL, 1975

Friedl, Ernestine. 1956. Persistence in Chippewa Culture and Personality. *American Anthropologist* 58: 814–825.

———. 1962. *Vasilika: A Village in Modern Greece.* New York: Holt, Rinehart and Winston.

———. 1970. Fieldwork in a Greek Village. In *Women in the Field*, Peggy Golde, ed. Chicago: Aldine.

———. 1975. *Women and Men: An Anthropologist's View.* New York: Holt, Rinehart and Winston.

———. 1995. The Life of an Academic: A Personal Record of a Teacher, Administrator, and Anthropologist. *Annual Review of Anthropology* 24: 1–19.

Hollingshead, Lynne M. 1989. Ernestine Friedl (1920–). In *Women Anthropologists: Selected Biographies*, Ute Gacs, Aisha Khan, Jerrie McIntyre, and Ruth Weinberg, eds. Urbana: University of Illinois Press.

WALTER R. GOLDSCHMIDT, 1976
Papers: UCLA

Durrenberger, E. Paul, and Kendall M. Thu. 1996. The Expansion of Large Scale Hog Farming in Iowa: The Applicability of Goldschmidt's Findings Fifty Years Later. *Human Organization* 55(4): 409.

Goldschmidt, Walter R. 1946. *As You Sow.* New York: Harcourt, Brace and Co.

———. 1959. *Man's Way: A Preface to the Understanding of Human Society.* New York: World Publishing Company and Holt, Rinehart, Winston.

——— 1966. *Comparative Functionalism: An Essay in Anthropological Theory.* Berkeley: University of California Press.

———. 1967. *Sebei Law* Berkeley: University of California Press.

———. 1979. *On Becoming an Anthropologist.* Washington DC: American Anthropological Association.

———. 1990. *The Human Career: The Self in the Symbolic World.* Cambridge MA: Basil Blackwell

Goldschmidt, Walter R., ed. 1954. *Ways of Mankind.* Boston: Beacon.

———, ed. 1979. *The Uses of Anthropology.* Washington DC: American Anthropological Association.

———, ed. 1983. *Anthropology and Public Policy: A Dialogue.* Washington DC: American Anthropological Association

Goldschmidt, Walter R., and Robert Edgerton. 1959. A Picture Technique for the Study of Values. *American Anthropologist* 63(1): 26–47.

Goldschmidt, Walter R., with Gale Goldschmidt. 1976. *Culture and Behavior of the Sebei: A Study in Continuity and Adaptation.* Berkeley: University of California Press.

Kennedy, John G., and Robert B. Edgerton. 1982. *Culture and Ecology: Eclectic Perspectives.* Washington DC: American Anthropological Association.

Labao, Linda M. 1990. *Locality and Inequality: Farm and Industry Structure and Socioeconomic Conditions.* Albany: State University of New York Press.

Louky, James P., and Jeffrey R. Jones. 1976. *Paths to the Symbolic Self: Essays in Honor of Walter Goldschmidt.* Berkeley: University of California Press.

Turner, Jonathan H., and Alexandra Maryanski. 1979. *Functionalism.* Menlo Park CA: Benjamin Cummings.

RICHARD N. ADAMS, 1977

Adams, Richard N. 1957. *Cultural Surveys of Panama-Nicaragua-Guatemala-El Salvador-Honduras.* Pan American Sanitary Bureau, Scientific Publications 33, Washington DC.

———. 1967. *The Second Sowing: Power and Secondary Development in Latin America.* San Francisco: Chandler.

———. 1970. *Crucifixion by Power: Essays on Guatemalan National Social Structure, 1944–66.* Austin: University of Texas Press.

———. 1975. *Energy and Structure: A Theory of Social Power.* Austin: University of Texas Press.

———. 1976. Ricocheting Through a Half Century of Revolution. Address on receiving the Kalman Silvert Award. *LASA Forum* 29(3): 14–20 (1998).

———. 1982. *Paradoxical Harvest: Energy and Explanation in British History, 1870–1914.* Cambridge: Cambridge University Press.

———. 1988. *The Eighth Day: Human Society as the Self-Organization of Energy Processes.* Austin: University of Texas Press.

———. 1996. *Etnica en evolución social: Estudios de Guatemala y Centroamérica.* Mexico: Universidad Autonoma Metropolitana, Unidad Iztapalapa.

Adams, Richard N., ed., with Dwight Health. 1965. *Contemporary Cultures and Societies of Latin America: A Reader.* New York: Random House.

Adams, Richard N., ed., with Raymond Fogelson. 1977. *The Anthropology of Power.* New York: Academic Press.

FRANCIS L. K. HSU, 1978

Hsu, Francis L. K. 1947. On a Technique for Studying Relationship Terms. *American Anthropologist* 49: 618–624.

———. 1948. *Under the Ancestors' Shadows: Chinese Culture and Personality*. New York: Columbia University Press.

———. 1952. *Religion, Science, and Human Crises: A Study of China in Transition and Its Implications for the West*. London: Routledge and Kegan Paul.

———. 1953. *American and Chinese: Two Ways of Life*. New York: Abelard-Shuman. Revised edition; New York: Natural History Press, 1970.

———. 1961. *Psychological Anthropology*. Homewood IL: Dorwood.

———. 1971. Psychosocial Homeostasis and Jen: Conceptual Tools for Advancing Psychological Anthropology. *American Anthropologist* 73: 23–44.

———. 1973. Prejudice and Its Intellectual Effect on American Anthropology: An Ethnographic Report. *American Anthropologist* 75: 1–19.

———. 1975. *Iemoto: The Heart of Japan*. Cambridge MA: Schenkman.

———. 1978. Passage to Understanding. In *The Making of Psychological Anthropology*, George D. Spindler, ed. Berkeley: University of California Press.

Hsu-Balzer, Eileen, Richard Balzer, and Francis Hsu. 1974. *China Day by Day*. New Haven: Yale University Press.

PAUL BOHANNAN, 1979
Papers: NAA

Bohannan, Paul. 1957. *Justice and Judgment among the Tiv*. Oxford: Oxford University Press.

———. 1960. *African Homicide and Suicide*. Princeton: Princeton University Press.

———. 1963. *Social Anthropology*. New York: Holt, Rinehart and Winston.

———. 1964. *Africa and Africans*. New York: Doubleday.

———. 1970. *Divorce and After*. New York: Doubleday.

———. 1980. You Can't Do Nothing. *American Anthropologist* 82(3): 508–524.

———. 1985. *All the Happy Families: Exploring the Varieties of Family Life*. New York: McGraw-Hill.

———. 1991. *We the Alien: An Introduction to Cultural Anthropology*. Prospect Heights IL: Waveland.

———. 1995. *How Culture Works*. New York: Free Press.

Bohannan, Paul, and Mark Glazer, eds. 1973. *High Points in Anthropology*. New York: Knopf.

Bohannan, Paul, and Margaret Gruter, eds. 1982. *Law, Biology, and Culture*. Santa Barbara: Ross-Erickson.

Bohannan, Paul, and Philip Curtin. 1995. *Africa and Africans*. Fourth edition. Prospect Heights IL: Waveland.

Bohannan, Paul, and Dirk Van Der Elst. 1998. *Asking and Listening: Ethnography as Personal Adaptation*. Prospect Heights IL: Waveland.

CONRAD M. ARENSBERG, 1980

Arensberg, Conrad M. 1937. *The Irish Countryman: An Anthropological Study*. Garden City NY: Natural History.

———. 1972. Culture as Behavior: Structure and Emergence. *Annual Review of Anthropology* 1: 1–26.

———. 1981. Cultural Holism through Interactional Systems. *American Anthropologist* 83: 562–581.

Arensberg, Conrad M., and Solon T. Kimball. 1965. *Culture and Community.* New York: Harcourt, Brace and World.

———. 1968. *Family and Community in Ireland.* Cambridge: Harvard University Press.

Arensberg, Conrad M., and Alan Lomax. 1977. A Worldwide Evolutionary Classification of Cultures by Subsistence Systems. *Current Anthropology* 18: 659–708.

Arensberg, Conrad M., and A. H. Niehoff. 1964. *Introducing Social Change: A Manual for Americans Overseas.* Chicago: Aldine.

Arensberg, Conrad M., Karl Polanyi, and H. W. Pearson, eds. 1957. *Trade and Markets in the Early Empires.* Glencoe IL: The Free Press.

Chapple, Eliot D., and Conrad M. Arensberg. 1940. Measuring Human Relations: An Introduction to the Study of the Individual. *Genetic Psychology Monograph* 23: 3–147.

Comitas, Lambros. 1997. Conrad M. Arensberg. *Anthropology Newsletter* 38(5): 18.

Lynch, O. M., ed. 1984. *Culture and Community in Europe: Essays in Honor of Conrad M. Arensberg.* Delhi: Hindustan.

Thomas, Robert. 1997. Conrad Arensberg 86 Dies: Hands-on Anthropologist. *New York Times.* 16 February, sec. 1, 51.

Warner, W. Lloyd. 1941. *Yankee City.* New Haven: Yale University Press.

WILLIAM C. STURTEVANT, 1981
Papers: NAA

Conklin, Harold C., and William C. Sturtevant. 1953. Seneca Indian Singing Tools at Coldspring Longhouse: Musical Instruments of the Modern Iroquois. *Proceedings of the American Philosophical Society* 97: 262–290.

Sturtevant, William C. 1955. The Mikasuki Seminole: Medical Beliefs and Practices. Ph.D. dissertation, Yale University.

———. 1960a. A Seminole Medicine Maker. In *In the Company of Man: Twenty Portraits by Anthropologists,* Joseph B. Casagrande, ed. New York: Harper.

———. 1960b. *The Significance of Ethnological Similarities between Southeastern North America and the Antilles.* Yale University Publications in Anthropology 64. New Haven: Yale University Press.

———. 1964. Studies in Ethnoscience. In *Transcultural Studies in Cognition. American Anthropologist Special Publication,* A. Kimball Romney and Roy Goodwin D'Andrade, eds., 66 (3, part 2). Washington: American Anthropological Association.

———. 1966. Anthropology, History and Ethnohistory. *Ethnohistory* 13: 1–51.

———. 1967. Seminole Men's Clothing. In *Essays on the Verbal and Visual Arts,* June

Helm, ed. Proceedings of the 1966 Annual Spring Meeting of the American Ethnological Society. Seattle: University of Washington Press.

——. 1971. Creek into Seminole. In *North American Indians in Historical Perspective*, Eleanor Burke Leacock and Nancy Oestreich Lurie, eds. New York: Random House.

——. 1973. Museums as Anthropological Data Banks. In *Anthropology beyond the University*, Alden Redfield, ed. Southern Anthropological Society Proceedings 7. Athens: University of Georgia Press.

——. 1977. *A Guide to Field Collecting of Ethnographic Specimens.* Second edition. Smithsonian Information Leaflet 503. Washington DC: Smithsonian Institution.

——. 1983. Tribe and State in the Sixteenth and Twentieth Centuries. In *The Development of Political Organization in Native North America,* Elisabeth Tooker, ed. Proceedings of the American Ethnological Society, 1979. Washington: American Ethnological Society.

——. 1984. A Structural Sketch of Iroquois Ritual. In *Extending the Rafters: Interdisciplinary Approaches to Iroquoian Studies*, Michael K. Foster, Jack Campisi, and Marianne Mithun, eds. Albany: State University of New York Press.

——. 1998. Tupinambá Chiefdoms? In *Chiefdoms and Chieftaincy in the Americas*, Elsa M. Redmond, ed. Gainesville: University of Florida Press.

Sturtevant, William C., ed. 1978–2001. *Handbook of North American Indians*, 12 vols. Washington DC: Smithsonian Institution.

M. MARGARET CLARK, 1982

Ames, Genevieve, and Joan Ablon. 1994. Margaret Clark: From Field Research to Theory Development. *Medical Anthropology Quarterly* 8(4): 355–559.

Browner, C. H. 1994. Margaret Clark's Enduring Contribution to Latino Studies in Medical Anthropology. *Medical Anthropology Quarterly* 8(4): 468–475.

Clark, Margaret. 1959. *Health in the Mexican-American Culture: A Community Study.* Berkeley: University of California Press.

——. 1973. Contributions of Cultural Anthropology to the Study of the Aged. In *Cultural Illness and Health*, L. Nader and T. W. Maretzki, eds. Anthropological Studies 9. Washington DC: American Anthropological Association.

Clark, Margaret and Barbara Gallatin Anderson. 1967. *Culture and Aging: An Anthropological Study of Older Americans.* Springfield IL: Charles C. Thomas.

DELL HYMES, 1983
Papers: APS

Baumann, Richard and Joel Scherzer, eds. 1974. *Explorations in the Ethnography of Speaking.* Cambridge: Cambridge University Press.

Gumperz, John, and Dell Hymes, eds. 1972. *Directions in Sociolinguistics: The Ethnography of Communication.* New York: Holt, Rinehart and Winston.

Hymes, Dell. 1963. Notes Toward a History of Linguistic Anthropology. *Anthropological Linguistics* 5: 59–103.

———. 1966. Two Types of Linguistic Relativity. In *Sociolinguistics*, W. Bright, ed. The Hague: Mouton.

———. 1973. Speech and Language: On the Origins and Foundations of Inequality in Speaking. *Daedalus* (summer): 59–86.

———. 1980a. In Five-Year Patterns. In *First Person Singular*, B. H. Davis and R. O'Cain, eds. Amsterdam: John Benjamins.

———. 1980b. *Language in Education: Ethnolinguistic Essays*. Washington DC: Center for Applied Linguistics.

———. 1981. *In Vain I Tried to Tell You*. Philadelphia: University of Pennsylvania Press.

———. 1983. *Essays in the History of Linguistic Anthropology*. Amsterdam: John Benjamins.

Hymes, Dell, ed. 1964. *Language in Culture and Society*. New York: Harper and Row.

———, ed. 1971. *Pidginization and Creolization of Language*. Cambridge: Cambridge University Press.

———, ed. 1972. *Reinventing Anthropology*. New York: Pantheon.

———, ed. 1974a. *Studies in the History of Linguistics: Traditions and Paradigms*. Bloomington: Indiana University Press.

———, ed. 1974b. *Foundations in Sociolinguistics: An Ethnographic Approach*. Philadelphia: University of Pennsylvania Press.

Hymes, Dell, and John Fought. 1975. *American Structuralism*. New York: Mouton, 1981.

NANCY O. LURIE, 1984–1985
Papers: UWM, MPM, NAA

Ganteaume, Cecile R. 1989. Nancy Oestreich Lurie. In *Women Anthropologists: Selected Biographies*, Ute Gacs, Aisha Khan, Jerrie McIntyre, and Ruth Weinberg, eds. Urbana: University of Illinois Press.

Lurie, Nancy Oestreich. 1961. *Mountain Wolf Woman, Sister of Crashing Thunder*. Ann Arbor: University of Michigan Press.

———. 1972. Two Dollars. In *Crossing Cultural Boundaries*, Solon Kimball and James Watson, eds. San Francisco: Chandler.

———. 1978. The Indian Claims Commission. *Annals of the American Academy of Political and Social Science* 436: 97–110.

———. 1981. Museumland Revisited. *Human Organization* 40(2): 180–187.

———. 1999. *Women and the Invention of American Anthropology*. Prospect Heights IL: Waveland.

Lurie, Nancy Oestreich, and Eleanor Burke Leacock, eds. 1971. *The North American Indian in Historical Perspective*. New York: Random House.

Lurie, Nancy Oestreich, and June Helm. 1966. *The Dogrib Handgame*. Anthropological Series 71, National Museum of Canada Bulletin 205.

Lurie, Nancy Oestreich, and Stuart Levine, eds. 1970. *The American Indian Today*. New York: Penguin.

Oestreich, Nancy. 1948. Trends of Change in Patterns of Child Care and Training among the Wisconsin Winnebago. *Wisconsin Archaeologist* 22(304): 40–140.

JUNE HELM, 1986–1987
Papers: NWT

Armstrong, Karen V. 1989. June Helm. In *Women Anthropologists: Selected Biographies*, U. Gacs, A. Khan, J. McIntyre, R. Weinberg, eds. Chicago: University of Chicago Press.

Helm, June. 1961. *The Lynx Point People: The Dynamics of a Northern Athabascan Band*. National Museum of Canada Bulletin 176.

———. 1965. Bilaterality in the Socioterritorial Organization of the Arctic Drainage Dene. *Ethnology* 4(4): 361–385.

———. 1978. Long Term Research among the Dogrib and other Dene. In *Long Term Field Research in Anthropology*, G. Foster, T. Scudder, E. Colson, R. Kemper, eds. Washington DC: University of America Press.

———. 1980. Female Infanticide, European Diseases, and Population Levels among the Mackenzie Dene. *American Ethnologist* 7: 361–385.

———. 1989. Matonabbee's Map. *Arctic Anthropology*. 25: 28–47.

———. 1994. *Prophecy and Power among the Dogrib Indians*. Lincoln: University of Nebraska Press.

———. 2000. *The People of Denendeh: Ethnohistory of the Indians of Canada's Northwest Territories*. Iowa City: University of Iowa Press and Montreal: McGill-Queen's University Press.

Helm, June, ed. 1966. *Pioneers of American Anthropology: The Uses of Biography*. Seattle: University of Washington Press.

———, ed. 1981. *Subarctic*. Vol. 6, *Handbook of North American Indians*. Washington DC: Smithsonian Institution.

———, ed. 1985. *Social Contexts of American Ethnology 1840–1984*. Proceedings of the American Ethnological Society, 1984. Washington DC: American Ethnological Society.

Helm, June, and Nancy O. Lurie. 1966. *The Dogrib Handgame*. National Museum of Canada Bulletin 205.

ROY A. RAPPAPORT, 1988–1989
Papers: NAA, UCSD, UM-B

Biersack, Aletta. 1999. Introduction: From the "New Ecology" to the New Ecologies. *American Anthropologist* 101: 5–18.

Hart, Keith, and Conrad Kottak. 1999. Roy A. "Skip" Rappaport (1926–1997). *American Anthropologist* 101: 159–161.

Kottak, Conrad P. 1999. The New Ecological Anthropology, *American Anthropologist* 101: 23–35.

Rappaport, Roy A. 1968. *Pigs for the Ancestors: Ritual in the Ecology of a New Guinea People*. New Haven: Yale University Press.

———. 1979. *Ecology, Meaning and Religion*. Richmond CA: North Atlantic Books.

———. 1993. The Anthropology of Trouble. *American Anthropologist* 95: 295–303.

———. 1999. *Ritual and Religion in the Making of Humanity*. Cambridge: Cambridge University Press.

Watanabe, John M., and Barbara B. Smuts. 1999. Explaining Religion Without Explaining it Away. *American Anthropologist* 101: 98–112.

JANE BUIKSTRA, 1990–1991

Buikstra, Jane. 1976. *Hopewell in the Lower Illinois River Valley: A Regional Approach to the Study of Biological Variability and Mortuary Activity*. Northwestern University Monograph 2.

———. 1977. Biocultural Dimensions of Archaeological Study: A Regional Perspective. In *Biocultural Adaptation in Prehistoric America*, Robert L. Blakely, ed. *Southern Anthropological Society Proceedings* 11: 67–84.

———. 1995. Tombs for the Living . . . or for the Dead: The Osmore Ancestors. In *Tombs for the Ancestors*, T. Dillehay, ed. Washington DC: Dumbarton Oaks Research Library and Collection.

Buikstra, Jane, ed. 1981. Prehistoric Tuberculosis in the Americas. Northwestern University Archaeological Program Research Paper.

Buikstra, Jane, and Douglas K. Charles. 1999. Centering the Ancestors: Cemeteries, Mounts and Sacred Landscapes of the North American Midcontinent. In *Archaeologies of Landscape: Contemporary Perspectives*, W. Ashmore and B. Knapp, eds. London: Blackwells.

Buikstra, Jane, and Della C. Cook. 1992. Palaeopathology: An American Account. *Annual Review of Anthropology* 9: 433–470.

Buikstra, Jane, and Claire C. Gordon. 1981. The Study and Restudy of Human Skeletal Series: The Importance of Long-Term Curation. *Annals of the New York Academy of Sciences* 31: 449–446.

Buikstra, Jane, and Lyle Konigsberg. 1985. Paleodemography: Critiques and Controversies. *American Anthropologist* 87: 316–333.

ANNETTE WEINER, 1992–1993

Beidelman, Thomas B. and Fred R. Myers. 1998. Obituary for Annette Weiner. *American Anthropologist* 39(2): 27.

Kirshenblatt-Gimblett, Barbara, and Fred R. Myers. 1997. Interview with Annette Weiner, 7 December 1997.

New York University. 1998. *A Book of Memories: Annette B. Weiner (1933–1997)*. New York: Department of Anthropology.

Weiner, Annette. 1976. *Women of Value, Men of Renown: New Perspectives in Trobriand Exchange*. Austin: University of Texas Press.

———. 1988. *The Trobrianders of Papua New Guinea*. Case Studies in Cultural Anthropology. New York: Holt, Reinhart and Winston.

———. 1992. *Inalienable Possessions: The Paradox of Keeping While Giving*. Berkeley: University of California Press.

Weiner, Annette, and Jane Schneider, eds. 1989. *Cloth and Human Experience*. Washington DC: Smithsonian Institution.

JAMES PEACOCK, 1994–1995

Peacock, James L. 1968. *Rites of Modernization: Symbolic and Social Aspects of Indonesian Proletarian Drama*. Chicago: University of Chicago Press.

———. 1975. *Consciousness and Change: Symbolic Anthropology in Evolutionary Perspective*. New York: Wiley.

———. 1978a. *Muslim Puritans: Reformist Psychology in Southeast Asian Islam*. Berkeley: University of California Press.

———. 1978b. *Purifying the Faith: The Muhammadijah Movement in Indonesian Islam*. Menlo Park CA: Benjamin Cummings.

———. 1986. *The Anthropological Lens: Harsh Light, Soft Focus*. Cambridge: Cambridge University Press.

———. 1998. Interview with Marilyn Grunkmeyer. Tapes and Transcript at the Southern Oral History Program, University of North Carolina, Chapel Hill.

Peacock, James L., and A. Thomas Kirsch. 1970. *The Human Direction: An Evolutionary Approach to Social and Cultural Anthropology*. New York: Appleton-Century-Crofts.

Peacock, James L., and Ruel W. Tyson Jr. 1989. *Pilgrims of Paradox: Calvinism and Experience among the Primitive Baptists of the Blue Ridge*. Washington DC: Smithsonian Institution.

YOLANDA T. MOSES, 1996–1997

American Association for Higher Education. 1999–2000. Yolanda T. Moses Named New AAHE President. *AAHE Bulletin* (*www.aahe.org/Bulletin/moses.htm*).

Bernstein, Richard. 1993. Excellence in an Age of Diversity. *New York Times*. 12 September, sec. 1, 47.

Journal of Blacks in Higher Education. 1993. Appointments, Tenure Decisions, and Promotions of African Americans in Higher Education. *Journal of Blacks in Higher Education*. (autumn): 113.

———. 1996/1997. Appointments, Tenure Decisions, and Promotions of African Americans in Higher Education. *Journal of Blacks in Higher Education*. (winter): 147.

McFadden, Robert D. 1993. More a Builder of Bridges Than a Typical Scholar. *New York Times*. 25 May, sec. 2, 2.

Moses, Yolanda T. 1989. *Black Women in Academe: Issues and Strategies*. Washington DC: Project on the Status and Education of Women, Association of American Colleges.

———. 1994/1995. Letter to the Editor. *Journal of Blacks in Higher Education*. (winter): 8–9.

———. 2001. Interview with L. Kaifa Roland, 29 January 2001.

Mydans, Seth. 1993. Taking the Challenge As City College Chief. *New York Times*. 31 May, sec. 1, 25.

Newman, Maria. 1993. A New President for City College. *New York Times*. 25 May, sec. 1, 1.

San Bernardino Valley College. 1998. Alumni Hall of Fame: Dr. Yolanda T. Moses. (*http://sbvc.sbccd.cc.ca.us/alumni/hall-of-fame/alumni/moses.htm*)

JANE H. HILL, 1998–1999

Blount, Ben, ed. 1995. *Language, Culture, and Society*. Second edition. Prospect Heights IL: Waveland.

Grillo, R. D. 1988. Review of *Speaking Mexicano*. *Man* 23(1): 199.

Hill, Jane. 1985. The Grammar of Consciousness and the Consciousness of Grammar. *American Ethnologist* 12(4): 725–737.

———. 1993. "*Hasta la vista*, Baby!" Anglo Spanish in the American Southwest. *Critique of Anthropology* 13(2): 145–176.

Hill, Jane H., and Kenneth C. Hill. 1986. *Speaking Mexicano: Dynamics of Syncretic Language in Central Mexico*. Tucson: The University of Arizona Press.

Hill, Jane, and Judith T. Irvine, eds. 1992. *Responsibility and Evidence in Oral Discourse*. New York: Cambridge University Press.

Hill, Jane H., P. J. Mistry, and Lyle Campbell, eds. 1998. *The Life of Language: Papers in Honor of William Bright*. New York: Mouton de Gruyter.

LOUISE LAMPHERE, 1999–2001

Abel, Emily. 1981. Collective Protest and Meritocracy: Faculty Women and Sex Discrimination. *Feminist Studies* 7: 505–538.

Lamphere, Louise. 1977. *To Run After Them: The Social and Cultural Bases of Cooperation in a Navajo Community*. Tucson: University of Arizona Press.

———. 1987. *From Working Daughters to Working Mothers: Immigrant Women in a New England Industrial Community*. Ithaca NY: Cornell University Press.

———. 1992. *Structuring Diversity: Ethnographic Persopectives on the New Immigration*. Chicago: University of Chicago Press.

———. MS. "Not So Much Worse Than Others": Forging a Career in the Context of a Title VII Suit.

Lamphere, Louise, and Michelle Rosaldo, eds. 1974. *Women, Culture, and Society*. Stanford: Stanford University Press.

Lamphere, Louise, Patricia Zavella, Felipe Gonzales and Peter B. Evans. 1993. *Sunbelt Working Mothers: Reconciling Family and Factory*. Ithaca NY: Cornell University Press.

Lamphere, Louise, Alex Stepick, and Guillermo Grenier, eds. 1994. *Newcomers in the Workplace: Immigrants and the Restructuring of the U.S. Economy*. Philadelphia: Temple University Press.

Lamphere, Louise, Helena Ragoné, and Patricia Zavella, eds. 1997. *Situated Lives: Gender and Culture in Everyday Life*. New York: Routledge.

Sizer, Lyde Cullen. 1991. "A Place for a Good Woman": The Development of Women Faculty of Brown. In *The Search for Equity: Women at Brown University, 1891–1991*, Polly Welts Kaufman, ed. Hanover: Brown University Press.

DONALD BRENNEIS, 2001–2003

Brenneis, Donald. 1978. The Matter of Talk: Political Performance in Bhatgaon. *Language in Society* 7: 159–170.

———. 1979. Conflict in Bhatgaon: The Search for a Third Party. In *The Indo-Fijian Experience*, Subramani, ed. St. Lucia: University of Queensland Press.

———. 1980. Straight Talk and Sweet Talk: Political Discourse in a Community of Equals. *Working Papers in Sociolinguistics* 71. Austin TX: Southwestern Educational Development Laboratory.

———. 1983. The Emerging Soloist: Kavvali in Bhatgaon. *Asian Folklore Studies* 42: 67–80.

———. 1984. Grog and Gossip in Bhatgaon: Style and Substance in Fiji Indian Conversation. *American Ethnologist* 11: 487–506.

———. 1985. Passion and Performance in Fiji India Vernacular Song. *Ethnomusicology* 29: 397–408.

———. 1987. Performing Passions: Aesthetics and Politics in an Occasionally Egalitarian Community. *American Ethnologist* 14: 236–250.

———. 1990. Shared and Solitary Sentiments: The Discourse of Friendship, Play and Anger in Bhatgaon. In *Language and the Politics of Emotion*, C. Lutz and L. Abu-Lughod, eds. New York: Cambridge University Press.

———. 1991. Aesthetics, Performance, and the Enactment of Tradition in a Fiji Indian Community. In *Gender, Genre, and Power in South Asian Expressive Traditions*, A. Appadurai, M. Mills, and F. Korom, eds. Philadelphia: University of Pennsylvania Press.

———. 1994. Discourse and Discipline at the National Research Council: A Bureaucratic Bildungsroman. *Cultural Anthropology* 9: 23–36.

———. 1995. Caught in the Web of Words: Performing Theory in a Fiji Indian Community. In *Everyday Conceptions of Emotions*, J. A. Russell et al., eds. Dordrecht: Kluwer Academic Publications.

———. 1999. New Lexicon, Old Language: Negotiating the "Global" at the National Science Foundation. In *Critical Anthropology Today*, George Marcus, ed. Santa Fe: School of American Research Press.

Illustration Credits

The AAA Centennial Commissions

Centennial Executive Commission

Chair: Regna Darnell

Lee D. Baker
Jennifer Brown
Raymond DeMallie
Frederic W. Gleach
Richard Handler (1999–2000)
Jonathan Marks
Stephen O. Murray

Ex officio

Jane Hill
Louise Lamphere
Don Brenneis
Carole Crumley

AAA Staff

Bill Davis
Susan Skomal

Centennial Advisory Commission

David Aberle
Richard Adams
John Aubrey
Willie Baber
William Balee

Paul Bohannan
C. Loring Brace
Jane Buikstra
Matti Bunzl
Harold Conklin

Gary Feinman
William Fenton
Raymond Fogelson
George Foster Jr.
Don Fowler
Richard Fox
Susan Tax Freeman
Ernestine Friedl
Walter Goldschmidt
Ward Goodenough
Carol Greenhouse
Richard Handler
Faye Harrison
June Helm
Jane Hill
Curtis Hinsley
Jake Homiak
W. W. Howells
Dell H. Hymes
Ira Jacknis
Alice Kehoe
Jack Kelso
Herbert Lewis
Leonard Lieberman
Nancy Lurie
David Maybury-Lewis
Irma McClaurin

Ann McMullen
Beatrice Medicine
William Merrill
Yolanda T. Moses
Nancy Parezo
James Peacock
Marvette Perez
Jeremy Sabloff
Vilma Santiago-Irizarry
Theresa Schenck
Joanna Scherer
Molly Schuchat
Daniel Segal
Bernard Siegel
Sydel Silverman
Richard Slobodin
George W. Stocking Jr.
William Sturtevant
Robert Sussman
Wesley Thomas
Arlene Torres
Bruce Trigger
Anthony Wallace
Gordon Willey
Nathalie F. S. Woodbury
Richard Woodbury
Anna Celia Zentella